364.1066
Y 88

JAN 2011

STUDIES OF THE AMERICAS

Edited by
James Dunkerley
Institute for the Study of the Americas
University of London
School of Advanced Study

Titles in this series are multi-disciplinary studies of aspects of the societies of the hemisphere, particularly in the areas of politics, economics, history, anthropology, sociology, and the environment. The series covers a comparative perspective across the Americas, including Canada and the Caribbean as well as the United States and Latin America.

Titles in this series published by Palgrave Macmillan:

Cuba's Military 1990–2005: Revolutionary Soldiers during Counter-Revolutionary Times
By Hal Klepak

The Judicialization of Politics in Latin America
Edited by Rachel Sieder, Line Schjolden, and Alan Angell

Latin America: A New Interpretation
By Laurence Whitehead

Appropriation as Practice: Art and Identity in Argentina
By Arnd Schneider

America and Enlightenment Constitutionalism
Edited by Gary L. McDowell and Johnathan O'Neill

Vargas and Brazil: New Perspectives
Edited by Jens R. Hentschke

When Was Latin America Modern?
Edited by Nicola Miller and Stephen Hart

Debating Cuban Exceptionalism
Edited by Bert Hoffman and Laurence Whitehead

Caribbean Land and Development Revisited
Edited by Jean Besson and Janet Momsen

Cultures of the Lusophone Black Atlantic
Edited by Nancy Priscilla Naro, Roger Sansi-Roca, and David H. Treece

Democratization, Development, and Legality: Chile, 1831–1973
By Julio Faundez

The Hispanic World and American Intellectual Life, 1820–1880
By Iván Jaksić

The Role of Mexico's Plural *in Latin American Literary and Political Culture: From Tlatelolco to the "Philanthropic Ogre"*
By John King

Faith and Impiety in Revolutionary Mexico
Edited by Matthew Butler

Reinventing Modernity in Latin America: Intellectuals Imagine the Future, 1900–1930
By Nicola Miller

Youth Violence in Latin America

Gangs and Juvenile Justice in Perspective

Edited by
Gareth A. Jones and Dennis Rodgers

palgrave
macmillan

First published in 2009 by
PALGRAVE MACMILLAN®
in the United States—a division of St. Martin's Press LLC,
175 Fifth Avenue, New York, NY 10010.

Where this book is distributed in the UK, Europe and the rest of the world,
this is by Palgrave Macmillan, a division of Macmillan Publishers Limited,
registered in England, company number 785998, of Houndmills,
Basingstoke, Hampshire RG21 6XS.

Palgrave Macmillan is the global academic imprint of the above companies
and has companies and representatives throughout the world.

Palgrave® and Macmillan® are registered trademarks in the United States,
the United Kingdom, Europe and other countries.

ISBN: 978–0–230–60056–0

Library of Congress Cataloging-in-Publication Data

Youth violence in Latin America : gangs and juvenile justice in
perspective / Gareth A. Jones and Dennis Rodgers (editors).
p. cm.—(Studies of the Americas)
Includes bibliographical references and index.
ISBN 0–230–60056–5
1. Juvenile delinquency—Latin America. 2. Violent crimes—Latin
America. 3. Gangs—Latin America. 4. Juvenile justice, Administration
of—Latin America. I. Jones, Gareth A. II. Rodgers, Dennis.

HV9110.5.A5Y68 2009
364.106'60835098—dc22   2009013899

A catalogue record of the book is available from the British Library.

Design by Newgen Imaging Systems (P) Ltd., Chennai, India.

First edition: November 2009

10 9 8 7 6 5 4 3 2 1

Printed in the United States of America.

Contents

Tables and Figures

Tables

Figures

Acknowledgments

There are many people to whom we owe thanks in bringing this volume to completion. First among them are the staff at Palgrave-Macmillan who exhibited endless patience and forbearance as we missed deadlines. Special thanks go to Gabriella Georgiades who provided the initial contract for the book, to Joanna Mericle who worked with us as draft chapters were received, and to Colleen Lawrie, Samantha Hasey, and Julia Cohen who took the final manuscript through production, and to Diana Pritchard for preparing the index. We are also extremely grateful to Donna DeCesare of the University of Texas at Austin for providing us with an example of her powerful photography to use as the cover.

The idea for this volume emerged from an international workshop on youth violence in Latin America held at the London School of Economics and Senate House, the University of London, in 2005. We would like to thank the sponsors of the workshop, the London School of Economics Crisis States Research Centre, the University of London Institute for the Study of the Americas, the Alistair Berkley Memorial Fund, the British Academy, the United Kingdom Foreign and Commonwealth Office, and the Society for Latin American Studies. Neither the workshop nor this volume would have been possible without the support of Professor James Dunkerley, former director of the University of London Institute for the Study of the Americas. We thank all participants at the workshop for their presentations and involvement in promoting lively constructive debate.

Finally, the participation of Wagner dos Santos in both the workshop and this volume was made possible thanks to Tim Cahill and Damian Platt, then at Amnesty International. Both Tim and Damian also assisted with the interpretation of the talk Wagner gave at the workshop, a recording of which forms the basis for the preface of this book, augmented by notes from an interview conducted by Julia Rochester, and translated by Fernanda Regaldo.

Preface: Wagner's testimony

It is an unfortunate fact that many people who live in or work in Latin America as academics, for civil society organizations, development agencies or government, have firsthand experience of violence. At the same time, however, although such experience can sometimes involve great risks, it is rare for researchers and practitioners to be the victims of violence to the same degree as those they are studying or working with. Amidst the scare-mongering surrounding youth violence in contemporary Latin America the voice of both victims and perpetrators are rarely heard, and we were therefore keen to have this volume opened by someone who could speak of violence from direct personal experience.

Wagner dos Santos was 22 years old on July 23, 1993, when hooded men opened fire on a group of young people who were sleeping rough near the Candelária church in the centre of Rio de Janeiro, Brazil. On most nights the area surrounding the church was a base for some 50 youths, and during the July attack, eight were killed, and dozens injured, including Wagner. Although several eyewitnesses came forward after the massacre, by the time the first Candelária case came to court only Wagner was still prepared to testify. Before being able to do so, however, he suffered a further attempt on his life in December 1994, despite having been placed in a "safe house." Following pressure from NGOs, the Federal government of Brazil sent Wagner to Europe for his own safety, but he courageously traveled back to Brazil in order to testify in trials against two policemen, Marcos Vinícius Borges Emanuel and Nelson Oliveira dos Santos Cunha, both of whom confessed to involvement in the Candelária killing after being identified by Wagner.

Wagner's account provides us with a firsthand insight of extreme violence suffered by a young person, whilst simultaneously highlighting the murky links that can exist between such violence and the justice system in Latin America. He begins by describing how he became homeless a few weeks before the massacre when police harassment forced him to leave the building in which he was living, and how he took to watching parked cars in the streets for money after losing his job as a street vendor. This activity only occasionally provided enough money to rent a bed for the night, so he would sleep rough, often around the Candelária church, seeking comfort and security in numbers with others who hung around there, some of whom he knew from having been brought up in Rio's orphanage system. His description of being shot and left for dead is harrowing, as is the subsequent account of the persecution he suffered, which ultimately culminated in his being shot and left for dead a second time. But his voice is powerfully moving, and stands as a unique warning against the consequences of violence and injustice.[1]

* * *

At the time, I lived in Vila do João,[2] with several former students.[3] We didn't have any family, and a friend had given us that place. I worked as a street vendor. One night, the police came in the middle of the night—it was around midnight, one in the morning—saying that we had to leave, that this was a drug trafficking location, although everyone knew that there was no trafficking going on there. The police came in and we started to shout, "But we have nowhere to live, we have no family, we are all former FUNABEM [*Fundações Nacional do Bem-Estar do Menor*] students." They left, but then they came back, over and over again, more policemen. One time they started beating everybody up, and then they would always hit us whenever they came. Then one day one of them said, "Listen, next time I come and find you here, I'll kill all of you." At that point I told the other kids, "We can't carry on like this. We'll have to each live our own lives." And so it was. I left and started looking after parked cars. When I could I would sleep in hostels, but sometimes on beaches, the Praça IV or Praça Mauá, sometimes on the streets in the Candelária.

The Candelária street youth would often get together, to play, or sniff glue. There was no set time. There was only a set time for sniffing glue. Otherwise they would come and go as they pleased, to get some food, to eat. Sometimes they would sit down, and everyone would play or sing. It was really interesting, they had no notion of time, of the hours, of what tomorrow would be like, or of the past, or what life might be like in 10 years, where I'll go from here—they never think about that. They live day to day. They have no sense of the dangers of life. So this is how it was. [But] It's interesting, sometimes they would put on theatre plays for themselves. There would always be something creative going on. So deep down despite their lack of knowledge they would be as creative as people that went to university.

The day of the massacre, we all went to the beach in the morning. There were too many of us so we had to split into groups and I joined one group. I was the only one to get to the beach, as the police told the other kids to get off the bus. I waited at the beach for the others but they never came, so around 4 or 6 pm, I went back to La Candelária, and I saw an argument between the kids and a policeman trying to arrest one of them.[4] I didn't get involved and when it was over I went to talk to the boys to find out what had happened. There was a guy called Neilton who had been a former student with me who had taken some boy's glue, and had been sniffing it when some policemen had come up and started beating him up. Neilton had said the glue was not his, that it was everybody's, and that instead of beating him, they should beat all of them. They didn't care. The police carried on hitting and hitting Neilton. One of the boys was so upset that he got a stone and threw it at the police car, breaking a window. I think a policeman also got hurt. The police took him to the police station, and he was detained until 7 pm. When he came back, he said that a policemen had told him that we should not stay in the Candelária because they would be coming back.

I then went with two other kids, Gambá and Paulo, to go and buy cigarettes, and as we walked back to the Candelária, we saw a car parked near the church, with its boot open. Some guy stopped the other two, and one of them went, "No, no, no!" I didn't know what was going on, so I kept walking. As I walked past, another guy said, "Police! Police!," and pulled out a gun. I stopped and put my hands up. He asked for my documents and asked if I was from here. I told him, "No, I live in Vila do João," and he said, "Let's go, even so." The policeman slapped me on the face, and I slapped him back, but then another one came up and he hit me on the head, and put a gun in my face, saying, "Remember me?" He asked us, "Where's Russo?," and Paulo told him, "He's in the Candelária." They then put us in the car and that's when they shot me.

I don't know how to explain the sensation...It's a bit like you're drowning...Like you're under the water...You go all numb...I remember one of the policemen shouting, "Let's take him to hospital," and the other kids in the car getting agitated, there were seven people in the car in total. Then I passed out. When I woke up, I was somewhere in Flamengo. Gambá was on one side of me, Paulo on the other. Neither of them was breathing, they were both dead. I got up and started to walk, and collapsed when I got to a gas station. The guy working there cried, "No! Don't fall there! What have you done?," but then a police patrol came along, and then the firemen, and I was taken to the hospital.

I didn't know what had happened in the Candelária, but when I was on a hospital trolley passing through the corridor, I was put next to "Come Gato" [a youth who was considered the leader of the Candelária group]. He was in a coma,[5] and although I stayed on the trolley in the hospital corridor, I knew something had happened. Then in the morning I heard about the massacre, that a lot of kids had died. The police asked me to give a description of the policemen who had shot me, to help them draw up an identikit picture. Then they took me to the police station to make identifications, and there I started recognizing people. I spent a year in hospital. The BOPE, the Special Police,[6] watched over me at first. They treated me respectfully, and one of them even gave me a radio. But after they left, this other guy came. He was sneaky, and he wanted to get to me psychologically. I can't remember which police force he was from, but he kept threatening me, he would say, "You fucker Wagner," "We'll get you," and so on. That was when I got Amnesty International to look into my case, and the police stopped threatening me.

After coming out of hospital I was put in a safe house with some of the other Candelária youth who had survived until the trial. The thing is that everybody knew where the safe house was, including the journalists, who were the first to give away the secret. The truth is that they had nowhere to put the Candelária witnesses, and were just improvising, you know, "Hey! Let's create a safe house." So I thought, "Forget about this," and went to Bahia instead, where I applied for a job at the Club Med. As I had some experience in catering, I got the job. It was wonderful! But after a few months I had to go down to Rio to identify some people. In Bahia they didn't know who I was, but when I went back to Rio everyone saw it on TV. Then people started to torment me, torment me, torment me. They would call me stuff like criminal, bandit, thief, street kid. So I said to myself, "I'm leaving. I'm not staying in this place." And I went back to the safe house in Rio.

Then one day I went out to visit a friend. I was close to the Central Station and this guy carrying a gun asked me, "Are you Wagner dos Santos?" I started running, but in order to get away I would have had to push over a small child who might have been hit by a bus, so I stopped running and they caught me. They handcuffed me to a lamppost and started to beat me up until I was all covered in blood. Everybody saw it, and people started saying, "Oh, it's the Candelária kid, what has he done?" The guys beating me said I had been stealing. One stuck his hand into my pocket and took out a bunch of money. People said, "Well, if he's been stealing you have to take him to the police station," and so they took me out, handcuffed, and we came to a police kiosk where they identified themselves as policemen! Everybody saw that, [and] they started taking me to the 2nd District Police Department. I was just thinking to myself, "Now I'm screwed" when they pushed me against the wall and fired the first shot. I fell, but the guy—*ta, ta, ta!*—kept shooting, and then I passed out.

After that, it was arranged by Amnesty International for me to leave the country, but I came back to testify. I did so because I don't agree with injustice. I have suffered so many injustices since I was a kid, it's made me see that it's so important to do the right thing. Despite all that's happened to me, despite the fact that they tried to kill me, it was necessary for me to testify against them, because they took away the right to life of all those kids. The way they did it was so dishonorable, and cowardly. What happened to me was political. The policemen who shot me are guilty, but it's more about politics than about them. They are victims too, deep down inside. When one is treated with respect, with care, one does not feel worthless. And deep down inside, they did what they did because what they do is seen as being of no value. Whether the police do a good job or not, nobody really cares in Brazil. There's no respect, no pride in their work, they do it only to maintain their families, and deep down, this ends up making them feel worthless... I believe in justice, but justice has to come from the human being's heart and from self-respect. When you respect yourself you can respect others. If people have no self-respect, then they will only exploit others.

*   *   *

Many people are surprised by Wagner's lack of anger toward what happened at Candelária. Despite an obvious emotion at the deaths of close friends and companions, he is keen to relate the massacre and its aftermath to a sense of justice—which he defines not in terms of a legal framework, but in terms of personal integrity and self-respect. He places the blame, not so much on the individual police who tried to kill him, but on a political culture in which it is hard to achieve self-respect. His disgust is mainly reserved for the politicians who fail to distribute Brazil's considerable wealth, and the systemic obstructions to justice. Wagner's trajectory since leaving Brazil merely adds grist to this mill. When Wagner was moved to Europe by the Federal government of Brazil, he was told that he would be doing courses in hotel management. Instead, no steps were taken to regularize his status and he had to work illegally in a restaurant kitchen. Eventually with the help of a Brazilian union lawyer and Amnesty International, his status was legalized, and he remained in Europe for his protection, particularly as the charges against most of those that he identified as his assailants and/or participants in the Candelária massacre were dropped following the convictions of Marcos Vinícius Borges Emanuel and Nelson Oliveira dos Santos Cunha, and threats have been made against Wagner. Indeed, all cases regarding the Candelária massacre have now been archived.[7]

As a result of the two attempts on his life, Wagner suffers partial paralysis of his face, damaged hearing, chronic pain, and still has two bullets lodged in his head that are causing lead poisoning. He was recently declared handicapped as a result of his injuries and is no longer able to work, but as of late 2008 has yet to receive full and final compensation for his injuries, despite successfully petitioning against the Federal government of Brazil at the Inter-American Human Rights Commission. One happy outcome, however, was that thanks to some irresponsible coverage of one of the trials in which Wagner testified, he was reunited with his older sister, whom he had not seen in 15 years. They then traced two other sisters who had been adopted out of the family when they were still babies, and Wagner is in regular contact with his rediscovered family. Not all survivors of La Candelária have been so fortunate, however. According to Amnesty International, over half of the young people who lived in Candelária had died violently by 2001.[8] The most famous of these tragic survivors is Sandro do Nascimento, who took bus passengers hostage in the Jardim Botânico area of Rio after a bungled robbery attempt on June 12, 2000, and was killed by a policeman in the car taking him to the police station after he had given himself up. The event was captured on television and eventually became the subject of the acclaimed 2002 documentary film, *Bus 174*.

When asked in London why he had come to talk at our workshop, Wagner explained that his "goal was to show things that are happening in the world and that people are not aware of. People are good. But we sit around in our houses, with our families, while other people are killing themselves. We don't know why these things happen, but if they are happening, it's good that a person, even when that person has a family, knows about it...What I saw in the workshop is that people are worried about what is going on, with all this violence in Latin America, because if this kind of thing is happening over there, one day it might happen over here." Joining with Wagner, we hope that this volume will contribute in some small way to this critical endeavor of informing people about the tragic reality and consequences of youth violence.

Notes

1. The text we present is taken from an interview given by Wagner to Julia Rochester and which expands upon a video of the original LSE talk. We have carried out some editing in order to facilitate the text's readability.
2. A favela in Rio de Janeiro.
3. Wagner uses the term "students" to describe friends who went through the government's orphanage system, the *Fundação Nacional do Bem-Estar do Menor* (FUNABEM). Wagner's parents died when he was young and he spent much of his early life in the FUNABEM.
4. On the day of the massacre there had been a large demonstration near the Candelária church which had led to a lot of police patrolling the area.
5. "Come Gato" died a few days later.
6. The *Batalhão de Operações Policiais Especiais*, or Special Police Operations Battalion.
7. A full discussion of the legal proceedings surrounding the Candelária massacre and Wagner's shootings, as well as obstruction of investigations by police and other organizations, can be found in Amnesty International's 2003 report, Rio de Janeiro 2003: Candelária and Vigário Geral 10 years on (AMR 19/015/2003), available online at http://web.amnesty.org/library/index/engamr190152003 (October 1, 2007).
8. Amnesty International, 2003, Rio de Janeiro 2003: Candelária and Vigário Geral 10 years on (AMR 19/015/2003), available online at http://web.amnesty.org/library/index/engamr190152003 (October 1, 2007), p. 13.

Chapter 1

Youth Violence in Latin America: An Overview and Agenda for Research

Dennis Rodgers and Gareth A. Jones

It is a little-noted fact that the world has recently undergone a momentous demographic transition, whereby almost half of the world's population is now under the age 25, with the overwhelming majority of these young people living in the developing world. The consequences of this situation are potentially enormous. As François Bourguignon, the World Bank's Chief Economist, pointed out at the press conference presenting the organization's 2007 World Development Report on the "Next Generation," "Such large numbers of young people living in developing countries present great opportunities, but also risks."[1] This World Bank report focuses mainly on the potential consequences of deficient education and skills training for a future work force, but there is also an increasingly widespread tendency to blame the so-called youth bulge for the rising levels of violence afflicting many parts of the developing world today (Goldstone 2001; Urdal 2007). Latin America is a case in point in this respect, with youth prominently associated with the region's high levels of violence, both as victims and perpetrators (Briceño-León and Zubillaga 2002; Koonings and Kruijt 1999, 2004; Weaver and Maddaleno 1999). Certainly, according to the United Nations' (UN) recently published *World Report on Violence against Children* (Pinheiro 2006: 357), Latin America suffers the highest regional youth homicide rate in the world. This trend is perhaps particularly evident in contemporary Central America; in El Salvador, for example, 93 percent of all homicide victims in 2005 were between 15 and 17 years old, while 15–24 year olds were deemed responsible for some 60 percent of all homicides in the same year (UNODC 2007).[2]

Although violence involving youth can take many other forms, including domestic abuse, attacks by death squads on street children and repressive juvenile justice systems,[3] this situation has been largely blamed on the widespread and very visible regional youth gang phenomenon (Barnes 2007; Rodgers 1999).[4] This is particularly the case in contemporary Central America, where gangs have come to the fore in an unprecedented manner during the past two decades (Arana 2005; Liebel 2004; Rodgers 2009).

Estimates of the total proportion of contemporary regional violence attributable to gangs vary widely from 10 to 60 percent (UNODC 2007: 64), as they have been accused of a whole slew of crimes and delinquency, ranging from mugging, theft, and drug dealing, to rape, assault, and kidnapping.[5] There have even been attempts to link them to revolution and global terrorism. A 2005 U.S. Army War College publication contended that Central American gangs constituted a "new urban insurgency" that had as an ultimate objective "to depose or control the governments of targeted countries" through *"coups d'street"* [sic],[6] for example, while Anne Aguilera, head of the Central America office of the International Narcotics and Law Enforcement Affairs branch of the U.S. State Department, asserted in an interview published in the Salvadoran newspaper *La Prensa Gráfica* on April 8, 2005, that gangs were "the greatest problem for national security at this time in Central America" (cited in Bruneau 2005).[7] Such concerns have legitimated a host of regional initiatives, including information sharing, secondment of police and military personnel, and the coordination of legislation, notably between Central America, Mexico, and the United States (Lara Klahr 2006).[8]

Although gangs are unquestionably a significant contemporary concern in the region, such sensationalist pronouncements—which are frequently echoed and fueled by the media (Briceño-León 2007; Huhn et al. 2006a; Penglase 2007)—suggest that they remain a profoundly misunderstood phenomenon. This is clearly partly due to the fact that both "youth" and "violence" are highly ambiguous categories. As Michael Taussig (1987: 241) points out, the latter is a "slippery" concept in that what counts as violence, and the meanings of such manifestations, can vary considerably within a given society, to say nothing of across cultures. To some extent, of course, most social scientists and policy makers can be said to rely on specific types of government compiled data—occasionally supplemented by reports from human rights groups—to capture the extent and nature of violence.[9] Such data tend to reduce violence to criminal categories of homicide and assault, and therefore miss phenomenological understandings of violence as an action or an effect (Cuadra 2003; Whitehead 2004). Without more nuanced understandings of violence, there is a danger of "naturalizing" the phenomenon as a general human condition—in the case of youth gangs, perhaps particularly characteristic of young people (Collins 2008)—which is something that clearly obscures the intimate links violence has to power, for example, especially in relation to the state (see Arendt 1970).

The notion of "youth" is similarly by no means clear cut. Although the UN has defined "youth" as persons falling between the ages of 15 and 24 years inclusive, some governments, such as those of El Salvador and Guatemala, bring the age limit down to 12 years, while in Mexico, the *Instituto Mexicano de la Juventud* pushes the category up to 29 years. Most researchers, however, would argue that what we understand as youth should include the sociocultural and institutional context, as well as individual attitudes, because even if "the experience of being young is universal, ... it takes many different forms, partly cultural and political, partly personal" (Wulff

1995: 6). Indeed, according to Comaroff and Comaroff (2005), the category of "youth" is a sign that inherently disrupts simplistic Panglossian readings of progress, a collective noun that is applied to the unruly and excluded, a plastic term that is difficult to shake off, especially for those at the margins. At the same time, however, the boundaries separating "youth" status from "adult" status are both highly variable and arbitrary, often relating to an individual's behavior patterns and activities, rather than his or her age, with individuals frequently not considered fully "adult" until they are seen to have taken on adult responsibilities and behaviors, for example. To this extent, as Pierre Bourdieu et al. (1986: 164) point out, the sociocultural category of "youth" is more of an ascribed social role than a physical state of being (see also Wyn and White 1997).

The ambiguities inherent to the issues of youth and violence have contributed to the particular slant of social science research on the topic in Latin America, something that is evident in relation to the gang phenomenon. Despite having long been a major topic of interest within the social sciences worldwide since the Chicago School of Sociology's pioneering studies of the 1920s and 1930s—see for example, Thrasher (1927), Shaw and McKay (1942), or Whyte (1943)—gangs as a topic of study have only recently appeared as a systematic focus of the Latin American social sciences. Even if there exist a number of individual studies of gangs in almost every country in Latin America—including for example DeFleur (1970) on Argentina, Reguillo (1991) on Mexico, or Salazar (1990) on Colombia (for overviews, see Rodgers 1999; Strocka 2006)—such in-depth studies remain rare and isolated phenomena, and there are perhaps only two real *bodies* of research, respectively concerning gangs in Brazil and Central America (for reasons undoubtedly to do with the local importance of the issue).[10] The present volume attempts to both deepen and broaden the coverage of study.

The Central American literature is clearly the most developed body of literature on Latin American gangs, partly because different studies are often carried out explicitly in conversation with others. The first in-depth investigation to focus specifically on gangs was Deborah Levenson's (1988) pioneering research with the *Asociación para el Avance de las Ciencias Sociales en Guatemala* (AVANCSO) on Guatemalan gangs, which Juan-Carlos Núñez (1996) drew on to conduct his early comparative research on gangs in Guatemala, El Salvador, and Nicaragua, and which also informed José Miguel Cruz and Nelson Portillo Peña's (1998) study of gangs in El Salvador, as well as Leticia Salomón, Julieta Castellanos, and Mirna Flores' (1999) study of gangs in Honduras. Similarly, the first ethnographic study of a Central American gang, carried out in Nicaragua in 1996–1997 by Rodgers (1997, 2000, 2007a), was built upon by Rocha (2000a, 2000b, 2003, 2005) during his own research on a different Managua gang in 1999–2000, with his results then taken up by Rodgers (2006a, 2007b) in order to calibrate new field research in 2002–2003, and further exchanges occurring for Rocha's continuing research in 2005–2006 and Rodgers' in 2007.[11] Since these early studies, there has been a proliferation of research by a range of investigators, including

Hume (2007a, 2007b), Savenije and Andrade-Eekhoff (2003) in El Salvador, Castro and Carranza (2001) in Honduras, Vermeij (2006) in Nicaragua, and Winton (2004) and Merino (2001) in Guatemala. A multivolume overview study was published in the early and mid 2000s by a conglomerate of Central American research institutes (ERIC et al. 2001, 2004a, 2004b), but the research panorama remains relatively sparse, with new research occurring only very sporadically, although there is a proliferation of articles based on secondary literature as the topic becomes very much in vogue.[12]

Research on Brazil has proceeded somewhat differently. It is interesting to note that in Janice Perlman's classic *The Myth of Marginality* there was no index reference to gangs or violence, and the limited attention to crime is largely to discuss its low levels and focus on property (Perlman 1976). By the middle of the 1980s, however, especially building upon the work of Alba Zaluar (1983, 1994), violence and gangs became an important theme of research. This approach motivated a series of other studies of gang-drug industry relations in Rio and other Brazilian cities (Soares et al. 2005), as well as on the politics of violence and crime (Adorno et al. 1998; Soares et al. 1996). Paulo Lins, author of *Cidade de Deus* (The City of God, 1997), produced perhaps the most powerful work on gangs, drugs, and violence, based on interviews conducted through a project with Zaluar. Further important studies followed, including studies on the drugs trade and gangs (Leeds 1996), gangs and youth identities (Abramovay et al. 2002), the relationships and effects that gangs have on community (Arias 2004, 2006; Goldstein 2003; Pereira Leite 2005), and ethnographies of people in close proximity to gangs (Gay 2005). By the time Perlman conducted a return study of Rio in 2001, crime and in particular violence through gangs had become the defining feature of favela life, affecting community participation and organization, livelihoods, and poverty (Perlman 2006).

The uneven research situation vis-à-vis gangs in Latin America is mirrored more generally at the level of youth violence, which is clearly often talked about but less frequently researched. Indeed, the lack of systematic and comparative research on the topic was specifically singled out by the UN *World Report on Violence against Children* as the most important factor preventing the elaboration of a coherent and comprehensive regional research and policy agenda on the issue (Pinheiro 2006: 23). To a certain extent, however, the situation is also partly due to the difficulties inherent to identifying what is a "gang." Perhaps more so than any other region in the world, there exist a large number of labels in Latin America referring to institutions that could conceivably be classified as gangs: *pandillas* in Mexico and Nicaragua,[13] *manchas* in Peru,[14] *barras* in Argentina (DeFleur 1970; Kuasñosky and Szulik 1996, 1997), *quadrilhas* and *galeras* in Brazil (Zaluar 1994, 1997), *maras* in Guatemala, Honduras, and El Salvador (Núñez 1996), or *chapulines* in Costa Rica (*Revista Centroamericana* 1994), to name but some examples. Comparing and contrasting between these different social forms is by no means easy, particularly considering that, as Herbert Covey (2003: 12) notes in his global survey of the gang literature, there is generally little in the way of a theoretical consensus concerning gangs.[15] Indeed, in many ways we have not improved substantially on Frederick Thrasher's (1927: 57) classic proposition that

> a gang is an interstitial group, originally formed spontaneously, and then integrated through conflict. It is characterized by the following types of behavior: meeting face to face, milling, movement through space as a unit, conflict, and planning. The result of this collective behavior is the development of tradition, unreflective internal structure, *esprit de corps*, solidarity, morale, group awareness, and attachment to a local territory.

At the same time, however, this is a definition that clearly covers a lot of ground. Certainly, it is well established that amongst the many practices of youth is the general tendency to congregate into peer groups and engage in collective behavior patterns; this is a universal aspect of the youth life cycle, during which young individuals learn to socialize and interact with their physical and social environment through the group, which provides definite referential parameters and behavioral codes (Amit-Talai and Wulff 1995; Dubet 1987; Mead 1928).[16] Sports and recreational clubs, friendship networks, and youth gangs all constitute different examples of such juvenile peer groups. While obviously conceptually distinct, many of these groups are interlinked and overlap considerably with each other, making them difficult to set apart in practice. Furthermore, although some of these groups do differ substantially from gangs, others can often also share many of the characteristics that Thrasher attributed to the latter in his definition: meeting face to face, "milling," displaying solidarity and group awareness, and attachment to a local territory can all apply to a football team or a close-knit group of neighborhood friends, for example.[17]

Perhaps the most widespread criteria considered to set youth gangs apart from other juvenile peer groups is their routine association with illegal and violent activities (Cohen 1990; Klein and Maxson 1989; Miller 1982; Spergel 1984; Vigil 1988).[18] Of course, such behavior is not the exclusive preserve of youth gangs and their members. Other youth groups can be involved in such activities, although most frequently on a lesser scale and scope, as well as less regularly, than youth gangs. More generally, juvenile delinquency is obviously much more than just a youth gang phenomenon, even if there is evidence to suggest that being a member of a gang increases the likelihood of delinquent behavior (see Curry and Spergel 1988; Fagan 1990). What differentiates the illegal and violent behavior of youth gangs from that of other delinquent groups and individuals is that it is considered by wider society to be something inherent to the youth gang. Although other youth groups can be violent or engage in criminal enterprise, this behavior is generally not perceived as normative; it might be seen as induced by alcohol, or a form of temporary rebellion against authority, for example. Youth gangs, on the other hand, are often seen as violent and criminal "by nature." Engaging in collective criminal and violent behavior patterns is to this extent a defining feature. Thus, even if many instances of illegal and violent behavior attributable to members of youth gangs are actually committed individually, or in small groups of two or three, rather than collectively (Erickson and Jensen 1977; Short 1968), they are considered to be causally linked to the fact of the perpetrator's or perpetrators' gang membership, and are therefore associated with the gang, rather than individual delinquency (Cohen 1990: 10; Miraglia 2005).

Such a conception of youth gangs is of course what underpins the widespread "criminalizing processes" that Jane and Peter Schneider (2008: 356) identify as perniciously shaping dominant modes of thinking about particular groups associated with criminal behavior patterns. The social sciences have put forward a variety of alternative approaches, the most influential of which is perhaps the "social ecology" argument, proposing that gangs are the result of the "social disorganization" of poor urban areas.[19] Within this framework, youth gangs are conceived as partial replacement structures for institutions such as families that have become dysfunctional as a result of the "social disorganization" of poverty and social exclusion (Whyte 1943). Other important theories include cultural explanations of gangs as reflections of lower class "subculture" (Cohen 1955), political visions of gangs as forms of resistance to "blocked" opportunities (Cloward and Ohlin 1960), economic conceptions treating gangs as informal business enterprises (Sánchez Jankowski 1991), and psychological interpretations of gangs either as the result of gang members' deviant sociopathological personality traits (Yablonsky 1963), or else as vehicles for youth maturation processes and identity creation (Bloch and Niederhoffer 1958; Katz 1988).

It is beyond the scope of this introduction to attempt to consider which of these approaches is most persuasive, and as Ruth Horowitz (1990: 53) has moreover sensibly pointed out, to a large extent they correspond to "different dimensions of the gang experience that cannot be easily separated in practice." Seen from this perspective, it is arguably more fruitful to provide a sense of the varied intertwined factors that underlie the emergence of gangs (rather than trying to establish any kind of bottom-line determination) and to appreciate both the positive contributions of research on youth violence and gangs in Latin America, as well as its possible blind spots. At the same time, however, it is interesting to note that most of the preceding theoretical literature refers to U.S. gangs. This suggests the potential for obvious contrasts with the Latin America context. Certainly, although there are numerous similarities between the extant research in both parts of the world, there are arguably also some notable differences—at least of degree—emerging from Latin America research.

First, numerous studies underscore the interplay of gangs and youth violence in Latin America with other forms of social behavior and the formation of identities. As most studies note that the overwhelming majority of youth gang members around the world are male, it is unsurprising that many Latin Americanist scholars have related youth gangs to machismo and conceptualizations of masculinity (Barker 2005; Zubillaga and Briceño-Leon 2001). Masculine identities are manifest as both male-on-male and male-on-female violence, as well as the use of "beating-in" inductions of new gang members and the use of rape in the induction of female gang members (Hume 2004).[20] The use of and iconography of tattoos, body piercings, and clothing styles and the lyrics to hip-hop are also associated with macho performances, extending cultural mores and adding explicit sexualized and violent overtones (Rocha 2003; Rubio 2007).[21] As such indicate the difficult task of organizations working to affect male identities, including enhancing esteem as "fathers" or "workers,"[22] and should also prompt us to question how far youth and gangs really do reflect what Hagedorn (2008) calls "resistance identities." Moreover gangs' uses of clothing, music, slangs, graffiti or tags, and other "cultural signs" are obviously vital to their identities (Cuerno 2000; Martel 2007), but also need to be appreciated as not inimical to youth sociability more generally (Castillo and Jones this volume). Finally, a number of studies have pointed to the role that ideas of "death" and religion play in relation to macho gang iconography and moral codes (see respectively Perea Restrepo 2007, and Alves 2002), as well as to religious conversion for young people leaving gang life and becoming *calmado* (see Riaño-Alcalá 2006; Vásquez and Marquardt 2003; Wolseth 2008).[23]

A second notable contribution of research on Latin American gangs and youth violence is a critical focus on their social "embeddedness." It is worth repeating that gangs and youth violence emerge from particular social contexts. The predominant interpretation of this gang-context relationship, however, is largely informed by the U.S. perspective, and stresses (or assumes) that gangs are the consequence of significant social disorganization. Hence, poverty, family breakdown, school dropout, and unemployment emerge time and again as likely predictors of gang membership, something that is seemingly only confirmed by signs of antisocial behavior including graffiti, vandalism, and open drug or alcohol use. Yet, while gangs are mostly associated with poorer neighborhoods, this is not exclusively the case as Portocarrero (1996) has explored for Peru.[24] Moreover, relationships between gangs and communities are often very strong and highly organized, if not necessarily with positive social and political outcomes (Zaluar 1997, 2000).[25] Arias (2006) and Pereira Leite (2005), for example, outline the negotiation and consequences of agreements between community leaders and gangs or leaders and police for violence management.[26] Similarly, an important set of studies reveal how communities can relate to gangs and violence (Arias 2004; Goldstein 2003; Rodgers 2000, 2006a), and also how gangs build reputations and extend their control through the enforcement of existing norms vis-à-vis certain criminal activities, domestic violence and child abuse, alcoholism, drug use, and property disputes (Arias and Davis Rodrigues 2006; Zaluar 2000). Indeed, gangs may organize to "defend" communities from outside incursion, construct networks with other gangs, and develop (hierarchical) structures for command and control (Dowdney 2005).

The nature of the social embeddedness of gangs is however clearly mutable. As some gangs have become more networked they have also become more mobile, for example.[27] The most obvious example are the *mara* gangs in Central America that have formed and reformed as a consequence of deportations from the United States. Many members have subsequently migrated "to return" north, becoming "transnational" or "global," and disrupting territorial loyalties and spatial identities (Reguillo 2005; Zilberg 2004, 2007). In a few cases, gangs of Latin American origin have emerged further afield as a result of migration, in Western and Southern Europe (Feixa et al. 2008; Hagedorn 2008). It is important however to distinguish between the flows of gang members, and the geographies of violence, and the "mobility" of the gang as an idea. As Reguillo (2005) has suggested, the *maras* have become central to a public imagination of fear, a convenient pariah or "other" easily called up to legitimate a host of anxieties and geopolitical responses. This is particularly obvious in relation to the infamous application of highly repressive antigang measures such as *Mano Dura* in Central America (González 2003; Hume 2007b; Lara Klahr 2006)—despite the fact that these are clearly not working (Aguilar 2006; Berkman 2005; see also Unger, this volume)—but also the growing extension of particular forms of "info-structure" for monitoring gangs, sometimes quite obviously, such as with the establishment of FBI (Federal Bureau of Investigation) offices in San Salvador or the new security provisions included in the 2008 Merida Initiative, or else more surreptitiously, through the specific targeting of USAID (United States Agency for International Development) and Millennium Challenge Funds donor flows to security-related projects, for example. An obvious question in this respect is to what extent the increased surveillance of Central America will extend to the rest of the continent, and how this will shape future societies in the region.

Partly for this reason, we feel that it is important to combine any analysis of a specific form of youth violence such as gangs with an exploration of various aspects of the juvenile justice systems that they encounter. In some parts of Latin America—Central America being a case in point—particular types of policies are arguably increasingly *the* key to understanding the critical shift that has occurred in the underlying nature of youth violence, which has become more violent and "disembedded" (see Rodgers et al. 2009). Seen from this perspective, particular forms of juvenile justice arguably embody deeper problems inherent within Latin American societies. Yet juvenile justice remains one of the Cinderella's of regional and international attention to young people in Latin America. UN agencies such as UNICEF (United Nations Children's Fund) have not afforded juvenile justice priority status, while the UN Coordination Panel on Juvenile Justice, which consists of WHO (World Health Organization), UNICEF, and UNHCHR (United Nations High Commissioner for Human Rights), has been largely ineffectual since its inception. Regional organizations such as the OAS (Organization of American States) and the Latin American Court for Human Rights have been more interested in reform of statute than ensuring practical interventions on the ground. Similarly, the rights agenda has had an uneasy relationship to juvenile justice—compared with the public discourses and agents lined up in other critical areas such as indigenous groups ("first rights," cultural patrimony), natural resources and environment, gender, race, and disability. Rights have only percolated through to the juvenile justice system in Latin America, and been picked up by the media in the breach, that is, in their abuse (Macaulay 2007).

Of particular importance in this regard is the role played by the state (see Frühling et al. 2003). It is an oft repeated fallacy that contemporary violence in Latin America is now more social and economic in nature, compared to the political brutality of the past, with the spread of democracy and the decline of counterinsurgent state violence held up as an exemplification of this process. Yet even if ideological struggles between states and guerrillas have undoubtedly waned, countering youth violence, whether manifest as gangs, through involvement in criminal networks, or as individual actions of "delinquency," retains the legitimation discourse of "defending" the state, the nation, and moral order (Huggins et al. 2002). The state therefore deploys resources against young people in extralegal forms, with impunity provided by tacit political support, a judicial system slanted in favor of the police and against victims' relatives, and acquiescence to popular opinion that condones "order" outside the parameters of the "law" (see Brinks 2008; also Caldeira 2002; Holston and Caldeira 1998; Godoy 2006; Perea Restrepo 2004; as well as Denyer Willis, this volume).[28] The question of who controls the state and why they might be deploying its apparatus in such a manner clearly goes to the heart of the underlying dynamics of the new political economy of violence in contemporary Latin America (see Rodgers, 2009).

These are "big issues" in every sense that we feel particularly require detailed study if we are truly to get to grips with the dynamics of the contemporary youth violence phenomenon in Latin America. Of course, there are potentially many other underexplored avenues for research. We remain surprised about the paucity of gang research in the region related to "race" and ethnicity and gangs, for example. There are also relatively few studies that provide a detailed account of what might be termed gang "cosmologies," that is, to say the multiple social, cultural, and historical repertoires they draw on, and how they both corrupt and reinvent them. The study of gangs as business organizations also requires greater tracing through both quantitative and qualitative studies; from knowing that few gang members are well off and that most get by, and that gangs may charge "taxes" on local business enterprises, there is little research indicating how the gangs legitimate business decisions, network with other organizations, and how the size and other characteristics of the gang may affect these rationale. Finally, and perhaps most importantly of all, we know little about circumstances in which gangs do not emerge despite the "standard" conditions propitious to their doing so, nor how certain youth successfully resist becoming involved in gangs in areas affected by them. We also know little about how gangs subside.

We do not, however, wish to use this volume to map out a set of categorical statements, prognoses, or issues about the emergence of gangs and youth violence in Latin America. Indeed, neither in our own work nor in that of most contributors would such certainty be justified. Rather, we present this volume as a first step toward the elaboration of a more coherent and focused research agenda on contemporary Latin American youth violence, that seeks to draw on the insights of preceding studies while also thinking about the specific dynamics of the present. It does so by focusing on gangs and state-sponsored systems of juvenile justice, but in as broad a fashion as possible, adopting different viewpoints and foci, and trying to draw links across different themes and issues. The current importance, both real and imagined, attributed to the gang phenomenon in Latin America makes it an inevitable center of attention, as is also the case of the infamous forms of juvenile justice that have been increasingly deployed in the region during the past decade. Yet gangs have existed in Latin America for many decades, even if— interestingly—the concern with "youth violence" is a recent one. Certainly, in a great many Latin American countries, there have been periods in the past where levels of violence have been extremely high, yet young people have not been its principal perpetrators or victims. Moreover, whereas Brazil, Colombia, Venezuela, and most of Central America are currently synonymous with gangs and violence, youth violence seems either much lower or much less documented elsewhere. To this extent, focusing explicitly on the contemporary gangs and the juvenile justice systems that they have engendered seem to us to constitute a potentially highly revealing lens through which to get to grips with the wider underlying processes that are currently shaping Latin American societies.

The volume is loosely organized into two parts. The first half is made up of studies that focus specifically on the dynamics of youth violence, considering violence as an action within social life, and most often in its gang or quasi-gang manifestation. The second half has contributions that focus on of different interventions relating to youth violence by both the state, including the police, and civil society organizations. All of our contributors adopt or are sympathetic to ethnographic styles of analysis, getting as close as is feasible to the young people in gangs or to those most directly affected by their actions. As Daiute and Fine (2003) note, it is rare to read about youth violence from the perspective of youth themselves, and a number of authors have noted the paucity of studies drawing from primary research and conducted with young people in their territories rather than on "neutral ground" or in prisons (Huhn et al. 2006b; Liebel 2004; Moser and McIlwaine 2004). They suggest that there is a real need for studies to broaden out from a concern with youth behavior to youth subjectivity and experience, and to consider the context of institutions, relations, and symbolic media. Wagner's story, which opens this volume, arguably does this in the most direct of manners, but most of the other contributions brought together in this collection can be said to attempt to do so as well.

Chapter 2 by Dennis Rodgers details the longitudinal evolutionary trajectory of Nicaraguan gangs between the 1990s and 2000s. Focusing specifically on a *pandilla* in *barrio* Luis Fanor Hernández, a poor neighborhood in Managua, the country's capital city, he traces how it originated as a form of local social structuration in the face of broader conditions of high crime, insecurity, and sociopolitical breakdown and then changed significantly over the course of a decade from a form of collective social violence to a more individually and economically motivated type of brutality organized around a nascent drugs trade. At the same time, however, Rodgers relates this transformation to wider structural processes, which he describes as coming together and precipitating a form of "social death" in contemporary

Nicaragua. Chapter 3 is a personally reflexive piece by Monique Sonnevelt on gangs in Guadalajara, Mexico, where she details the way that different local actors, both violent and nonviolent, interact with each other, and how the actions of one have consequences for the other. In describing what might be understood as a "market for security," she outlines how dealing with youth violence is framed by broader governance and policing issues, which lead the local community to turn to gang members for the resolution of disputes. Sonnevelt's study reveals "security" not as an antonym of "violence," but rather as two closely entwined conditions, with the latter providing legitimacy to agents able to deliver the former even if they are involved in violent actions themselves. An emphasis on social organization in a context of violence, and how personal experience of brutality relates to identity construction and cultural form is also central to Chapter 4 by Jon Wolseth. Recounting the lives of young people on the streets of Santo Domingo, in the Dominican Republic, Wolseth shows how violence both cuts across social relationships and also forms a vital component of patterns of solidarity amongst them, both practically and discursively. The bonding, manifest as the sharing of drugs and care, suggests a potential for the constitution of a "proto-gang" identity, albeit one that is fragile in the face of competition for drug sales, space, and personal rivalries.

It is often said that violence is central to the identities of gang members, and youth, but rarely is this relationship explicitly mapped out. This is something that Chapter 5 by Verónica Zubillaga explicitly attempts to do, focusing on "young men of a violent life" in poor Caracas *barrios*. She explores the content of their discourses about their "search for respect," suggesting that these need to be understood as exemplifying a subjective management of a threatened and negated identity. Zubillaga then goes on to draw out connections between different types of demands for respect and their associated brutality, showing how violence constitutes an attempt to obtain a form of personal recognition, before then going on to explore the life trajectories of young men who previously led violent lives but managed to forge new, nonviolent lifestyles. Chapter 6 by Cordula Strocka similarly explores approaches through which to turn youth away from violence; indeed, the study that she presents explicitly aimed to change the behavior and attitudes of participating youth gang members in Ayacucho, Peru, through the application of the classic Robber's Cave social psychology experiment. Although this intervention was initially successful, Strocka suggests that it can ultimately only lead to short-term results, because gang membership is highly fluid and people inevitably "mature out," and it moreover leaves the structural causes of formation and adoption of violent actions untouched.

Chapter 7 by Dominique P. Béhague considers benefits and limitations of a different type of alternative, more medicalized intervention that has been deployed to tackle youth violence in Pelotas, Brazil. She points out that "classic" juvenile justice systems have a tendency to vilify youth involved with violence, and that this has been increasingly challenged by medicalized approaches based on psychiatric diagnoses. These however are not unproblematic, often ignoring the socioeconomic and political conditions surrounding violence, and pathologizing violence through the creation of psychiatric categories such as "antisocial behaviour" and "conduct disorder." Brazil has been at the forefront of attempts to construct a politically sensitive medicalized framework that neither vilifies nor pathologizes youth violence, and Béhague traces the practical dilemmas that "psi" professionals attempting to implement such a framework in Pelotas have faced. In particular, she highlights the contingent nature of the various meanings attributed to youth violence within such a conceptual framework, and critiques the professionals' sometimes uncritical construction of "expert knowledge," showing how class and other standpoint positions can often filter through as a result.

José Luis Rocha Gómez's Chapter 8 explores the differing underlying logics and dynamics of the two main Nicaraguan governmental organizations dealing with youth violence, the National Police and the Office of the Special Ombudsman for Children and Adolescents. Rocha highlights how and why these organizations often have extremely contradictory discourses and practices. He traces the existence of incongruent interest groups and objectives within both organizations, and their consequences, as well as also describing the methodological means through which these were concretely mapped out. Using a perspective informed by the work of Jürgen Habermas, Rocha explores how law and practice diverge under pressure from party, corporate, and individual interests. Rather than see deficiencies in the system of juvenile justice as a problem of converting policy principles to practice, he provides us with a rich understanding of the way that different elements of a same state apparatus can construct their legitimacy in often contradictory manners, and the potential consequences of such a disjuncture.

Chapter 9 by Graham Denyer Willis focuses on the rise and dynamics of the *Primeiro Comando da Capital* (PCC), a "gang-cartel" that was originally founded as a self-protection organization in the prisons of São Paulo, Brazil, during the early 1990s, but which has since spread to a large number of poor peripheral urban communities. He traces this particular genesis to the introduction of zero tolerance policies on the one hand, but also the partial absence of the state in peripheral neighborhoods, arguing that these have combined to create spaces for the PCC to consolidate a grip over local communities. At the same time, however, Denyer Willis rejects the argument that the PCC represents a form of "parallel power" (Leeds 1996), contending instead that it is symbiotically linked to the state in both real and imagined ways. This, he suggests, is leading to the emergence of societal perceptions of violence that are particularly ominous for the future, as is well reflected in the emergence of a discourse calling for the revocation of the human rights of the poor and the violent, despite the fact that these categories do not necessarily overlap.

As Héctor Castillo Berthier and Gareth Jones discuss in Chapter 10, to most residents of Mexico City it seems incredible that less than a decade ago the mayor announced that this was *La Ciudad de la Esperanza* (The

City of Hope). They describe how Mexico City today is apparently racked by crime and violence, a highly unequal city in which anxiety and fear are a "shared idiom." The *banda*, a term once used to describe socially amorphous associations of young people, has been replaced by the *pandilla*, itself a term increasingly synonymous with organized crime, "delinquency," and the *maras*. Castillo Berthier and Jones outline how the Mexican state has deployed zero tolerance and antigang measures, and shifted policy from enhanced policing to a militarization of "public security." They argue that this constitutes a raising of the stakes by the state, which thus discursively folds gangs and other forms of youth behaviors into a single category of violence—that also encapsulates drug cartel brutality and transnational organized crime—that is deemed system-threatening, and therefore a new "political violence." The chapter considers how such a youth-gang-security nexus influences the "sociological imagination" of young people, including how they understand their present lives through the medium of violence and the state's reaction to violence.

Finally, we close with Chapter 11 by Mark Unger, which focuses on the tensions that exist between repressive and preventive approaches to policing youth, describing how these can largely be said to be the result of the region's varying political and socioeconomic conditions. Unger draws comparatively on a broad range of examples, including Honduras, Peru, Bolivia, Colombia, Brazil, and Argentina in order to explore three key issues related to juvenile justice, namely legal responsibility, public space, and gangs, each of which he argues highlight particular aspects of the extreme difficulties inherent to moving beyond the opposing paradigms of repression and prevention in addressing youth violence in Latin America. He concludes however on a more optimistic note, describing a range of promising community-oriented programs that are beginning to be enacted throughout the Latin American region.

Notes

1. See http://go.worldbank.org/L889ZRIN20 (accessed October 14, 2008).
2. The overall homicide rate in Latin America, according to the UN, is just over 25 per 100,000, with the rate in El Salvador, Guatemala, and Venezuela about 100 per 100,000. The rate among 10–29 year olds for Latin America is 34.6 per 100,000 compared to a global average of 9.2 (WHO 2002).
3. Best estimates put the number of children victims of domestic violence in Latin America at six million (see Barker 2005; Buvinic et al. 1999). For studies of death squad and/or police killings of street children see Godoy (1999) and Huggins and De Castro (1996).
4. The high levels of youth violence in Latin America can be linked to more structural factors, such as to the social, cultural, and economic conditions in which most of the region's 140 million youth live—almost half of youth in the region are estimated to live in conditions of poverty—as well as to the availability of firearms and effects of the drug trade (see Briceño-León and Zubillaga 2002; Fajnzylber et al. 2002; Kruijt 2008; Moser and McIlwaine 2004; Saraví 2004). See Kessler (2004) for a nuanced analysis of the way such

factors impact on youth violence in contemporary Argentina, as well as more generally, Sánchez (2006).

5. A report by the Dutch organization IKV Pax Christi (2008) indicates that five of the top ten countries for kidnap worldwide are in Latin America, both in terms of total kidnap numbers and in terms of kidnaps as a proportion of population. Mexico tops the list for total kidnaps, and is superseded only by Iraq for kidnaps as a proportion of total population. Other countries to register are Brazil, Ecuador, Venezuela, and Colombia.

6. See Manwaring (2005; 2006). A follow-up report by the same author published in 2008 further contended that gang violence constituted "another kind of war (conflict) within the context of a "clash of civilizations" . . . being waged . . . around the world" (Manwaring, 2008: 1).

7. Similarly emotive—occasionally verging on alarmist—coverage of gangs, their transnationality, and their potential for networks with terrorist organizations or drug cartels include Arana (2005), Papachristos (2005), and Sullivan (2006). It is interesting to note that despite the "gang threat" thus being seen by policy makers as "political", asylum determination systems refuse to recognize those escaping gang related violence as having credible claims (Corsetti 2006).

8. Measures have included fast-track deportations of gang members and transfer of prisoners; the establishment of a Transnational Anti-Gang Unit involving agencies of the Central American and the U.S. government in 2007; information sharing coordinated by the FBI National Gang Intelligence Center Task Force; and the inclusion of gangs in security assessments (see Joint Operating Environment 2008). In 2008 the U.S. Congress also approved the U.S.$ 1.6 billion Plan Mérida to enhance border control enforcement as a regional security strategy.

9. There have been numerous attempts to use these data as a means to "cost" violence in Latin America (see Buvinic et al. 1999; Londoño and Guererro 1999; Morrison et al. 2004).

10. By contrast, Bolivia, Chile, Paraguay, and Uruguay have particularly few studies of gangs or youth violence.

11. Nicaragua is probably the country which has been studied in greatest empirical depth as a result of this rather unique process of longitudinal ethnographic conversation between Rocha and Rodgers (see Rocha and Rodgers 2008).

12. Four further, somewhat uneven overview studies have also been published: Demoscopía (2007), Rubio (2007), USAID (2006), and the work of the "Pandillas juveniles transnacionales en Centroamérica, México y Estados Unidos" project coordinated by the Instituto Tecnológico Autónomo de México's (ITAM) Centro de Estudios y Programas Interamericanos (CEPI), whose output is available online at http://interamericanos.itam.mx/maras/index.html (accessed June 4, 2009).

13. See the contributions to this volume by Castillo Berthier and Jones, Rodgers, and Sonnevelt, for example.

14. See the contribution to this volume by Strocka, for example.

15. See Hagedorn (2008) for a useful discussion of the difficulties in adopting a gang "ideal" type, and which institutions such definitions usefully serve. Hagedorn himself suggests that the best definition is an "amorphous one: they are simply alienated groups socialized by the streets or prisons, not conventional institutions" (2008: 31).

16. In a related manner, one aspect of youth gang membership that is almost universally agreed upon is that it is a finite social role (even if it has been observed that occasionally individuals do remain associated with the gang beyond a "normal" age range—see Whyte 1943: 10). It has been noted all over the world that youth gang members inevitably "mature out" of the gang and more often than not integrate mainstream society, by taking a job or founding a family (something that is often the cause of "maturing out") (Hagedorn 1988; Vigil 1988; Whyte 1943: 35).

17. Similarly, while some gangs display clear leadership figures, well-developed lines of authority, and other organizational features (see Chin 1990; Dowdney 2005; Harris 1988; Moore 1978), many are less cohesive (Stafford 1984), although it should be noted that just as with any social group, gang membership can often be categorized as either "core" or "peripheral", with the former more implicated in collective group activities than the latter, something that can make precisely delimitating a gang an inexact science (see Klein 1995: 59–62).

18. The degree of criminal and violent activity is not the issue. The Brazilian *quadrilhas* are deeply implicated in drug dealing and display regular patterns of extremely violent behavior, including murder, for example (see Zaluar 1994; 1997), whereas Peruvian *pandillas* seem to engage principally in low-level violence, such as street brawls or muggings and pickpocketing (Cánepa 1993). Yet, both are considered to be youth gangs by wider society because they are both inherently associated with behavior patterns perceived as predominantly revolving around illegal and violent activities. Generally, as these two examples suggest, the types of illegal and violent activities youth gangs engage in can vary considerably, and, as John Hagedorn (2008: xxv) points out, can be highly mutable, insofar as "today's youth gang might become a drug posse tomorrow, even transform into an ethnic militia or a vigilante group the next day."

19. The original proponent of such a view was Frederick Thrasher (1927). It has been taken up by a variety of subsequent researchers, including Horowitz (1983), Shaw and McKay (1942), Short and Strodtbeck (1965), Suttles (1968; 1972), and Whyte (1943), for example.

20. By contrast, portrayals of female gang members have tended to highlight a status as exploited sex objects (see, for example, Hopper and Moore 1990; Gay 2005 offers a different perspective, however), even if there often exist empowered female members (*hainas*), and all-female youth gangs have also been noted to exist in Guatemala, Nicaragua, and Mexico (Cummings 1994; Rodgers 2006a; Winton 2007) as well as the United States (Campbell 1984; Giordano 1978; Harris 1988; Miranda 2003).

21. Curiously, there are relatively few Latin American studies that provide a detailed account, brief mention aside, of gang uses of cultural symbols, from the iconography of tattoos and the "meanings" attached to clika names to the music associated with gang culture.

22. See, for example, the work of Puntos de Encuentro (http://www.puntos.org.ni), Promundo (http://www.promundo.org.br), Luta pela Paz (Fight for Peace) (http://www.fightforpeace.net) and Homies Unidos (http://homiesunidos.org).

23. There are few studies, however, indicating how people come to terms with fear and distress in circumstances of violence, although the popularity of spiritism and devotion to "death religions" such as Santa Muerte are clearly one route (see Ferrándiz 2004; Jones et al. 2007).

24. Similarly, a recent study in Guatemala City found that neighborhoods falling within the metropolis' bottom quartile in terms of impoverishment suffered less gang-related crime than neighborhoods falling within the second-to-last quartile (see PNUD 2007).

25. Zaluar shows how gang formations in Rio de Janeiro's *favelas* controlled the territories and the drug trade in a way that she terms "perverse integration," thereby highlighting the highly violent dynamics of processes that converted small scale gangs (*galeras*) into larger *comandos*, which in turn forced communities (and men) to support and defend a territory from the rival *comandos* and the police.

26. Some studies have in fact argued that gangs can often represent "parallel" forms of governance (Leeds 1996; Penglase 2005; Rodgers 2006b).

27. The widespread assumption that a "critical mass" of youths located in close proximity is necessary for a gang to emerge, and hence the argument that gangs are mainly an urban phenomenon, still holds despite this new trend, partly because the evidential base of studies of youth gangs almost exclusively concerns cities. We have very little knowledge of youth violence or gangs in smaller towns and the countryside despite the general impression that rural areas can be more violent, if differently, from cities (see Kay 2001).

28. Certainly, in spite of numerous and expensive exercises in police reform throughout the region, it is still the state that is often identified generally and by youth themselves as the primary perpetrators of violence in Latin America.

Bibliography

Abramovay, M., J. J. Waiselfisz, C. C. Andrade, and M. das Graças Rua. 2002. *Guangues, Galeras, Chegados e Rappers: Juventude, Violência e Cidadania nas Cidades da Periferia de Brasília*, Rio de Janeiro: Garamond.

Adorno, S., R. S. de Lima, D. Feiguin, F. Biderman, and E. Bordini. 1998. O adolescente e a criminalidade urbana em Sao Paulo, *Revista Brasileira de Ciencias Criminais*, vol. 6, no. 23, pp. 189–204.

Aguilar, J. 2004. La mano dura y las "políticas" de seguridad, *Estudios Centroamericanos*, vol. 667, pp. 439–449.

Alves, J. C. S. 2002. Violência e religião na baixada fluminense: Uma proposta teórico metodológica, *Revista Rio de Janeiro*, vol. 8, pp. 59–80.

Amit-Talai, V., and H. Wulff. 1995. *Youth Cultures: A Cross-Cultural Perspective*, London: Routledge.

Arana, A. 2005. How the street gangs took Central America, *Foreign Affairs*, vol. 84, no. 3, pp. 98–110.

Arendt, H. 1970. *On Violence*, London: Allen Lane.

Arias, E. D. 2004. Faith in our neighbors: Networks and social order in three Brazilian favelas, *Latin American Politics and Society*, vol. 46, no. 1, pp. 1–38.

Arias, E. D. 2006. *Drugs & Democracy in Rio de Janeiro: Trafficking, Social Networks, & Public Security*, Chapel Hill: University of North Carolina Press.

Arias, E. D., and C. Davis Rodrigues. 2006. The myth of personal security: Criminal gangs, dispute resolution, and identity in Rio de Janeiro's favelas, *Latin American Politics and Society*, vol. 48, no. 4, pp. 53–81.

Barker, G. T. 2005. *Dying to Be Men: Youth, Masculinity and Social Exclusion*, London: Routledge.

Barnes, N. 2007. Executive summary: Transnational youth gangs in Central America, Mexico and the United States, *Transnational Study on Youth Gangs*, Washington: Washington Office on Latin America.

Berkman, H. 2006. The politicization of the judicial system of Honduras and the proliferation of *Las Maras, Journal of International Policy Solutions*, vol. 4, pp. 5–15.

Bloch, H. A., and A. Niederhoffer. 1958. *The Gang: A Study in Adolescent Behavior*, New York: Philosophical Library.

Bourdieu, P., J. C. Passeron, and J. C. Chamboredon. 1986. *Le Métier de Sociologue*, Paris: EHESS.

Briceño-León, R. 2007. *Sociología de la Violencia en América Latina*, Quito: Facultad Latinoamericana de Ciencias Sociales (FLACSO) and Municipio Metropolitano de Quito.

Briceño-León, R., and V. Zubillaga. 2002. Violence and globalization in Latin America, *Current Sociology*, vol. 50, no. 1, pp. 19–37.

Brinks, D. M. 2008. *The Judicial Response to Police Killings in Latin America: Inequality and the Rule of Law*, Cambridge: Cambridge University Press.

Bruneau, T. 2005. The maras and national security in Central America, *Strategic Insights*, vol. 4, no. 5, http://www.ccc.nps.navy.mil/si/2005/May/bruneauMay05.pdf [accessed April 24, 2007].

Buvinic, M., A. Morrison, and M. Shifter. 1999. *Violence in Latin America and the Caribbean: A Framework for Action*, Sustainable Development Department, Washington: Inter-American Development Bank.

Caldeira, T. P. R. 2002. The paradox of police violence in democratic Brazil, *Ethnography*, vol. 3, no. 3, pp. 235–263.

Campbell, A. 1984. *The Girls in the Gang: A Report from New York City*, Oxford: Basil Blackwell.

Cánepa, M. A. (ed.). 1993. *Esquinas, Rincones, Pasadizos: Bosquejos sobre Juventud Peruana*, Lima: Instituto Bartolomé de las Casas.

Castro, M., and M. Carranza. 2001. Las maras en Honduras, in ERIC, IDESO, IDIES, and IUDOP (eds.), *Maras y Pandillas en Centroamérica*, vol. 1, Managua: UCA Publicaciones, pp. 219–332.

Chin, K. 1990. Chinese gangs and extortion, in C. R. Huff (ed.), *Gangs in America*, Newbury Park: Sage, pp. 129–145.

Cloward, R. A., and L. E. Ohlin. 1960. *Delinquency and Opportunity: A Theory of Delinquent Gangs*, New York: Free Press.

Cohen, A. K. 1955. *Delinquent Boys: The Culture of the Gang*, New York: Free Press.

Cohen, A. K. 1990. Foreword and overview, in C. R. Huff (ed.), *Gangs in America*, Newbury Park: Sage.

Collins, R. 2008. *Violence: A Micro-Sociological Theory*, Princeton: Princeton University Press.

Comaroff, J., and J. Comaroff. 2005. Reflections on youth, from the Past to the Postcolony, in A. Honwana, and F. De Boeck (eds.), *Makers and Breakers: Children and Youth in Postcolonial Africa*, London: James Currey, pp. 19–30.

Corsetti, J. D. 2006. Marked for death: The maras of Central America and those who flee their wrath, *Georgetown Immigration Law Journal*, vol. 20, no. 3, pp. 407–436.

Covey, H. C. 2003. *Street Gangs throughout the World*, Springfield: Charles C. Thomas.

Covey, H. C., S. Menard, and R. J. Franzese. 1992. *Juvenile Gangs*, Springfield: Charles C. Thomas.

Cruz, J. M., and N. Portillo Peña. 1998. *Solidaridad y Violencia en las Pandillas del Gran San Salvador: Más Allá de la Vida Loca*, San Salvador: UCA Editores.

Cuadra, S. 2003. Globalization and the capacity of violence to transform social spaces: Some critical points about the Latin America debate, *Crime, Law & Social Change*, vol. 39, no. 2, pp. 163–173.

Cuerno, L. 2000. El lado oscuro de la calle: El caso extremo de las maras, *JOVENes: Revista de Estudios sobre Juventud*, vol. 4, no. 10, pp. 62–77.

Cummings, L. L. 1994. Fighting by the rules: Women street-fighting in Chihuahua, Chihuahua, Mexico, *Sex Roles*, vol. 30, no. 3/4, pp. 189–198.

Curry, G. D., and I. A. Spergel. 1988. Gang homicide, delinquency and community, *Criminology*, vol. 26, no. 3, pp. 381–405.

Daiute, C., and M. Fine. 2003. Youth perspectives on violence and injustice, *Journal of Social Issues*, vol. 59, no. 1, pp. 1–14.

DeFleur, L. B. 1970. *Delinquency in Argentina: A Study of Córdoba's Youth*, Pullman: Washington State University.

Demoscopía. 2007. *Maras y Pandillas, Comunidad y Policía en Centroamérica*, San José: Demoscopía.

Dowdney, L. 2005. *Neither War nor Peace: International Comparisons of Children and Youth in Organised Armed Violence*, Rio de Janeiro: Coalition in Organized Armed Violence.

Dubet, F. 1987. *La Galère: Jeunes en Survie*, Paris: Fayard.

ERIC, IDESO, IDIES, and IUDOP. 2001. *Maras y Pandillas en Centroamérica*, vol. 1, Managua: UCA Publicaciones.

ERIC, IDESO, IDIES, and IUDOP. 2004a. *Maras y Pandillas en Centroamérica: Pandillas y Capital Social*, vol. 2, San Salvador: UCA Publicaciones.

ERIC, IDESO, IUDOP, NITLAPAN, and DIRINPRO. 2004b. *Maras y Pandillas en Centroamérica: Políticas Juveniles y Rehabilitación*, vol. 3, Managua: UCA Publicaciones.

Erickson, M. L., and G. F. Jensen. 1977. Delinquency is still group behavior! Toward revitalizing the group premise in the sociology of deviance, *Journal of Criminal Law and Criminology*, vol. 68, no. 2, pp. 262–273.

Fagan, J. 1990. Social processes of delinquency and drug use among urban gangs, in C. R. Huff (ed.), *Gangs in America*, Newbury Park: Sage, pp. 183–219.

Fajnzylber, P., D. Lederman, and N. Loayza. 2002. Inequality and violent crime, *The Journal of Law and Economics*, vol. 45, no. 1, pp. 1–39.

Feixa, C., N. Canelles, L. Porzia, C. Recio, and L. Giliberti. 2008. Latin kings in Barcelona, in F. van Gemert, D. Peterson, and I. L. Lien (eds.), *Street Gangs, Migration and Ethnicity*, Cullompten: Willan, pp. 63–78.

Ferrándiz, F. 2004. The body as wound: Possession, malandros and everyday violence in Venezuela, *Critique of Anthropology*, vol. 24, no. 2, pp. 107–133.

Frühling, H., J. S. Tulchin, and H. A. Golding. 2003. *Crime and Violence in Latin America: Citizen Security, Democracy, and the State*, Baltimore: John Hopkins University Press.

Gay, R. 2005. *Lucia: Testimonies of a Brazilian Drug Dealer's Woman*, Philadelphia: Temple University Press.

Giordano, P. C. 1978. Girls, guys, and gangs: The changing context of female delinquency, *Journal of Criminal Law and Criminology*, vol. 69, no. 1, pp. 126–132.

Godoy, A. S. 1999. "Our right is the right to be killed": Making rights real on the streets of Guatemala City, *Childhood*, vol. 6, no. 4, pp. 423–442.

Godoy, A. S. 2006. *Popular Injustice: Violence, Community, and Law in Latin America*, Stanford: Stanford University Press.

Goldstein, D. 2003. *Laughter out of Place: Race, Class, Violence and Sexuality in a Rio Shantytown*, Berkeley: University of California Press.

Goldstone, J. A. 2001. Demography, environment, and security, in P. F. Diehl, and N. Petter Gleditsch (eds.), *Environmental Conflict*, Boulder: Westview Press, pp. 84–108.

González, L. A. 2003. El plan "mano dura": Burda politización de un problema social, *Estudios Centroamericanos*, vol. 658, pp. 783–787.

Hagedorn, J. 1988. *People and Folks: Gangs, Crime and the Underclass in a Rustbelt City*, Chicago: Lakeview Press.

Hagedorn, J. 2008. *A World of Gangs: Armed Young Men and Gangsta Culture*, Minneapolis: University of Minnesota Press.

Harris, M. G. 1988. *Cholas: Latino Girls and Gang*, New York: AMS Press.

Holston, J., and T. P. R. Caldeira. 1998. Democracy, law, and violence: Disjunctions of Brazilian citizenship, in F. Agüero and J. Stark (eds.), *Fault Lines of Democracy in Post-transition Latin America*, Coral Gables: North-South Center Press/ University of Miami, and Boulder: Lynne Rienner Publishers, pp. 263–296.

Hopper, C. B., and J. Moore. 1990. Women in outlaw motorcycle gangs, *Journal of Contemporary Ethnography*, vol. 18, no. 4, pp. 363–387.

Horowitz, R. 1983. *Honor and the American Dream: Culture and Identity in a Chicano Community*, New Brunswick: Rutgers University Press.

Horowitz, R. 1990. Sociological perspectives on gangs: Conflicting definitions and concepts, in C. R. Huff (ed.), *Gangs in America*, Newbury Park: Sage, pp. 37–54.

Huggins, M. K., and M. M. P. De Castro. 1996. Exclusion, civic invisibility and impunity as explanations for youth murders in Brazil, *Childhood*, vol. 3, no. 1, pp. 77–98.

Huggins, M. K., M. Haritos-Fatouros and P. G. Zimbardo. 2002. *Violence Workers: Police Torturers and Murderers Reconstruct Brazilian Atrocities*, Berkeley: University of California Press.

Huhn, S., A. Oettler, and P. Peetz. 2006a. *Exploding Crime? Topic Management in Central American Newspapers*, German Institute of Global and Area (GIGA) Studies Working Paper No. 33, Hamburg: GIGA.

Huhn, S., A. Oettler, and P. Peetz. 2006b. *Construyendo Inseguridades: Aproximaciones a la Violencia en Centroamérica desde el Análisis del Discurso*, German Institute of Global and Area Studies Working Paper No. 34, Hamburg: GIGA.

Hume, M. 2004. "It's as if you don't know, because you don't do anything about it": Gender and violence in El Salvador, *Environment and Urbanization*, vol. 16, no. 2, pp. 63–72.

Hume, M. 2007a. (Young) men with big guns: Reflexive encounters with violence and youth in El Salvador, *Bulletin of Latin American Research*, vol. 26, no. 4, pp. 480–496.

Hume, M. 2007b. Mano dura: El Salvador responds to gangs, *Development in Practice*, vol. 17, no. 6, pp. 739–751.

IKV Pax Christi. 2008. *Kidnapping is Booming Business: A Lucrative Political Instrument for Armed Groups Operating in Conflict zones*, http://www. ikvpaxchristi.nl/files/Documenten/LA%20Colombia/English%20Colombia/ Eng%20brochure_Opmaak%201.pdf [accessed January 14, 2009].

Joint Operating Environment (JOE). 2008. *Challenges and Implications for the Future Joint Force*, Suffolk: United States Joint Forces Command, https//us.jfcom.mil/sites/J5/j59/default.aspx [accessed January 14, 2009].

Jones, G. A., E. Herrera, and S. Thomas de Benítez. 2007. Tears, trauma and suicide: Everyday violence among street youth in Puebla, Mexico, *Bulletin of Latin American Research*, vol. 26, no. 4, pp. 462–479.

Katz, J. 1988. *Seductions of Crime*, New York: Basic Books.

Kay, C. 2001. Reflections on rural violence in Latin America, *Third World Quarterly*, vol. 22, no. 5, pp. 741–775.

Kessler, G. 2004. *Sociología del Delito Amateur*, Buenos Aires: Paidós.

Klein, M. W. 1995. *The American Street Gang: Its Nature, Prevalence, and Control*, New York: Oxford University Press.

Klein, M. W., and C. L. Maxson. 1989. Street gang violence, in N. A. Weiner, and M. E. Wolfgang (eds.), *Violent Crime, Violent Criminals*, Newbury Park: Sage, pp. 198–234.

Koonings, K., and D. Kruijt. (eds.). 1999. *Societies of Fear: The Legacy of Civil War, Violence and Terror in Latin America*, London: Zed.

Koonings, K., and D. Kruijt. (eds.). 2004. *Armed Actors: Organised Violence and State Failure in Latin America*, London: Zed.

Kruijt, D. 2008. Violencia y pobreza en América Latina: Los actores armados, *Pensamiento Iberoamericano*, no. 2, pp. 57–70.

Kuasñosky, S., and D. Szulik. 1996. Desde los márgenes de la juventud, in M. Margulis (ed.), *La Juventud es Más que una Palabra: Ensayos sobre Cultura y Juventud*, Buenos Aires: Editorial Biblos, pp. 47–68.

Kuasñosky, S., and D. Szulik. 1997. Los extraños de pelo largo: Vida cotidiana y consumos culturales, in M. Margulis (ed.), *La Cultura de la Noche: La Vida Nocturna de los Jóvenes en Buenos Aires*, 2nd edition, Buenos Aires: Editorial Biblos, pp. 263–292.

Lara Klahr, M. 2006. *Hoy te Toca la Muerte: El Imperio de las Maras Visto desde Adentro*, Mexico City: Planeta.

Leeds, E. 1996. Cocaine and the parallel polities in the Brazilian urban periphery: Constraints on local-level democratization, *Latin American Research Review*, vol. 31, no. 3, pp. 47–83.

Levenson, D. (with the assistance of N. M. Figueroa and M. Y. Maldonado Castilla). 1988. *Por Sí Mismos: Un Estudio Preliminar des las "Maras" en la Ciudad de Guatemala*, Cuaderno de Investigación No. 4, Guatemala: Asociación para el Avance de las Ciencias Sociales en Guatemala (AVANCSO).

Liebel, M. (2004). Pandillas juveniles en Centroamérica o la difícil búsqueda de justicia en una sociedad violenta, *Desacatos*, no. 14, pp. 85–104.

Lins, P. 1997. *Cidade de Deus*, São Paulo: Companhia das Letras.

Londoño, J. L., and R. Guererro. 1999. *Violencia en América Latina: Epidemiología y Costos*, Research Network Working Paper R-375, Washington: Inter-American Development Bank.

Macaulay, F. 2007. Knowledge production, framing and criminal justice reform in Latin America, *Journal of Latin American Studies*, vol. 39, no. 3, pp. 627–651.

Manwaring, M. G. 2005. *Street Gangs: The New Urban Insurgency*, Carlisle: Strategic Studies Institute, U.S. Army War College.

Manwaring, M. G. 2006. Gangs and coups d'streets in the new world disorder: Protean insurgents in post-modern war, *Global Crime*, vol. 7, no. 3–4, pp. 505–543.

Manwaring, M. G. 2008. *A Contemporary Challenge to State Sovereignty: Gangs and Other Illicit Transnational Criminal Organizations (TCOs) in Central America,*

El Salvador, Mexico, Jamaica, and Brazil, Carlisle: Strategic Studies Institute, U.S. Army War College.

Martel Trigueros, R. 2007. Las maras Salvadoreñas: Nuevas formas de espanto y control social, in J. M. Valenzuela Arce, A. Nateras Domínguez, and R. Reguillo Cruz (eds.) *Las Maras: Identidades Juveniles al Limite,* Mexico City: Universidad Autónoma Metropolitana Iztapalapa, pp. 83–126.

Mead, M. 1928. *Coming of Age in Western Samoa,* New York: William Morrow & Co.

Merino, J. 2001. Las maras en Guatemala, in ERIC, IDESO, IDIES, and IUDOP (eds.), *Maras y Pandillas en Centroamérica,* vol. 1, Managua, UCA Publicaciones, pp. 109–217.

Miller, W. B. 1982. *Crime by Youth Gangs and Youth Groups in the United States,* Washington: Office of Juvenile Justice and Delinquency Prevention.

Miraglia, P. 2005. *Between me and you and among us: Homicides, gangs and individuals in the periphery of São Paulo,* paper presented at the conference on Youth Violence in Latin America: Gangs, Street Children, and Juvenile Justice in Perspective, London School of Economics and University of London Institute for the Study of the Americas, May 26–27.

Miranda, M. 2003. *Homegirls in the Public Sphere,* Austin: University of Texas Press.

Moore, J. 1978. *Homeboys: Gangs, Drugs, and Prison in the Barrios of Los Angeles,* Philadelphia: Temple University Press.

Morrison, A., M. Ellsberg, and S. Bott. 2004. *Addressing Gender-Based Violence in theLatin American and Caribbean Region: A Critical Review of Interventions,* World Bank Policy Research Working Paper No. 3438, Washington: World Bank.

Moser, C. O. N., and C. McIlwaine. 2004. *Encounters with Violence in Latin America: Urban Poor Perceptions from Colombia and Guatemala,* London: Routledge.

Núñez, J. C. 1996. *De la Ciudad al Barrio: Redes y Tejidos Urbanos en Guatemala, El Salvador y Nicaragua,* Ciudad de Guatemala: Universidad Rafael Landívar/ PROFASR.

Papachristos, A. V. 2005. Gang world, *Foreign Policy,* no. 147, pp. 48–55.

Penglase, B. 2005. The shutdown of Rio de Janeiro, *Anthropology Today,* vol. 21, no. 5, pp. 3–6.

Penglase, B. 2007. Barbarians on the beach: Media narratives of violence in Rio de Janeiro, Brazil, *Crime, Media, Culture,* vol. 3, no. 3, pp. 305–325.

Perea Restrepo, C. M. 2004. Pandillas y conflict urbano en Colombia, *Desacatos,* vol. 14, pp. 15–35.

Perea Restrepo, C. M. 2007. Pandillas y sociedad contemporánea, in J. M. Valenzuela Arce, A. Nateras Domínguez, and R. Reguillo Cruz (eds.) *Las Maras: Identidades Juveniles al limite,* Mexico City: Universidad Autónoma Metropolitana Iztapalapa, pp. 271–306.

Pereira Leite, M. 2005. Miedo y representación Comunitaria en las favelas de Rio de Janeiro: Los invisibles exiliados de la violencia, in R. Reguillo and M. Godoy Anativia (eds.), *Ciudades Translocales: Espacios, Flujo, Representación. Perspectivas desde las Américas,* Tlaquepaque: ITESO, pp. 365–392.

Perlman, J. E. 1976. *The Myth of Marginality: Urban Poverty and Politics in Rio de Janeiro,* Berkeley: University of California Press.

Perlman, J. E. 2006. The metamorphosis of marginality: Four generations in the favelas of Rio de Janeiro, *The ANNALS of the American Academy of Political and Social Science,* vol. 606, no. 1, pp. 154–177.

Pinheiro, P. S. 2006. *World Report on Violence against Children*, Geneva: United Nations.

PNUD (Programa de las Naciones Unidas para el Desarrollo—United Nations Development Programme). 2007. *Informe Estadístico de la Violencia en Guatemala*, Ciudad de Guatemala: PNUD.

Portocarrero, B. 1996. El lumpen pituco: Bad boys, *QueHacer*, no. 104, pp. 70–73.

Reguillo, R. 1991. *En la Calle Otra Vez: Las Bandas Juveniles, Identidad Urbana y Usos de la Comunicación*, Guadalajara: ITESO.

Reguillo, R. 2005. La mara: Contingencia y afiliación con el exceso, *Nueva Sociedad*, vol. 200, pp. 70–84.

Revista Centroamericana. 1994. Violencia juvenil en Centroamérica, *Revista Centroamericana*, no. 2, pp. 4–9.

Riano-Alcala, P. 2006. *Dwellers of Memory: Youth, Memory, and Violence in Medellin, Colombia*, New Brunswick: Transaction Publishers.

Rocha, J. L. 2000a. Pandilleros: La mano que empuña el mortero, *Envío*, no. 216, pp. 17–25.

Rocha, J. L. 2000b. Pandillas: Una cárcel cultural, *Envío*, no. 219, pp. 13–22.

Rocha, J. L. 2003. Tatuajes de pandilleros: Estigma, identidad y arte, *Envío*, no. 258, pp. 42–50.

Rocha, J. L. 2005. El traido: Clave de la continuidad de las pandillas, *Envío*, no. 280, pp. 35–41.

Rocha, J. L., and D. Rodgers. 2008. *Bróderes Descobijados y Vagos Alucinados: Una Década con las Pandillas Nicaragüenses 1997–2007*, Managua: Envío.

Rodgers, D. 1997. Un antropólogo-pandillero en un barrio de Managua, *Envío*, no. 184, pp. 10–16.

Rodgers, D. 1999. *Youth Gangs and Violence in Latin America and the Caribbean: A Literature Survey*, Latin America and Caribbean Region Sustainable Development Urban Peace Program Working Paper No. 4, Washington: World Bank.

Rodgers, D. 2000. *Living in the Shadow of Death: Violence*, Pandillas, *and Social Disintegration in Contemporary Urban Nicaragua*, unpublished PhD dissertation, Department of Social Anthropology, University of Cambridge, United Kingdom.

Rodgers, D. 2006a. Living in the shadow of death: Gangs, violence, and social order in urban Nicaragua, 1996–2002, *Journal of Latin American Studies*, vol. 38, no. 2, pp. 267–292.

Rodgers, D. 2006b. The state as a gang: Conceptualising the governmentality of violence in contemporary Nicaragua, *Critique of Anthropology*, vol. 26, no. 3, pp. 315–30.

Rodgers, D. 2007a. Joining the gang and becoming a *broder*: The violence of ethnography in contemporary Nicaragua, *Bulletin of Latin American Research*, vol. 26, no. 4, pp. 444–461.

Rodgers, D. 2007b. When vigilantes turn bad: Gangs, violence, and social change in urban Nicaragua, in D. Pratten and A. Sen (eds.), *Global Vigilantes*, London: Hurst, pp. 349–370.

Rodgers, D. 2009. Slum Wars of the 21st Century: Gangs, *Mano Dura*, and the New Geography of Conflict in Central America, *Development and Change*, forthcoming.

Rodgers, D., R. Muggah, and C. Stevenson. 2009. *Gangs of Central America: Causes, Costs, and Interventions*, Small Arms Survey Occasional Paper no. 23, Geneva: Small Arms Survey.

Rubio, M. 2007. *De la Pandilla a la Mara: Pobreza, Educación, Mujeres y Violencia Juvenil*, Bogotá: Universidad Externado de Colombia.

Salazar Jaramillo, A. 1990. *No Nacimos Pa' semilla*, Medellín: Corporación Región.

Salomón, L., J. Castellanos, and M. Flores. 1999. *La Delincuencia Juvenil: Los Menores Infractores en Honduras*, Tegucigalpa: CEDOH.

Sánchez Jankowski, M. 1991. *Islands in the Street: Gangs and American Urban Society*, Berkeley: University of California Press.

Sánchez, M. 2006. Insecurity and violence as a new power relation in Latin America, *The ANNALS of the American Academy of Political and Social Science*, vol. 606, no. 1, pp. 178–195.

Saraví, G. A. 2004. Juventud y violencia en América Latina: Reflexiones sobre exclusión social y crisis urbana, *Desacatos*, no. 14, pp. 127–142.

Savenije, W., and K. Andrade-Eekhoff. (eds.). 2003. *Conviviendo en la Orilla: Violencia y Exclusión Social en el Area Metropolitana de San Salvador*, San Salvador: FLACSO.

Schneider, J., and P. Schneider. 2008. The anthropology of crime and criminalization, *Annual Review of Anthropology*, vol. 37, pp. 351–373.

Shaw, C. R., and H. D. McKay. 1942. *Juvenile Delinquency and Urban Areas*. Chicago, University of Chicago Press.

Short, Jr., J. F. 1968. *Gang Delinquency and Delinquent Subcultures*, New York: Harper and Row.

Short, Jr., J. F., and F. Strodtbeck. 1965. *Group Process and Gang Delinquency*, Chicago: University of Chicago Press.

Soares, L. E., J. T. S. Sé, J. Rodrigues, and L. Piquet Cerneiro. 1996. *Violencia e Politica no Rio de Janeiro*, Rio de Janeiro: Editora Relume.

Soares, L. E., M. V. Bill, and C. Athayde. 2005. *Cabeca de Porco*, Rio de Janeiro: Editora Objetiva.

Spergel, I. A. 1984. Violent gangs in Chicago: In search of social policy, *Social Service Review*, vol. 58, no. 2, pp. 199–226.

Stafford, M. 1984. Gang delinquency, in R. E. Meier (ed.), *Major Forms of Crime*, Beverly Hills: Sage, pp. 167–190.

Strocka, C. 2006. Youth gangs in Latin America, *SAIS Review*, vol. 26, no. 2, pp. 133–146.

Sullivan, J. P. 2006. Maras morphing: Revisiting third generation gangs, *Global Crime*, vol. 7, no. 3, pp. 487–504.

Suttles, G. D. 1968. *The Social Order of the Slum: Ethnicity and Territory in the Inner City*, Chicago: University of Chicago Press.

Suttles, G. D. 1972. *The Social Construction of Communities*, Chicago: University of Chicago Press.

Taussig, M. 1987. *Shamanism, Colonialism, and the Wild Man: A Study in Terror and Healing*, Chicago, University of Chicago Press.

Thrasher, F. M. 1927. *The Gang: A Study of 1313 Gangs in Chicago*, Chicago: The University of Chicago Press.

UNODC (United Nations Office on Drugs and Crime). 2007. *Crime and Development in Central America: Caught in the Crossfire*, Vienna: UNODC.

Urdal, H. 2007. The demographics of political violence: Youth bulges, insecurity and conflict, in L. Brainard and D. Chollet (eds.), *Too Poor for Peace? Global Poverty, Conflict and Security in the 21st Century*, Washington: Brookings Institution Press, pp. 90–100.

USAID. 2006. *Central America and Mexico Gangs Assessment*, Washington: USAID.

Vásquez, M. A., and M. F. Marquardt. 2003. *Globalizing the Sacred: Religion across the Americas*, New Brunswick: Rutgers University Press.

Vermeij, P. J. 2006. *That's Life: Community Perceptions of Informality, Violence, and Fear in two Spontaneous Human Settlements in Managua, Nicaragua*, unpublished MA thesis, Latin American and Caribbean Studies programme, Utrecht University, Holland.

Vigil, J. D. 1988. *Barrio Gangs: Street Life and Identity in Southern California*, Austin: University of Texas Press.

Weaver, K., and M. Maddaleno. 1999. Youth violence in Latin America: Current situation and violence prevention strategies, *Revista Panamericana de Salud Pública*, vol. 5, no. 4–5, pp. 338–343.

Whitehead, N. L. 2004. On the poetics of violence, in N. L. Whitehead (ed.), *Violence*, Santa Fe: School of American Research, pp. 55–77.

WHO (World Health Organization). 2002. *World Report on Violence and Health*, Geneva: WHO.

Whyte, W. F. 1943. *Street Corner Society: The Structure of an Italian Slum*, 2nd edition (enlarged), Chicago: University of Chicago Press.

Winton, A. 2004. Young people's view on how to tackle gang-violence in "post-conflict" Guatemala, *Environment and Urbanization*, vol. 16, no. 2, pp. 83–99.

Winton, A. 2007, Using "participatory" methods with young people in contexts of violence: Reflections from Guatemala, *Bulletin of Latin American Research*, vol. 27, no. 4, pp. 497–515.

Wolseth, J. 2008. Safety and sanctuary: Pentecostalism and youth gang violence in Honduras, *Latin American Perspectives*, vol. 35, no. 4, pp. 96–111.

Wulff, H. 1995. Introducing youth culture in its own right: The state of the art and new possibilities, in V. Amit-Talai and H. Wulff (eds.), *Youth Cultures: A Cross-Cultural Perspective*, London, Routledge, pp. 1–18.

Wyn, J., and R. D. White. 1997. *Rethinking Youth*, London: Sage.

Yablonsky, L. 1963. *The Violent Gang*, New York: Macmillan.

Zaluar, A. 1983. Condomínio do diabo: As classes populares urbanas e a lógica do "Ferro" e do fumo, in P. S. Pinheiro (ed.), *Crime, Violência e Poder*, São Paulo: Brasiliense, pp. 251–277.

Zaluar, A. 1994. *Condomínio do Diabo*, Rio de Janeiro: Editora Revan/UFRJ.

Zaluar, A. 1997. Gangues, galeras e quadrilhas: Globalização, juventude e violência, in H. Vianna (ed.), *Galeras Cariocas: Territórios de Conflitos e Encontros Culturais*, Rio de Janeiro: Editora UFRJ, pp. 17–57.

Zaluar, A. 2000. Perverse integration: Drug trafficking and youth in the favelas of Rio de Janeiro, *Journal of International Affairs*, vol. 53, no. 2, pp. 653–671.

Zilberg, E. 2004. Fools banished from the kingdom: Remapping geographies of gang violence between the Americas (Los Angeles and San Salvador), *American Quarterly*, vol. 56, no. 3, pp. 759–779.

Zilberg, E. 2007. Gangster in guerrilla face: A transnational mirror of production between the USA and El Salvador, *Anthropological Theory*, vol. 7, no. 1, pp. 37–57.

Zubillaga, V., and R. Briceño-León. 2001. Exclusión, masculinidad y respeto: Algunas claves para entender la violencia entre adolescentes en barrios, *Nueva Sociedad*, vol. 173, pp. 34–48.

Chapter 2

Living in the Shadow of Death: Gangs, Violence, and Social Order in Urban Nicaragua, 1996–2002

Dennis Rodgers

Introduction

The past two decades have seen crime increasingly recognized as a critical social concern. Crime rates have risen globally by an average of 50 percent over the past 25 years, and the phenomenon is widely considered to contribute significantly to human suffering all over the world (Ayres 1998). This is particularly true in Latin America, where contemporary violence has reached unprecedented levels due to rising crime and delinquency (Londoño et al. 2000). This trend has been widely linked to a perceived shift in the political economy of violence in post–Cold War Latin America, with the most visible expressions of brutality no longer stemming from ideological conflicts over the nature of politics, as in the past, but from more "prosaic" forms of everyday violence (Caldeira 1996: 199). Violence in Latin America has arguably "democratized," ceasing to be "the resource of only the traditionally powerful or of the grim uniformed guardians of the nation and increasingly appear[ing] as an option for a multitude of actors in pursuit of all kinds of goals" (Kruijt and Koonings 1999: 11). These new dynamics are seen to be linked to a regional "crisis of governance," whereby economic liberalization, weak democratization, and intensifying globalization have undermined states and their ability to command a monopoly over the use of violence. The emergence of "disorderly" forms of criminal violence epitomizes this declining political authority, and signals a rising social chaos (de Rivero 2001).

This chapter develops a contrary argument and contends that far from embodying incipient anarchy, certain manifestations of this so-called disorderly violence can be conceived as coherent modes of social structuration in the face of processes of state and social breakdown. This claim is made particularly in relation to the most emblematic form of brutality within the new Latin American political economy of criminal violence, namely youth gang violence. The lack of statistical data makes it impossible to determine the exact proportion of criminal violence attributable to youth gangs in Latin America, but they are widespread throughout the region, and as such, constitute a potentially illuminating lens through which to explore the nature of contemporary violence. This chapter presents a case study of a Nicaraguan youth gang, or *pandilla*, based on ethnographic research conducted in *barrio* Luis Fanor Hernández,[1] a low-income neighborhood in Managua, the capital city of Nicaragua.[2] It begins by providing an overview of crime in Nicaragua, including a description of its social consequences, and then continues with an account of the *barrio* Luis Fanor Hernández *pandilla* as it existed in 1996–1997, and then in 2002. A theoretical discussion of the dynamics of *pandillerismo* follows, first situating the phenomenon within its wider sociocultural context before outlining how it can be conceived as a form of local-level social structuration in the face of sociopolitical breakdown.

Crime in Contemporary Nicaragua

Violence is not new to Nicaragua. The country suffered the longest-running dictatorship in modern Latin American history, that of the Somoza dynasty, which was finally overthrown after 45 years in 1979 by the famous *Sandinista* revolution. The triumph of the revolution led to an attritional civil war against the U.S. supported *Contras*, which only came to an end in 1990 following the electoral defeat of the *Sandinistas*. Although the country has formally been at peace since, violence remains an overwhelming reality, particularly in urban areas. Certainly, there has been an explosion in criminal violence during the past 15 years. According to Nicaraguan National Police statistics, crime levels have risen by an average of 10 percent per year since 1990, compared to just 2 percent during the 1980s. The absolute number of crimes more than tripled between 1990 and 2000, with violent crimes such as homicides, rapes, and assaults rising by over 460 percent (Serbin and Ferreyra 2000: 185). Although this upward trend is undoubtedly accurate, the official statistics must be treated with caution (see Godnick et al, 2002: 26).[3] This is particularly true of the homicide rate, which during the 1990s stood at an average of just 16 deaths per 100,000 persons, a suspiciously low level when considered in a regional perspective.[4] I tallied nine crime-related deaths in *barrio* Luis Fanor Hernández in 1996–1997, which works out to a rate of 360 deaths per 100,000 persons. While this calculation is unsystematic and only reflects the situation in one neighborhood, it is nevertheless suggestive that official statistics are underestimations.

Numerous alternative indicators attest to the high levels of crime in contemporary Nicaragua. A CID-Gallup survey conducted in April 1997 reported that one in four inhabitants of Managua had been victims of crime during the previous four months (*La Tribuna* May 2, 1997: 4). Similarly, respondents to a national survey conducted by the NGO *Ética y Transparencia* in 1999 singled out crime as the principal problem affecting the country by a margin of over 30 percent (Cajina 2000: 177). Crime and delinquency were also clearly cardinal preoccupations in *barrio* Luis Fanor Hernández, both in

1996–1997 and 2002. Almost all my informants had been victims of crime at some point, and there was a pervasive sense of insecurity, as *Doña* Yolanda reflected well in an interview in 2002:

> There's so much delinquency, it's impossible to live...they'll kill you for a watch...they'll kill you for a pair of shoes...they'll kill you for your shirt...they're everywhere, you've got to watch out...they could be your neighbor, even your friend, you can never be sure...you can't go out any more, you can't wear rings, bracelets, nice shoes, anything that makes us look a little better than we really are...how can we live? It's not possible...

This insecurity had dramatic effects on local social organization, with the erosion of the social fabric reaching such proportions that it is no exaggeration to talk of a veritable "atomization" of social life (Nitlapán-Envío team 1995).[5] Traditional institutions of social solidarity such as the extended family or *compadrazgo* had shattered, and there were few community networks of trust and mutual aid, as *Don* Sergio described in 1997:

> Nobody does anything for anybody anymore, nobody cares if their neighbor is robbed, nobody does anything for the common good. There's a lack of trust, you don't know whether somebody will return you your favors, or whether he won't steal your belongings when your back is turned. It's the law of the jungle here; we're eating one another, as they say in the Bible...

In 2002, the situation was no better, as *Doña* Yolanda made clear:

> You never feel safe in the *barrio*, because of the lack of trust. There always has to be somebody in the house, because you can't trust anybody to look out for you, for your things, to help you, nothing. People only look out for themselves—everyone, the rich, the poor, the middle class...Life is hard in Nicaragua, and you've just got to look out for yourself and try and survive by hook or by crook. It was the same five years ago; nothing has changed, except that we're now five years on, and the future didn't get any better...

The most prominent actors within this panorama of insecurity are undoubtedly the *pandillas* that roam the streets of Nicaraguan cities, robbing, beating, and frequently killing. The aforementioned *Ética y Transparencia* survey found that gangs were considered the most likely perpetrators of crime by over 50 percent of respondents (Cajina 2000: 177), and over half of all those arrested in Nicaragua in 1997 were young males aged between 13 and 25 years old, which corresponds to a typical *pandillero* age and gender profile, although obviously not all were gang members (Rocha 2000: 20). More discursively, people in *barrio* Luis Fanor Hernández often prefaced their complaints about crime with an expressive "*¡estas pandillas, me matan, te digo, me matan!*" (these gangs, they kill me, I tell you, they kill me!). Indeed, gangs have largely come to symbolically epitomize crime in contemporary Nicaragua, with the words *pandilla* and *pandillerismo* often used interchangeably with "criminality" or "delinquency."[6] At the same time, the word *pandilla* denotes a very definite social institution, consisting of a variably sized group of generally male youths ranging between 7 and 23 years old, who engage in illicit and violent behavior—although not all their activities are illicit or violent—and who have a particular territorial dynamic. Most notably, a *pandilla* tends to be associated with a specific urban neighborhood,[7] although larger neighborhoods often have more than one gang and not all have one, as there clearly needs to be a critical mass of youth in a neighborhood for a gang to emerge, and they tend not to develop in richer neighborhoods.

Although *pandillas* can be traced back to the 1940s in Nicaragua, they were small scale and relatively innocuous youth aggregations until the early 1990s, when their numbers increased massively and they became much more violent. By 1999, the Nicaraguan Police estimated that there were 110 *pandillas* in Managua alone, incorporating 8,500 youths (Policia Nacional de Nicaragua 2001), double the number in 1996, and five times that in 1990, although these statistics undoubtedly err on the low side. The evidence as to whether *pandillerismo* has increased or declined since 1999 is contradictory. The Police insist that the phenomenon is in decline, but Nicaraguan public opinion, media reports, and my informants in *barrio* Luis Fanor Hernández all suggest that gangs are an increasingly overwhelming feature of urban Nicaragua. It has been hypothesized that while the total number of youths involved in *pandillerismo* in Nicaragua may be declining in absolute terms, gangs have simultaneously become smaller in size, such that while there are less *pandilleros*, there are an increasing number of *pandillas* (Sosa Meléndez and Rocha 2001). The case study of the *barrio* Luis Fanor Hernández *pandilla* presented next supports this conjecture, but also suggests that the nature of Nicaraguan *pandillerismo* is not what it is widely thought to be. In particular, gangs emerge less as contributors to the disorder that characterizes contemporary urban Nicaragua and more as attempts to mitigate this ambient insecurity.

The *Barrio* Luis Fanor Hernández *Pandilla* in 1996–1997

In 1996–1997, the barrio Luis Fanor Hernández *pandilla* was made up of about 100 youths, all males aged between 7 and 22 years old. Gang members originated indiscriminately from richer and poorer households, and other stereotypical "determinants," such as family fragmentation, domestic violence, migration, or parental alcoholism, did not seem significant in explaining membership. The only element that systematically affected membership was religious, insofar as there were no evangelical Protestant youths in the *pandilla*. In many ways, this is hardly surprising since many of the activities associated with being a *pandillero*—being violent, stealing, drinking, smoking, or taking drugs—are in contradiction with the tenets of evangelical Protestantism. Furthermore, the totalizing nature of Evangelical Protestantism means that churches often tended to provide a complete organizational framework for their members—more so than the Catholic Church—and thereby constituted an alternative institutional form to the gang for youth. Beyond the gang, Evangelical Protestant churches, small networks of friends, and intermittent groups coming together to play basketball or baseball, however, there was little in the way of alternative local collective social forms for non-*pandillero* youth in *barrio* Luis Fanor Hernández.[8]

The neighborhood gang was subdivided into distinct age and geographical subgroups. There were three age cohorts—the 7–12 years olds, the 13–17 years olds, and those 18 years old and over—and three geographical subgroups, respectively associated with the central area of the neighborhood, the *abajo* (West) side of the neighborhood, and the *arriba* (East) side of the neighborhood. Groups were approximately of equal size: geographically, they ranged between 25–35 individuals, and within this each of the subgroups divided into three age cohorts of 7–14 individuals each. The different geographical subgroups had distinct names, respectively *los de la Calle Ocho* (named after the alleyway where this group congregated), *los Cancheros* (because of a *cancha*, or playing field on that side of the *barrio*) and *los Dragones* (because all its members sported a dragon tattoo). These subgroups generally operated separately, except in the context of gang warfare, when they would come together in order to defend the neighborhood or attack another. At the same time, even if the different groups were very autonomous, individual gang members qualified themselves as members of a generic neighborhood *pandilla*, which was called *Los Sobrevivientes*, in reference to *La Sobrevivencia*, the neighborhood's prerevolutionary name. There also existed a notion of generic neighborhood *pandilla* territory, despite its variable occupation by different geographical subgroups and age cohorts. Moreover, none of the subgroups, whether age- or geography-determined, ever fought each other.

Although *pandilla* behavior patterns often involved violence, not all did. For example, there existed a distinct *pandillero* sartorial "fashion," which included wearing one's t-shirt inside out, sporting an earring and tattoo, and having a partially shaved head. Such practices were to a large extent shared with various segments of the non-*pandillero* youth population, however, as were other nonviolent gang activities such as smoking marijuana, sniffing glue, drinking heavily, or hanging out on street corners, and as such, they did not constitute distinguishing features of *pandillerismo*. In many ways, this is hardly surprising, as *pandilleros* were inevitably situated within a wider youth culture. But while they naturally engaged in the usual activities of youth—they talked, joked, exchanged stories, listened to music, danced, drank, smoked—they also regularly engaged in violent and socially disruptive activities, and it is this that distinguished them from other youth.

There were two major forms of gang violence: delinquency and warfare. Different age groups were involved in different delinquent activities, from low-level pickpocketing and stealing by the youngest, mugging and shoplifting by the middle group, to armed robbery and assault by the oldest. A golden "rule" of delinquency common to all groups, however, was not to prey on local neighborhood inhabitants, and in fact to actively protect them from outside thieves, robbers, and *pandilleros*. This happened frequently, although the *barrio* gang members were not always effective in providing protection. During the course of my fieldwork in the *barrio* in 1996–1997, three inhabitants of the neighborhood died as a result of delinquency by *pandilleros* from other *barrios*. In addition, one *barrio* Luis Fanor Hernández *pandillero* died whilst attempting an assault in another neighborhood. The dynamics of delinquency were clearly social rather than economic. Even if the revenue from delinquent activities was not inconsiderable, amounting on average to about 450 *córdobas* (U.S.$ 50) per month, it was not as important as having a tale to tell the rest of the gang afterwards, with whatever had been stolen becoming a sign of the deed for all to see. Moreover, *pandilleros* never contributed any of their illicit income to their family economy, but always spent it quickly, on cigarettes, alcohol, glue, or marijuana, to be consumed communally with other gang members. Such collective activity contributed to the construction of a sense of identity, based on common emotions and shared pleasures.

Although gang delinquency was more prevalent than gang warfare, the latter was undoubtedly more spectacular, as rival gangs fought each other with weaponry ranging from sticks, stones, and knives to AK-47 automatic rifles, fragmentation grenades, and homemade mortars, with frequently dramatic consequences for both gang members and local populations. During 1996–1997, there were 14 gang wars in *barrio* Luis Fanor Hernández, which left three gang members and two neighborhood inhabitants dead (as well as several hundred injured). Although these gang wars initially seemed highly chaotic, they in fact displayed very regular patterns, almost to the point of being ritualized. The *pandilleros* organized themselves into "companies," and operated in a strategic manner. There was generally a "reserve force," and although weapons were an individual's own property, each gang member was distributed amongst the different "companies" in order to balance out firepower, except when a high powered "attack commando" was needed for a specific tactical purpose. Conflicts revolved around either attacking or protecting a neighborhood, with fighting generally focused either on harming or limiting damage to both neighborhood infrastructure and inhabitants, as well as injuring or killing symbolically important *pandilleros* (their fame being based on having killed a certain number of people or having a distinguishing physical characteristic or mode of behavior, for example).

The first battle of a *pandilla* war typically involved fighting with stones and bare hands, but each new battle involved an escalation of weaponry, first to sticks and staffs, then to knives and broken bottles, then mortars, and eventually to guns, AK-47s, and fragmentation grenades. Although the rate of escalation could vary, its sequence never did, and *pandillas* never began their wars immediately with mortars, guns, or AK-47s. Moreover, battles involved specific patterns of behavior on the part of gang members, intimately linked to what they called "living in the shadow of death" (*ser muerte arriba*). This expression reflected the very real fact that gang members often found themselves in dangerous situations, but it was also about gang members' attitudes and practices. For them, "living in the shadow of death" entailed displaying specific behavior patterns in battle, including flying in the face of danger and exposing oneself purposefully in order to taunt the enemy, taking risks and displaying bravado, whatever the odds and consequences, daring death to do its best. It meant not asking questions or calculating chances, but just going ahead and acting in a cheerfully exuberant manner, with style and panache. In many ways, the idea of "living in the shadow of death" was thus a primary constitutive practice for the *pandilleros*, playing a fundamental role in the construction of the individual gang member self. Gang wars furthermore also contributed to the constitution of the gang as a group, reaffirming the collective unit by emphasizing the distinction between "us" and "them." But *pandilla* warfare was also about a broader form of social construction that related to the wider neighborhood community. Indeed, the *pandilleros* justified their fighting other gangs as an "act of love" for their neighborhood. As one of them called Julio put it, "You show the neighborhood that you love it by putting yourself in danger for people, by protecting them from other *pandillas*...You look after the neighborhood; you help them, keep them safe..."

This is not as implausible as it may initially seem. The ritualized nature of *pandilla* warfare can be conceived as a kind of restraining mechanism; escalation is a positive constitutive process, in which each stage calls for a greater but definite intensity of action, and is always therefore under the actors' control. At the same time, the escalation process also provided local neighborhood inhabitants with a framework through which to organize their lives, acting as an "early warning system." As such, *pandilla* wars can be thought of as having constituted "scripted performances" which offered a means of circumscribing the "all-pervading unpredictability" of violence (Arendt 1969: 5). Although *pandilla* wars had negative effects for the local population, these were indirect, as gangs never directly victimized the local population of their own neighborhood, protecting them instead. The threat to local neighborhood populations stemmed from *other* gangs, whom the local gang would engage with in a prescribed manner, thereby limiting the scope of violence and creating a predictable "safe haven" for local inhabitants. In a wider context of chronic violence and insecurity, this function was a positive one, and local neighborhood inhabitants recognized it as such, even if it was not always 100 percent effective. Although there was deep ambivalence toward gangs among local neighborhood inhabitants, they distinguished between *pandillerismo* in general and the local manifestation of the gang. As *Don* Sergio put it,

> The *pandilla* looks after the neighborhood and screws others; it protects us and allows us to feel a little bit safer, to live our lives a little bit more easily...Gangs are not a good thing, and it's their fault that we have to live with all this insecurity, but that's a problem of *pandillerismo* in general, not of our gang here in the *barrio*. They protect us, help us—without them, things would be much worse for us.[9]

At the same time, however, this positive view of the gang did not only stem from its violent "care" for the neighborhood and the concomitant sense of security it provided. There also existed a clear sense of identification with the local gang and its violent exploits, which was particularly evident in the "communal aesthetic pleasure" (Bloch 1996: 216) that *barrio* inhabitants derived from swapping stories about the gang, exchanging eyewitness accounts, spreading rumors, and retelling various incidents over and over again. The gang thereby became a symbolic index of the neighborhood that furthermore provided a concrete medium through which to enact an otherwise absent form of collective community identity in the *barrio*, and as such, stood in sharp contrast to the ambient atomization and social breakdown.

The *Barrio* Luis Fanor Hernández *Pandilla* in 2002

The *pandilla* had changed radically when I returned to *barrio* Luis Fanor Hernández in 2002, and was now constituted by a single unitary group of just 18 youths aged 17–23 years old known as *Los Dragones* (all of whom had belonged to the *Sobrevivientes* gang *Dragones* subgroup cohort of 13–17 year olds in 1996–1997). Although certain patterns of behavior persisted, such as the *Dragones pandilla's* continued occupation of the *Sobrevivientes pandilla's* territory, others had evolved, including in particular the nature of the group's violent and illicit activities. Gang warfare had disappeared, levels of gang-related violence had increased, and the gang was now intimately connected with a new and thriving local neighborhood cocaine-based drug economy.[10] Cocaine began to be traded in the *barrio* around mid-1999, initially on a small scale by just one individual but rapidly expanding into a three-tiered pyramidal drug economy by the first half of 2000. At the top of the pyramid was the "*narco*," who brought cocaine into the neighborhood. The *narco* only wholesaled his goods, among others to the half a dozen "*púsheres*" who resold the cocaine in smaller quantities or else "cooked" it into crack[11] which they sold from their houses, mainly to a regular clientele which included "*muleros*," the bottom rung of the drug dealing pyramid. *Muleros* sold crack to all-comers on *barrio* street corners, generally in the form of small "*paquetes*" costing 10 *córdobas* (U.S.$ 0.70) each and containing two fixes, known as "*tuquitos*." There were 19 *muleros* in *barrio* Luis Fanor Hernández; 16 were *Dragones pandilleros*—the two non-*mulero pandilleros* were brothers of one who was, and shared in his profits—and the other three were ex-members of the gang.

The *Dragones muleros* hung about on neighborhood street corners as a group, waiting for potential clients to come by, and taking turns selling them drugs. The rewards of such small-scale dealing were substantial: an individual *mulero* could make between 5,000 and 8,500 *córdobas* (U.S.$ 350–600) profit per month, equivalent to between three and five times the average Nicaraguan wage, and considerably higher than a *pandillero's* average income from delinquency in 1996–1997. The spending habits of *pandilleros* had also changed compared to the past. Although a significant proportion of gang members' delinquent income was still spent on items such as alcohol, drugs, and cigarettes, they also bought new items of "conspicuous consumption" such as gold chains, rings, expensive watches, powerful hi-fi systems, and wide-screen televisions, and moreover, a sizeable proportion was also being used to improve the material conditions of gang members' lives and their families. This was reflected in the infrastructural disparities that had developed between drug dealer and non–dealer homes in *barrio* Luis Fanor Hernández, with the former displaying major improvements or having been completely rebuilt. Overall, some 40 percent of the neighborhood seemed to be benefiting from the drug economy, either through direct involvement, or else indirectly, by being related to or employed by somebody involved.

Despite many in the neighborhood benefiting from the drugs trade, there also existed a generalized wider ambivalence toward it. This was partly due to the physical effects of regular crack consumption. Crack is a powerfully addictive drug that can have serious consequences for the health of users. At least half a dozen addicts in *barrio* Luis Fanor Hernández had died since 1999, and those who hadn't often displayed grotesque wasting effects, to the extent that they were popularly referred to as *gárgolas* (gargoyles). But a more important factor contributing to the generalized ambivalence about the drugs trade was the fact that crack consumption had heightened levels of insecurity in the neighborhood. Although marijuana had been widely smoked by the *pandilleros* in 1996–1997, it is a drug that has very different effects from crack; in particular, crack makes users extremely violent, as a *pandillero* called Chucki emphasized:

> This drug, crack, it makes you really violent, I tell you…when I smoke up and somebody insults me, I immediately want to kill them, to get a machete and do them in, to defend myself…I don't stop and think, talk to them, ask them why or whatever…I don't even recognize them, all I want to do is kill them…it's the drug, I tell you, that's where the violence comes from…

Not surprisingly, perhaps, there were more acts of spontaneous public violence occurring in *barrio* Luis Fanor Hernández in 2002 than in 1996–1997, and the majority of them were linked to crack consumption, as Adilia explained:

> The problem is that now, anybody could be a potential danger, if they've smoked some crack, any time…you can't know what they're going to do, with this drug people become more violent, more aggressive, they don't care about anything, they don't recognise you…you don't know what they're thinking or even if they're thinking at all, they could just kill you like that, without a thought…

Although not the only crack users in the *barrio*, the gang was a privileged site of crack consumption, and *pandilleros* were deeply involved in such drug-related violence. At the same time, however, this heightened sense of insecurity and the concomitant ambivalence toward the gang were the consequence of more than just their crack consumption. The *pandilleros* in 2002 were a much more intimidating and threatening presence in the neighborhood, in no small part because the gang was longer imbued with an ethos of "loving" the *barrio*, as one *pandillero* called Roger made clear:

> We couldn't give a fuck about the *barrio* inhabitants anymore...If they get attacked, if they're robbed, if they have problems, who cares? We don't lift a finger to help them anymore, we just laugh instead, hell, we even applaud those who are robbing them...Why should we do anything for them? Now we just hang out in the streets, smoke crack, and rob, and nothing else!

Although crack consumption clearly influenced this changed behavior pattern, it was arguably more a consequence of the gang's intimate association with the local drugs trade per se. In addition to being *muleros*, the gang as a group acted to ensure the proper functioning and protection of the *barrio* drug economy, providing security services to the *narco* and to *púsheres*, roughing up recalcitrant clients or guarding drug shipments as they were moved both within and outside the *barrio*, for example, but also making sure that clients could enter the neighborhood unmolested. Because they would have made it difficult for clients to come into the *barrio*, the ritualized gang wars of the past had therefore disappeared, while at neighborhood level, the gang had instituted a veritable regime of terror. *Pandilleros* would strut about the streets, menacingly displaying guns and machetes, repeatedly verbally warning *barrio* inhabitants of potential retribution if they denounced them or others involved in the drugs trade, and frequently backing these threats up with random acts of violence. *Doña* Yolanda summarized the overall situation in the following way:

> Five years ago, you could trust the *pandilleros*, but not anymore...They've become corrupted due to this drug crack...They threaten, attack people from the *barrio* now, rob them of whatever they have, whoever they are...They never did that before...They used to protect us, look out for us, but now they don't care, they only look out for themselves, for their illegal business (*bisnes*)...People are scared, you've got to be careful what you say or what you do, because otherwise they'll attack you...Even if you say nothing, they might still come and rob you, come into your home, steal a chair, food, some clothes, whatever they can find...They often do, you know it's them, but you can't blame them, otherwise they'll come and burn your house down...It's their way of telling you to be careful...If you say anything to them, if you do anything, if you denounce them, then they'll come at night and wreak their vengeance...We live in terror here in the *barrio*, you have to be scared or else you're sure to be sorry...It's not like it used to be when you were here last time, Dennis, when the *pandilleros* were kids we could be proud of because of what they did for us and for the *barrio*...They're like strangers to us now, they just

do things for themselves and never for the good of the community like before...

Gangs, Violence, and Social Order in Urban Nicaragua

There exist a number of competing theories within the social sciences purporting to explain why youth gangs emerge. These include social ecology arguments that gangs are partial replacement structures for institutions such as families that have become dysfunctional as a result of the "social disorganization" of poverty and social exclusion (Whyte 1943), cultural theories that gangs are reflections of lower class "subculture" (Cohen 1955), political visions of gangs as forms of resistance to "blocked" opportunities (Cloward and Ohlin 1960), economic conceptions treating gangs as informal business enterprises (Sánchez Jankowski 1991), and psychological interpretations of gangs either as the result of gang members' deviant sociopathological personality traits (Yablonksy 1963), or else as vehicles for youth maturation processes and identity creation (Bloch and Niederhoffer 1958). It is beyond the scope of this chapter to attempt to consider which of these approaches is most persuasive. Moreover, as Ruth Horowitz (1990: 53) has sensibly pointed out, to a large extent they correspond to different dimensions of the gang experience that cannot be easily separated in practice. Seen in this way, rather than trying to establish any kind of bottom-line determination about gangs, it is perhaps more fruitful to attempt to provide a sense of the varied intertwined factors that underlie them instead, examining how these interact and specifically influence their emergence.

This is an especially appropriate strategy to adopt in relation to Nicaraguan *pandillerismo* considering the way it is a social form that is very evidently embedded within wider sociocultural norms and structures. Perhaps the most immediately obvious is the long history of violence that characterizes Nicaragua. There are clear links between the dynamics of *pandilla* violence and the war in Nicaragua during the 1980s, for example. The *barrio* Luis Fanor Hernández *pandilla's* militaristic organization into "companies" and "commandoes" during gang warfare is an obvious example, as is the gang members' familiarity with firearms and other weapons usually associated with martial situations. Sometimes the association is more subtle, though, such as the fact that *pandilleros* rarely went into battle against other gangs drunk or high on drugs, maintaining (quite rightly) that this reduced their capabilities, thereby echoing a similar norm proscribing drinking on combat duty maintained by *Sandinista* guerrillas during the years of revolutionary insurrection. At the same time, however, the history of violence does not explain the emergence of gangs as such. As previously mentioned, *pandillerismo* in Nicaragua has antecedents going back to the 1940s, which was a period of relative peace in the country. The phenomenon moreover almost completely disappeared during the war years of the 1980s, partly due to military conscription, as well as the extensive organized neighborhood vigilance promoted by the *Sandinista* regime, but reemerged with the end of the civil war in 1990. The early 1990s in fact saw an explosion in gang formation, suggesting that the phenomenon was less a consequence of the war but rather of the advent of peace.

This was strongly supported by interviews conducted with ex-*pandilleros* from this period in *barrio* Luis Fanor Hernández and in another neighborhood called *barrio* 3–80 that was established by postwar returnee *Contras* and their families in 1990–1991. The vast majority of these ex-*pandilleros* had been 16- to 20-year-old youths in 1990, freshly demobilized from the *Sandinista* Popular Army and the *Contra* forces. They systematically mentioned three basic reasons for joining a gang during this period. Firstly, the change of regime in 1990 led to a devaluation of their social status, which as conscripts defending the Nation, or as "freedom fighters," had been high within their respective social contexts, and becoming *pandilleros* had seemed a means of reaffirming themselves vis-à-vis a wider society that seemed to very rapidly "forget" them. Secondly, becoming *pandilleros* had been a way of recapturing some of the dramatic, yet marking and almost addictive, adrenaline-charged experiences of war, danger, and death, as well as of comradeship and solidarity that they had lived through as conscripts or guerrillas, and which were rapidly becoming scarce commodities in postwar Nicaragua. Finally, becoming *pandilleros* had seemed to many a natural continuation of their previous roles as conscripts or guerrillas. The early 1990s had been highly uncertain times, marked by political polarization, violence, and spiraling insecurity, and by joining a gang these youths felt they could "serve" their friends and families by "protecting" them more effectively than as individuals.

These motivations for forming a gang could be interpreted as providing substance to an interpretation of *pandillerismo* as something of a perverse "subculture of violence" resulting from the trauma and reintegration difficulties of (young) ex-combatants. A crucial aspect of *pandillerismo* that cautions against such an analysis, however, is that being a gang member in Nicaragua is a finite social role. Generally, at some point between 18 and 23 years of age *pandilleros* "mature out" of the gang,[12] either integrating mainstream society or else becoming *tamales* (professional criminals). Most-about 85–90 percent in the case of the *barrio* Luis Fanor Hernández *pandilleros*—join the mainstream rather than turning to full-time crime, but either way, the process of "maturing out" means that by the mid-1990s the majority of the demobilized ex-*Sandinista* Popular Army and ex-*Contra* conscripts who had made up the first wave of post-1990 *pandillerismo* were no longer gang members, and had been replaced by new youths who had no direct experiences of the traumas of civil war. The fact that most *pandilleros* do eventually integrate into mainstream life and society implies that they actually share mainstream values, and that *pandillerismo* is therefore not a perverse "subculture."

This is not to say that a *pandilla* does not constitute a locus of particular values, however. As Ulf Hannerz (1969) has argued, an individual's "cultural repertoire" is largely situational. Because *pandilleros* are embedded within larger social contexts and do not socialize solely within the gang—but also with their families and wider *barrio* inhabitants, for example—they are also exposed to mainstream social practices. These enter their individual repertoires and indeed are often "used" in relation to situations that do not touch directly on gang activities. While individuals are in the *pandilla*, however, their *pandillero* social role will be their primary one, and the corresponding cultural repertoire will be dominant, with their mainstream "cultural repertoire" constituting a secondary resource. Seen in this way, what "maturing out" of the gang signals is a reversal of an individual's hierarchy of repertoires, with the mainstream one becoming dominant. This was well illustrated by Elvis's response when I asked him in 2002 why he was not longer a gang member:

> The majority of those who were *pandilleros* then now have children, Dennis, and when you have children, you of course want to distance yourself from the whole *pandilla* thing, you know that you have to work in order to support your family, you've got to become like everybody else and you can't hang out in the streets anymore.

It might be tempting to interpret *pandillerismo* as something of a rite of passage for Nicaraguan youth. Certainly, there is a long-standing association between youth and violence in Nicaragua. In the late 1920s, one of the rebel general Augusto César Sandino's lieutenants was the 17-year-old Santos López, for example, and a striking feature of the *Sandinista* Revolution noted by many commentators was the youthfulness of the *Sandinista* fighters. It is doubtful, though, whether either violence in general, or *pandillerismo* in particular, constitute features of a general Nicaraguan youth life cycle, because not all Nicaraguan youth are violent nor do they all join *pandillas* (about 15 percent of *barrio* Luis Fanor Hernández youth joined the gang in 1996–1997, and much less in 2002). A similar logic arguably applies to the relationship between *pandillerismo* and another major structural feature of Nicaraguan society with which it is often associated, namely *machismo*. The concept of *machismo* encompasses a number of traditional ideas about masculinity and femininity, drawing them together into an ideological system that provides templates for accepted and acceptable social behavior patterns on the part of both men and women. As noted above, Nicaraguan gangs are almost exclusively constituted of male youths, and this gender bias certainly derives partly from the fact that being a *pandillero* involves behavior patterns that revolve around activities that are "very much the essence of machismo's ideal of manhood" (Lancaster 1992: 195), such as taking risks or displaying bravado in the face of danger, and therefore inherently challenges Nicaraguan *machismo's* ideal of womanhood, which is associated with subordination and "domestic roles, especially mothering" (Montoya 2003: 63). Seen in this way, *pandillerismo* can arguably be considered a heightened expression of *machismo*.

While this is no doubt the case up to a point, it should also be noted that female gang members are not completely unknown in Nicaragua. According to newspaper reports and urban legend there were two all-female *pandillas* in Managua in 1997, one in *barrio* 19 de Julio, and the other in the *Ciudad* Sandino satellite city. Moreover, although the *barrio* Luis Fanor Hernández *pandilla* was all male in both the mid-1990s and early 2000s, there had been a female member in the gang in the early 1990s. Her femininity was very obviously downplayed whenever contemporary *pandilleros* talked about her, however. She was invariably described as having been extremely violent and fearless, both of which reflected the *machismo*-inspired ideal of what a gang member should be, and therefore arguably had something of a "masculinized" status, which implicitly suggests an absence of female roles within the *pandilla*. Although this "masculinization" process can be said to support the notion of a link between *machismo* and *pandillerismo* up to a point, it also highlights the dangers of making blanket assertions about the potential relationship between a structural feature and a specific social practice, however.

Simply attributing *pandillerismo* to patriarchal domination within Nicaraguan society fails to capture the way in which such social processes are never unmediated structural outcomes but rather the result of dynamic interplay between structure, agency, and practice. Although *pandillerismo* is readily associable with certain features of *machismo*, it is necessary to consider the specific contexts, social agents, relations, and changing everyday manifestations that shape it as a social practice in order to grasp the underlying nature of the phenomenon. This also applies more generally. Ultimately wider sociocultural norms and structures such as a long history of violence or *machismo* can only be seen as contributing to rather than determining the institutional development of Nicaraguan *pandillerismo*. They constitute "building blocks" that are drawn upon by social actors in variable ways through a process of "institutional bricolage" (Douglas 1987: 66), whereby institutions emerge as a result of the *ad hoc* combination of different elements of preexisting social forms. Seen in this way, although the actual "building blocks" are important in their own right, they do not necessarily explain the underlying dynamics of the institutions that they are brought together to constitute. Rather, it is necessary to consider not only the context but also the primary institutional function of gangs in contemporary urban Nicaragua, and in this respect, although at one level it is undeniable that *pandillas* are violent institutions that contribute to the general insecurity of life, they are clearly also fundamental socially structuring institutions.

This is particularly clear with respect to the material presented on the *barrio* Luis Fanor Hernández *pandilla*. Although the gang obviously represented a source of violence and danger that frequently disrupted everyday lives in the *barrio*, it also generated significant measures of order. This is especially obvious in relation to the 1996–1997 expression of the gang, which promoted an explicitly "solidaristic" form of collective social organization that drew together the whole neighborhood, both practically and symbolically, but it is also true of the *pandilla*'s 2002 incarnation. Although this latter manifestation of the gang upheld a much more "exclusive" order focused specifically on the management of a limited process of capital accumulation based on the local drugs trade, it nevertheless affected and constrained the whole *barrio* population and not just those involved in the drug economy. In both cases the gang and its violent practices can therefore be said to have constituted the institutional means for the construction and maintenance of localized forms of collective social organization, providing a sense of order, laying down practical and symbolic rules and norms, which provided individuals and groups within the *barrio* Luis Fanor Hernández community with a framework through which to manage their existences within a wider context of insecurity and social breakdown. Admittedly, in both 1996–1997 and 2002 *pandillerismo* constitutes a rather limited form of social construction, but as Charles Taylor (2002: 91 & 106) has underlined, the primary measure of any form of collective organization is not so much its magnitude, but rather whether or not it is imbued with a "social imaginary." This refers to the self-understandings that are constitutive of a collective unit: "It is what enables, through making sense of, the practices of a society." It is "the ways in which people imagine their social existence, how they fit together with others, how things go on between them and their fellows, the expectations that are normally met, and the deeper normative notions and images that underlie these expectations." These are precisely the kinds of social processes the *barrio* Luis Fanor Hernández *pandilla* achieved in both 1996–1997 and 2002, symbolically and through its socially organizing violent practices.

The traditional institutional purveyor of social imaginary in the modern era is generally considered to be the nation-state (Anderson 1983). Its Nicaraguan expression is, however, clearly deficient, as its incapacity to routinely ensure security within its boundaries due to its limited reach over society demonstrates (Isbester 1996). Although gangs and their violence are restricted forms of social imagination, they are among the few working forms of collective organization in the wider contemporary Nicaraguan context. As such, they can be conceived as exemplifications of Ulrich Beck's (1996) notion of "subpolitics." This describes small-scale social practices that are imbued with political authority—which Beck defines as the ability to structure "living conditions"—despite not pertaining to the formal, state-centered political sphere. Subpolitical institutions are therefore normatively nonpolitical informal institutions that become political by exercising influence over the social order in response to the limitations of formal politics. The obvious question such an analysis brings up, however, is to what extent such forms of social construction are sociologically viable. In this regard, Robert Latham's (2000: 2–3) notion of "social sovereignty"—which extends the classical Weberian conception of the sovereign state by contending that sovereignty can be "understood as an attribute not just of states but of other forms of social organization as well, operating within and across national boundaries"—offers a useful conceptual lens through which to consider *pandillerismo*. Latham claims that forms of nonstate social structuration can be considered "sovereign" if they are institutional arrangements possessing final political authority over a given community—which the *pandilla* clearly was in relation to the *barrio* in both 1996–1997 and 2002—and that such forms of social sovereignty can constitute viable foundations for the establishment of stable political systems in their own right in circumstances where state-based forms of social organization extend very irregularly. To this extent, the idea of social sovereignty goes beyond the idea of subpolitics in that it effectively constitutes gangs as forms of social structuration that are ontologically equivalent to state-based forms of sovereignty.

Although intuitively attractive as a conceptual framework, the nature of the *barrio* Luis Fanor Hernández *pandilla*'s transformation between 1997 and 2002 suggests that ultimately *pandillerismo* cannot be thought of as a form of "social sovereignty" on a par with state forms of sovereignty. In fact, it could be argued that the situation is quite the reverse insofar as the gang's evolution effectively constitutes a reversal of Charles Tilly's (2002 [1985]) famous characterization of the rise of European states as resulting from the gradual development of encompassing interests by warlords over the areas they dominate, as their ties with these become increasingly ties of systematic economic extraction as opposed to one-off plunder. Tilly's idealized sequence involves warlords incidentally establishing the institutional trappings of statehood within their domains as they provide autonomous rights to their subjects in order to maximize their own economic interest through decentralized collective economic coordination. The *barrio* Luis Fanor Hernández gang's evolutionary trajectory is almost precisely the opposite. In 1996–1997, the *pandilla* was imbued with an encompassing interest for the neighborhood that generated explicitly solidaristic behavior patterns, both symbolic and practical. By 2002, however, this had changed such that the gang no longer displayed any solidarity for the neighborhood, and had instead imposed a predatory regime of terror that served its new drugs-related economic interests.

This particular transformation can generally be linked to an overarching process whereby the sociological basis of collective social life in contemporary urban Nicaragua has been shrinking during the course of the past two decades, contracting initially from the nation-state to the *barrio* (Núñez 1996), and now from the *barrio* to the gang group. It is a process that bears comparison with the notion of "social death" that Ghassan Hage (2003) develops in his thought-provoking analysis of Palestinian suicide bombing, which arguably also provides a more general framework for conceptualizing *pandillerismo*. Hage contends that suicide bombing in Palestine/Israel is a coherent response to what he portrays as the systematic destruction of the institutions of collective life in the Palestinian territories under Israeli rule. He characterizes this process as a form of "social death," because it closes off traditional channels for becoming "socially recognized beings," thereby reducing the "possibilities of a worthy life," particularly among youth (Hage 2003: 78). Suicide bombers "exchange" their meaningless physical existences for lasting "symbolic" ones as fêted martyrs known to all. In doing so they not only escape individually from constrained circumstances, but by becoming societal reference points they also force a degree of collective sociability upon the vacuum of "social death," and constitute themselves doubly as an act of political resistance against Israeli occupation. Without pushing the analogy too far, it can be contended that the circumstances of insecurity and social breakdown in urban Nicaragua, and the continued economic crisis, political corruption, and high levels of disillusion, despair, and apathy, have all combined to create conditions that are comparable to a context of "social death." The possibilities of collective social life, particularly at the local level, have undergone a process of steady erosion, and *pandillerismo* can therefore also be seen as a fundamentally constitutive social practice attempting to counter these conditions of "social death" in an analogous manner to suicide bombing in Palestine/Israel. Drawing on "building blocks" such as *machismo* and violence, *pandillerismo* improvises a social order that is enacted in multiple ways—ritualized gang warfare, drug dealing entrepreneurship, symbolizing community—and at multiple levels—the individual gang member, the gang group, the local neighborhood community. As such, *pandillerismo* constitutes itself as a socially structuring institution that can be seen literally as a desperate form of "living in the shadow of death" in contemporary urban Nicaragua.

Conclusion

I have argued that *pandillas* and their violence constitute a form of subpolitical social structuration in contemporary urban Nicaragua, rather than the source of chaotic disorder they are generally perceived to be. The case study presented of the *barrio* Luis Fanor Hernández gang explored how this social structuration took on different institutional forms in 1996–1997 and 2002. In both cases, however, I suggest they can be conceived as a form of "street-level politics"—in other words, a type of Beckian "subpolitics"—that establish localized regimes of order and security in wider conditions of social and state breakdown, constrained economic circumstances, and uncertainty. Nicaraguan *pandillerismo* can therefore be seen as a desperate response to the shrinking range of social possibilities in contemporary urban Nicaragua, analogous to Hage's analysis of Palestinian suicide bombing as a response to "social death," that can be characterized as a form of "living in the shadow of death." The fact that the gang is a social form that has changed over time, from a form of collective social violence in 1996–1997 to a more individual economic violence in 2002, suggests that *pandillerismo* is not a sustainable form of social structuration, however. In opposition to the "positive" form of social organization that the state constitutes in the modern era, *pandillerismo* can be categorized as a "negative" form of social structuration, in the sense that the social structuration *pandillas* have provided in Nicaragua during the past decade is a process of "scaling down" rather than "scaling up." The obvious question that this raises is "what next?," and in this respect, the phenomenon of *pandillerismo* allows for little in the way of optimism, insofar as it is ultimately an epiphenomenal reflection of a broader and inexorable shift in the underlying nature of Nicaraguan society, which is increasingly characterized by an emergent model of elite-sponsored exclusion and segregation (see Rodgers 2004b). From this perspective, what the *pandillas* arguably represent are portents of a dystopian future.

Notes

This is an abridged version of the article "Living in the Shadow of Death: Gangs, Violence, and Social Order in Urban Nicaragua, 1996–2002," *Journal of Latin American Studies*, vol. 38, no. 2, pp. 267–292, 2006. Reprinted by permission of Cambridge University Press.

1. This name is a pseudonym, as are all the names of informants mentioned in this article.

2. The first period of fieldwork was carried out July 1996–July 1997. The second period was conducted in February 2002–March 2002 as part of the London School of Economics Crisis States Programme, which also sponsored a further visit in December 2002–January 2003.

3. Statistical underreporting is mainly due to the Nicaraguan Police's incapacity to systematically collect data. Since 1990, the Police has been reduced in size and budget, to the extent that it is absent in 21 percent of Nicaraguan municipalities. This situation is compounded by a lack of funds, with the Nicaraguan Police having the lowest number of personnel per capita and per crime, the lowest budget per crime, the lowest budget per officer, and the lowest salaries in Central America (Cajina 2000: 174).

4. There were almost three times as many homicides in Honduras and over six times as many in Guatemala and El Salvador during the same period (Moser and Winton 2002: 47). Having said this, while Nicaragua is clearly more violent than official statistics would suggest, levels of violence are by all accounts lower than those affecting Honduras, El Salvador, or Guatemala.

5. Nicaragua's predicament can be linked to other factors, including the legacy of war and structural adjustment, but it was violence that emerged most forcefully as a key issue in discourses in both 1996–1997 and 2002.

6. This association is clearly reinforced by sensationalist reporting in the Nicaraguan media. Nevertheless, gangs are a real source of insecurity in Nicaragua, and it would be inaccurate to characterize them as a "moral panic."

7. *Pandillas* are overwhelmingly an urban phenomenon principally found in Managua, although media reports do signal their presence in other urban centers, including Chinandega, Estelí, Granada, León, and Matagalpa.

8. The labor market and schooling constituted partial exceptions to this at the macro level, although due to the high levels of unemployment in Nicaragua, most youths' experiences of work tended to be sporadic, and the school dropout rate was extremely high, especially after primary school.

9. It should be noted that local inhabitants never called the police about gang members, although it must be said that the police rarely came unless the caller accepted to "pay for the gasoline." Police patrols in the *barrio* were generally infrequent in 1996–1997, as Police Commissioner Franco Montealegre admitted in a 2001 interview, youth gangs frequently outgunned the police, making effective patrolling difficult (Nicaragua Network News, vol. 9, no. 6, February 5–11, 2001).

10. For details on the emergence of the cocaine trade in Nicaragua, see Rodgers (2004a).

11. Cocaine is distributed either as cocaine hydrochloride powder or as "crack," a mix of cocaine and sodium bicarbonate. Crack is much less expensive than cocaine powder and is known as "the poor man's cocaine."

12. The process of "maturing out" seems to be universal to youth gangs around the world and is likely part of the inherent dynamics of youth groups (Covey et al. 1992).

Bibliography

Anderson, B. 1983. *Imagined Communities: Reflections on the Origin and Spread of Nationalism*, London: Verso.

Arendt, H. 1969. *On Violence*, New York: Harcourt Brace.

Ayres, R. 1998. *Crime and Violence as Development Issues in Latin America and the Caribbean*, World Bank Latin American and Caribbean Studies Viewpoint Studies Series, Washington: The World Bank.

Beck, U. 1996. World risk society as cosmopolitan society? Ecological questions in a framework of manufactured uncertainties, *Theory, Culture & Society*, vol. 13, no. 4, pp. 1–32.

Bloch, H. A., and A. Niederhoffer. 1958. *The Gang: A Study in Adolescent Behavior*, New York: Philosophical Library.

Bloch, M. 1996. La "consommation" des jeunes hommes chez les Zafimaniry de Madagascar, in F. Héritier (ed.), *De la Violence*, Paris: Odile Jacob, pp. 201–222.

Cajina, R. J. 2000. Nicaragua: De la seguridad del Estado a la inseguridad ciudadana, in A. Serbin and D. Ferreyra (eds.), *Gobernabilidad Democrática y Seguridad Ciudadana en Centroamérica: El Caso de Nicaragua*, Managua: CRIES, pp. 157–183.

Caldeira, T. P. R. 1996. Crime and individual rights: Reframing the question of violence in Latin America, in E. Jelin and E. Hershberg (eds.), *Constructing Democracy: Human Rights, Citizenship, and Society in Latin America*, Boulder: Westview Press, pp. 197–211.

Cloward, R., and L. Ohlin. 1960. *Delinquency and Opportunity: A Theory of Delinquent Gangs*, Glencoe: Free Press.

Cohen, A. K. 1955. *Delinquent Boys: The Culture of the Gang*, Glencoe: Free Press.

Covey, H. C., S. Menard, and R. J. Franzese. 1992. *Juvenile Gangs*, Springfield: Charles C. Thomas Publisher.

de Rivero, O. 2001. *The Myth of Development: The Non-viable Economies of the 21st Century*, London: Zed.

Douglas, M. 1987. *How Institutions Think*, London: Routledge.

Godnick, W., R. Muggah, and C. Waszink. 2002. *Stray Bullets: The Impact of Small Arms Misuse in Central America*, Small Arms Survey Occasional Paper No. 5, Geneva: Small Arms Survey.

Hage, G. 2003. "Comes a time we are all enthusiasm": Understanding Palestinian suicide bombers in times of exighophobia, *Public Culture*, vol. 15, no. 1, pp. 65–89.

Hannerz, U. 1969. *Soulside: Inquiries into Ghetto Culture and Community*, New York: Columbia University Press.

Horowitz, R. 1990. Sociological perspectives on gangs: Conflicting definitions and concepts, in C. R. Huff (ed.), *Gangs in America*, Newbury Park: Sage, pp. 37–54.

Isbester, K. 1996. Understanding state disintegration: The case of Nicaragua, *The Journal of Social, Political and Economic Studies*, vol. 21, no. 4, pp. 455–476.

Kruijt, D., and K. Koonings. 1999. Introduction: Violence and fear in Latin America, in K. Koonings and D. Kruijt (eds.), *Societies of Fear: The Legacy of Civil War, Violence and Terror in Latin America*, London: Zed, pp. 1–27.

Lancaster, R. 1992. *Life is Hard: Machismo, Danger, and the Intimacy of Power in Nicaragua*, Berkeley: University of California Press.

Latham, R. 2000. Social sovereignty, *Theory, Culture & Society*, vol. 17, no. 4, pp. 1–18.

Londoño, J. L., A. Gaviria, and R. Guerrero (eds.). 2000. *Asalto al Desarrollo: Violencia en América Latina*, Washington: Inter-American Development Bank.

Montoya, R. 2003. House, street, collective: Revolutionary geographies and gender transformation in Nicaragua, 1979–99, *Latin American Research Review*, vol. 38, no. 2, pp. 61–93.

Moser, C., and A. Winton. 2002. *Violence in the Central American Region: Towards an Integrated Framework for Violence Reduction*, Overseas Development Institute Working Paper No. 171, London: ODI.

Nitlapán-*Envío* team. 1995. The crisis is bordering on the intolerable, *Envío* (in English), no. 167, June, pp. 3–13.

Núñez, J. C. 1996. *De la Ciudad al Barrio: Redes y Tejidos Urbanos en Guatemala, El Salvador y Nicaragua*, Ciudad de Guatemala: Universidad Rafael Landívar/PROFASR.

Policía Nacional de Nicaragua (Nicaraguan National Police). 2001. *Boletín de la Actividad Delictiva*, no. 32, http://www.policia.gob.ni/boletin32.htm [accessed April 3, 2002].

Rocha, J. L. 2000. Pandillero: La mano que empuña el mortero, *Envío*, March, http://www.uca.edu.ni/publicaciones/revistas/envio/2000/esp/MARZO/Pandilleros.htm [accessed April 3, 2002].

Rodgers, D. 2004a. La globalización de un barrio desde abajo: Emigrantes, remesas, taxis, y drogas, *Envío*, no. 264, March, pp. 23–30.

Rodgers, D. 2004b. Disembedding the city: Crime, insecurity, and spatial organisation in Managua, Nicaragua, *Environment and Urbanization*, vol. 16, no. 2, pp. 113–124.

Sánchez Jankowski, M. 1991. *Islands in the Street: Gangs and American Urban Society*, Berkeley: University of California Press.

Serbin, A., and D. Ferreyra (eds.). 2000. *Gobernabilidad Democrática y Seguridad Ciudadana en Centroamérica: El Caso de Nicaragua*, Managua: CRIES.

Sosa Melendez, J. J., and J. L. Rocha. 2001. Las pandillas en Nicaragua, in ERIC, IDESO, IDIES, and IUDOP (eds.), *Maras y Pandillas en Centroamérica*, vol. 1, Managua: UCA Publicaciones, pp. 333–430.

Taylor, C. 2002. Modern social imaginaries, *Public Culture*, vol. 14, no. 1, pp. 91–124.

Tilly, C. 2002. War making and state making as organized crime, in C. Besteman (ed.), *Violence: A Reader*, New York: Palgrave Macmillan [Orig. 1985], pp. 35–60.

Whyte, W. F. 1943. *Street Corner Society: The Structure of an Italian Slum*, Chicago: University of Chicago Press.

Yablonsky, L. 1963. *The Violent Gang*, New York: Macmillan.

Chapter 3

Security at Stake: Dealing with Violence and Public (In)Security in a Popular Neighborhood in Guadalajara, Mexico

Monique Sonnevelt

Introduction

Startled and still a little drowsy I look around me, and realize where I am. Despite the heat, the bumping and the shaking, I dozed off in the 639 bus, which leaves from near the San Juan de Dios market in down town Guadalajara to Colonia Jalisco on the periphery. Slightly uphill in front of me looms what I now call "my neighborhood": Colonia Jalisco. The streets here, some paved some not, are dusty, full of pot holes and large stones. They are lined with simple houses and occasionally a car wreck. Graffiti on the walls spells out the names of the youth gangs who are marking their territory in this part of the neighborhood. There are a lot of these gangs here, with varying levels of infamy. The bus turns a steep left at Totatiche street, one of the few asphalted streets. We then turn into the direction of the central plaza of Colonia Jalisco, where the main church is located, as well as the *delegación*, the police station and some small shops.

I get off the bus and walk the last couple of blocks to my destination. It is four o'clock, and a couple of street vendors are setting up stalls where they sell pirate CD's with *banda* and *reggeaton* and the latest Hollywood blockbuster. Others sell the regular popular snacks: hotdogs, hamburgers and of course everything containing vitamin T, which comprises a wide variety of tacos, tamales, *tortas ahogadas*, and tostadas. Some older men sit side by side on one of the various benches on the central square, neighbors get together to exchange the latest gossip, families go for a snack and groups of teenagers hang out and flirt. However, after dark it quiets down quickly in the *colonia* and the atmosphere turns grimmer, and the streets more dangerous.

The above extract from my field notes provides a brief impression of Colonia Jalisco, a popular neighborhood in Mexico's second largest city, Guadalajara.

It is an area with a bad reputation for violence and public insecurity, a feature it shares with many other so-called *colonias populares* in Mexico's cities. Yet it is also a place that many people call home and therefore have to cope with the challenges that living there implies.

Violence and insecurity are of great concern to many Mexican citizens, and the number one concern for many people in Colonia Jalisco. The ineffectiveness of the police, corruption, and widespread impunity provide spaces for nonstate armed actors such as youth gangs and drug dealers to emerge, and to compete with the state for control over a certain territory. As a result, a market for security opens up (see Bandiera 2003; Elwert 1999; Shah 2006; Volkov 2002). Both legitimate and illegitimate "violence entrepreneurs" (Volkov 2002) dive into the void to provide protection and even forms of privatized justice. However, the market process surrounding security is more complicated than the basic economic principle of offer and demand. Coercion by armed actors, but also the social contextual dimension of the relationship between local residents and violence entrepreneurs, who often originate from the areas they end up protecting, influence the security market (see Rodgers 2006a; Sánchez Jankowski 1991; Venkatesh 1997 for examples of examinations of the influence of gang–community relations on gang behavior patterns).

Various authors have dealt with the rise of alternative strategies or parallel structures[1] of public security in low income areas in Latin America, a process that is sometimes also called the "informalization" of public security because it occurs in the absence of effective and legitimate government policies and actions (see, for example, Caldeira 2000; Goldstein 2004; Koonings and Kruijt 2007; Leeds 1996; Moser and McIlwaine 2004). Few have explored how emergent markets of security actually operate, however, and this chapter seeks to describe the ways in which the residents of Guadalajara's low income community of Colonia Jalisco[2] maneuver between formality and informality, legitimacy and illegitimacy, in their quest for security. The chapter is divided into three sections. In the first, I explore the theoretical framework of the market for security. In the second section, I offer an overview of Colonia Jalisco's security market, detailing the different actors within the neighborhood's particular political economy of violence. The third section zooms in on a specific fieldwork episode that sheds light on the complicated nature of the relations between the local community, the local youth gang as a source both of violence but also protection, and the local police in the context of the local security market

The State and Violence Entrepreneurs

Brutal *narco* violence, one of the world's highest rate of kidnappings, the widespread presence of youth gangs make public insecurity a dominant feature of everyday life in contemporary Mexico, especially in the larger cities. This reality is at odds with the assumption that it is the duty of the state to protect its citizens against basic dangers,[3] both internal and external, real or perceived, legitimate or fabricated. The state is normally supposed to monopolize and concentrate the means of violence (Weber 1995: 310, 311; 1972: 121, 122; Tilly 1985). Although this monopoly of violence is seldom absolute in practice, violence by nonstate actors is generally considered to be an exception, not the rule.

When the monopoly of violence disintegrates and the state does not adequately fulfill its protective role, spaces open up to violence, and so-called violence fields emerge (Elwert 1999). This opening generates (violent) competition among various armed actors for control, material benefits, or services, which also increases citizens' need to enhance their security. These services often end up being offered by the same protagonists that initially cause the increase in violence. Security in other words becomes a valuable commodity, and consequently, a security market with an array of both legitimate and illegitimate violence entrepreneurs emerges.[4] This is particularly obvious in low income areas; as Sánchez Jankowski's (1991: 22) has noted, "low income areas [. . .] are organized around an intense competition for, and conflict over, the scarce resources that exist in these areas." Security is one of these scarce resources, as it is a basic condition for survival.

The provision of security as a commodity does not depend solely on the level of demand and available choices. "The marketing strategy of private enforcers, once called 'the offer one cannot refuse,' implies that the initiative all too often belongs to force-wielding organizations rather than economic subjects" (Volkov 2002: 20). This does not necessarily mean coercion, but rather the creation of a field of pregiven possibilities. The point is well illustrated by Bandiera (2003) and Shah's (2006) research, respectively, in Italy and India. The former focuses on land reform, and the way the Sicilian Mafia acted both as an enforcer of security and an extorter. Shah (2006), for her part, illustrates how the "terrorist" Maoist movement in Jharkhand, India, did not simply offer protection from competing political groups, but also from itself. In both cases, however, the interaction of various armed actors also brought about a system that limited and governed the activities of violence entrepreneurs, creating relative order (Volkov 2002: 21).

The relationship between the community and illegitimate violence entrepreneurs is complicated. The entrepreneurs might provide some level of security to the community, within which they frequently live and where they have personal ties. However, it remains a relationship that in the end has a negative outcome for the wider community, a form of perverse social capital (see Moser and McIlwaine 2004: 158). Drug lords or (youth) gangs might offer some protection, but also remain a source of violence and social problems. For example, gangs and drug dealers can instill fear in a community that undermines democratic grassroots initiatives (Leeds 1996). Or else violence entrepreneurs might stop providing protection if it interferes with other (more profitable) interests, as illustrated by Rodgers (2006a, 2006b), who describes how a youth gang in Managua first protected local neighborhood inhabitants against violence and crime, but over time became involved with drug trafficking and lost interest in protecting local residents, terrorizing them instead in order to protect their drug-related economic activities.

The police force occupies an ambiguous position within the security market. On the one hand the police force is formally the state institution bestowed with the legal and legitimate means to maintain law and order. On the other hand, as Denissen (2008: 29) points out, drawing upon the examples of Russia, the United States, and Brazil, police corruption and brutality is widespread, and the police force systematically operates in the margins of illegality and illegitimacy. The Mexican police force is widely viewed as incompetent, corrupt, and often involved in crime in order to supplement their meager salaries (Suárez de Garay 2006: 13). Features such as corruption and the involvement in crime create a situation in which the boundary between the police and criminal activity becomes blurred, and consequently citizens no longer know whom they can trust. When a policeman is involved in corruption, he oversteps the boundaries of the legitimate power attributed to him as a policeman. One can wonder whether this policeman is still a representative of the legitimate state, or a criminal disguised as a state agent. On the other hand, this policeman invokes the power attributed to him by the state for his illegitimate business, and citizens will perceive this actor through his uniform as a representative of the state.

As Leeds (2007: 24) has pointed out in her study of the violence in Brazilian *favelas*, the permeable demarcation between unlawful and "official" violence has created a perverse dynamic whereby low income populations often perceive greater protection from the criminals than the police. In Latin America's socially divided societies, Kruijt (2008) describes how these practices enhance the gradual expansion of a gray zone between the formal and the informal, decency and illegality, respect for the law and criminality, civil society and "uncivil" society.[5] This zone of indifference and indefinition generates hybrid forms of injustice within legality, insecurity within the framework of the law, and informality within the institutions of order. Several scholars have therefore considered the continuity between the state and nonstate actors of violence (see, for example, Leach 1977; Shah 2006; Sluka 2000; Tilly 1985).

This line of thought does not necessarily mean that the situation in *colonias populares* such as Colonia Jalisco is the result of a weak state, with the violence fields the result of "governance voids."[6] Corruption by policemen and other government officials, as well as random police arrests, are everyday events that remind the *colonia*'s citizens that the state is arbitrary but also powerful (see Rodgers 2006b). Legitimate and effective governance might be limited but is not absent in the *colonias*, and the state continues to be perceived as a strong entity. These limited levels of legitimacy and effectiveness do however strengthen other social actors, and allow for competition to emerge, as I elaborate in the next section in relation to Colonia Jalisco.

Colonia Jalisco as a Security Market

Colonia Jalisco is a large *colonia popular* located on the periphery of the *Zona Metropolitana de Guadalajara* (ZMG). The community emerged in

1980 on the lands of *ejido*[7] *Zalatitan* as an illegitimate settlement, at a time when shantytowns mushroomed on the periphery of many Latin American cities. It was an era of economic crisis and restructuring through neoliberal reforms and, consequently, poverty grew and the gap between the rich and poor became more pronounced. At the same time, violence rose significantly in Guadalajara and in Mexico generally. From the 1980s on, organized, professional, and effective gang activity increased in Guadalajara. Drug trafficking activities proliferated and started to penetrate all social sectors and political institutions, especially following the rerouting of cocaine smuggling through Guadalajara. Together with the crime and violence, feelings of public insecurity increased dramatically among the general population (Ramírez Sáiz and Chávez Sevilla 1998: 198; Regalado Santillán 2001: 160).

Regardless of the initial privations and lack of public goods and services in Colonia Jalisco, residents believed this was the first stage of upward mobility for them. The community was seen as a place of hardship, but one in which improvements were possible and which would consolidate as an urban neighborhood over time. During the administration of President Carlos Salinas (1988–1994), Colonia Jalisco was selected as a model neighborhood for the National Solidarity Program (PRONASOL). "Solidarity" was presented as a poverty alleviation program directed at the urban poor, but was above all meant to establish a host of new relationships outside traditional patron-client mechanisms, and restore the legitimacy of Salinas and the ruling *Partido Revolucionario Institucional* (Institutional Revolutionary Part, PRI) party (Haber 1994: 278–279). Colonia Jalisco received several public goods and services under this program, such as running water, electricity, schools, and a police station. Previously, policing had been virtually absent in this community.

Despite these developments, the community never fully consolidated as an urban area. The urban goods and services were insufficient to cater to the whole population or turned out to be of low quality. To this day, many houses remain unfinished and the Colonia remains an area where the urban underclass reside and which is stigmatized for its violence, youth gangs, drugs dealing, and social problems.[8] Indeed, it became very clear during my fieldwork that despite the presence of many other social and economic problems, violence and insecurity, most notably in the form of youth gangs and drugs related violence, were the main concerns of the people living in Colonia Jalisco.[9] Although the police post on the *colonia*'s central plaza ensured there was a round-the-clock police presence, it was no guarantee for effective policing.

Indeed, the inhabitants of Colonia Jalisco generally had a very critical view of the police whom they described as corrupt, involved in crime, incompetent, and not having the interests of the population at heart. They felt that they always deliberately arrived too late whenever they were called, once the real trouble was already over, and more often than not making up an excuse for not interfering usually by referring to an event as "a private matter" (something that was often said in relation to cases of domestic violence). It was universally reported that policemen were often visibly drunk or drugged on duty, and generally displayed an arrogant attitude, frequently stopping and searching neighborhood inhabitants without legal ground. Indeed, they would often randomly arrest people, in order to extract a bribe from them for their release (sometimes in the form of spot "confiscations" of items of interest such as alcohol, cigarettes, and the likes), or else to have some "fun" with them.

The absence of effective policing meant that the *colonia* was very much an Elwertian "field" open to all sorts of violence, as various armed actors competed for control, material benefits, or services within its territory. Apart from the criminalized police, there were also some 20 different youth gangs, four or five of which are considered particularly dangerous and violent.[10] These youth gangs fought each other and other "enemies." There were also various small-scale drug dealers, who all had their own territory for (local) retailing, which they defended with violence. They themselves usually worked for drug lords higher up the hierarchy who lived elsewhere, but also employed people in the *colonia* to work as "body guards" or traffic small quantities of drugs from one part of town to another. There were also elements of organized crime present, for example, in the form of older, former youth gang members who had joined more professionally organized criminal gangs. These violent actors were complemented by a range of small-time individual criminals such as thieves, pimps, and so on.

As if the mere presence of all these different competing armed actors was not confusing enough, they and the community's residents were linked to each other in a network of multiple, but opaque, relations. Certain gang members, for example, worked together with drug dealers, who could be older sisters or brothers of a gang member. A drug dealer could have an agreement with a pimp for exclusiveness of drug sales in his brothel, while at the same time ensuring that the pimp was not bothered by other dealers. Members of different youth gangs might put aside their battles to work together on a lucrative "business project," or fight the police together. Gang members and drug dealers could also have protection agreements with policemen.

At the same time, there were also big differences between the various actors. Drug dealers in Colonia Jalisco were, for example, usually not involved in the security market in the same way as described in some studies of Brazilian *favelas,* where they have been depicted as maintaining strong networks of regulatory control over entire communities (see Gay 2005; Leeds 1996, 2007; Zaluar 2004). Rather, they simply sought to ensure that nothing interfered with their business, although they did sometimes provide broader forms of protection to their friends and family in certain cases. Youth gangs, on the other hand, provided security to the residents of their territory much more broadly and regularly—although not always systematically. They did so especially from individual thieves and robbers, and did so in exchange for loyalty among local residents, whom they expected to look the other way whenever they became involved in some illegal business, or else not denounce them in case of trouble with the police. As a result of such loyalty, the police often stressed that their efforts to improve security in Colonia Jalisco were fruitless because the local population did not cooperate with them.

The police were clearly a particularly important actor within the Colonia Jalisco security market, operating along different stages of both the legitimacy—illegitimacy and legality—illegality continuums. There were policemen who would come to the rescue whenever residents call them, while others would only watch out for their relatives or neighbors. Others still perhaps kept a keener eye over a particular shop, because the owner regularly provided them with coffee or a snack for free. There were of course also the policemen who provided protection to criminals, in exchange for goods or money. This "service" was often forced upon illegal entrepreneurs in order to avoid prosecution. In most of these cases, the incentive for the policemen was economic, but in some cases the existence of a personal relationship was important. This was quite paradoxical considering that according to the police the population of Colonia Jalisco generally displayed a hostile attitude toward officers. Indeed, many policemen argued that the residents of Colonia Jalisco tended to be "on the other side of the law" and talked about the security problems in the *colonia* as an "us vs. the people" stalemate. As a policeman I interviewed in Colonia Jalisco puts it, "We try to do our job and to improve things around here, but they [the residents] don't want to, they don't cooperate. So what can we do? You arrive at the scene, and no one has seen anything, knows about anything, nothing…Meanwhile they provide shelter in their houses [to the gang members]."[11]

It is the coexistence of multiple actors with complex sets of relationships to the security market that makes the situation in Colonia Jalisco opaque. It is hard to know exactly who is protected by whom, under what circumstances, and how effective the protection is. This situation leaves citizens very vulnerable in the face of violence and insecurity, as a resident of Colonia Jalisco called *Doña* Lupe described:[12]

> I sell tacos in front of my house every morning, here at the corner. At some point some gang members started to deal drugs here right at this same corner. It bothered me because it interfered with my business. I asked them a couple of times if they would take into account that I try to make a living here, but they kept coming back. I then called the police and denounced that drugs were being sold right here. A couple of days later the police came by. They were talking to the gang members. They seemed very friendly, and at some point I saw them […] giving money to the police. The police left, but they told the gang member who had made the complaint. From then on they started threatening me. […] For example, they would come and say to me that they exactly knew that my eldest daughter was attending school at night, what bus she took and what time she came back. They said they would wait for her and gang rape her between all of them.

The gang members in this example do not care about *Doña* Lupe or protect her as a neighbor living in their territory. She tries to solve her problem with them in an informal way by asking the gang members to take their business elsewhere, but they are unwilling to take her situation into account. When she tries to interfere with the lucrative business of the gang members by notifying the police, they start to threaten her and her family. *Doña* Lupe initially hoped to solve her problem with the gang members in an informal way. She did not complain about the drug dealing per se, even though she was not happy with that, but about the fact that it affected her business. When this strategy did not work, she notified the police, hoping that they would protect her. Instead, the police provided security to the highest bidder: the gang members.

Policemen in Colonia Jalisco readily admitted to this kind of protection deal (although such confessions of course always concerned other policemen, never themselves).[13] The fact that *Doña* Lupe notified the police also indicates that there was a chance that the police could have acted in her interest, however. Or, as another informant explained, you need to know a "good" cop, one that takes care of your interests. If you had such a relation, it did not matter whether the interests for which you sought their protection were legal or illegal.

Security in Colonia Jalisco was thus a complicated matter that left residents in a vulnerable position since policing was inadequate and their options to buy security were limited due to the paucity of resources. Any formal initiative among neighbors to develop alternative security strategies was likely to interfere with the interests of armed actors in the *colonia*, and many residents therefore preferred to simply mind their own business and avoid such initiatives because they were afraid of getting into trouble. The next section explores some of these fears and ambiguities relating to the workings of the security market in Colonia Jalisco by focusing on the local youth gang as a violence entrepreneur.

The Gang as a Violence Entrepreneur

Participant observation provides the researcher with a unique opportunity to observe the subjects that are studied in their own environment. As such, research is not a controlled experiment; one is not able to fully control situations. This exposes the researcher to a certain risk and presents a range of ethical dilemmas in situations of chronic insecurity (see Rodgers 2007). Nevertheless, even though such participant observation can sometimes become a rather unpleasant experience it can be very insightful, as the fieldwork episode presented below illustrates well.

It was a Thursday afternoon when I walked down to Maria's house in Colonia Jalisco. It was sunny and the streets were quiet. Some children greeted me. As I turned around the corner, a guy known as *el alacrán* [the scorpion] came walking towards me. I did not really know him, except from seeing him in the street. He was a drug addict who often hung around with the guys of the youth gang here. He was not exactly a teenager anymore, although his precise age was hard to guess. His body showed several tattoos. A large image of the virgin of Guadalupe, right in the middle of his chest, was the most striking one. He greeted me and stopped me in the middle of the street by blocking my way. He had a plastic cup in his hand and said that he wanted to give it to me. I told him that was very kind, but that it was not necessary. That he should keep it. I told him I had to go, but all of a sudden his mood seemed to change. It all happened so quickly and just when the alarm bells in my head started ringing, it was too late, and he grasped my arm firmly. He was surprisingly strong, and maneuvered me in such a position that I could not move anymore. I told him to let me go, but he just responded by twisting my arm further and further. He started to feel me up. "This is really getting out of hand," I thought. "What do I remember from the self-defense class? Is he armed? I have to..."

"Hey, you son of a bitch, what the hell do you think you are doing! Let her go!" shouted some very angry neighbors, who came running towards us. *El alacrán* was startled by the women who suddenly appeared and finally let me go. I was relieved when the women took me by the arm, leading me towards their houses down the road, while they were still swearing at my assailant and tried to comfort me at the same time. How could this happen! What did he do? Was there no one around to help you? You have to be careful! Questions and advice were bestowed upon me. We all sat down in front of Martha's house and I had to tell them precisely what happened. "It is such a disgrace! Looked what happened to you! And we do not even know who he is. He does not even live around here, that scumbag! And he is always so dirty, hanging around in the street. Our children play here in the street too. Today it is you, next thing you know he will do something to our children! This has to stop, we need to do something."

Something needed to be done, that was for sure. All the women agreed that action should be undertaken. It was not really up to me anymore if I wanted something to be done, it was a decision already made. So we deliberated on the options. It basically came down to two possibilities. We could either inform the police and see if they would do something about it or we could go talk to "the boys," the gang members, to see if they would help.

The neighbors who saved me wanted to undertake action for two reasons. On the one hand, because I had good personal relationships with several of them, and they felt responsible for my security in their community. On the other hand, action was also required because of what they felt could potentially happen to them or to their children if nothing were done. Security in this case thus proved to be a community issue, not just something individual. Beyond these motives, the neighbors considered two courses of actions to be potentially suitable means of dealing with the incident. One was reporting it to the police, the second one was to notify the local youth gang.

Discussions about these two options seemed highly paradoxical at times. The neighbors clearly considered policemen to be incompetent good-for-nothings, the "bad guys" whom they labeled "dogs," criminals even. They considered that the police would not necessarily help because they were "lazy," "afraid," "did not take an interest," or "had some kind of deal with criminals." Indeed, there was a palpable fear that notifying the police might even backfire. Going to the police would also mean engaging in a bureaucratic procedure, that would probably take up a lot of time. Bearing in mind such attitudes toward the police, and the bad experiences that many local residents of Colonia Jalisco had had with them, it is remarkable that filing a complaint with the police was regarded a viable option at all. At the same time, however, the police were clearly seen as having the legitimate power to arrest criminals, and for this reason it was thought that they might perhaps be able to intervene. There was also a sense that there was little to lose in this particular case. Not only was it "the right thing to do," since it was the official and legal means of handling such issues, but *el alacrán* was also not likely to enjoy police protection, so there was little risk that notifying the police would be counterproductive.

This deliberation over whether to call the police in this case was not an exception, as I was able to ascertain later through individual interviews. Local residents all suggested that whenever a violent event occurred in the *colonia*, for example, a fight between gang members or a dispute among neighbors, witnesses always considered the option of whether or not to call the police, asking questions such as the following: "Should I call the police?," "Has someone called the police yet?," or "Why has no one called the police yet?." Even if the authorities were not called in the end, the option was almost always considered. Despite the low opinion people had of the police in general it is important that the police were not "out of the game," so to speak. They were always perceived as a potential player within the wider security market.

No decision had been reached in the case of *el alacrán* when by coincidence a police patrol showed up at the other end of the street:

> While still talking about the possibilities of both solutions, we saw a patrol car with four policemen coming around the corner on the far end of the street. In the house on the corner lives a policeman and the patrol car could often be seen parked in front of the house, while the policemen would go in to get a drink or something to eat. Since they were here now anyway, we might as well go talk to them about the situation, Emilia suggested. Two of the neighbors accompanied me to the police car. The cops had parked the car and just got out when we approached them.
>
> "Excuse me sir, we have a problem, maybe you can help," Martha said. The policeman stood there in front of us, his body straight up, his legs somewhat apart, and holding his machinegun across his chest with both

hands. Dark sunglasses hid his eyes when he looked at us. "What's up?" he said, with a short nod of the head. His colleagues stood on the other side of the car, listening to our conversation. We explained to the policeman what happened. "Hmmm, so, but no one died, right? Nothing really happened, no crime was committed..." "He felt her up!" Martha exclaimed "Something did happen!" "Well, there is not much we can do now. Call us if you see the guy, or if something happens again. This is the phone number of the station," the policeman said while he handed out a small card. I tried to describe what *el alacrán* looked like, so maybe they could look out for him, but the policeman started laughing. "A large tattoo of the virgin of Guadalupe in the middle of his chest! That could be anyone!" As there was nothing more the cops could do for us, we thanked the policemen for their attention and went back to the other women.

"We should have known! This was a waste of time! Who could have thought they would really do something? They are useless." Some swearwords followed out of Martha's mouth. She was worked up about the policemen's behavior and their arrogant attitude; showing no compassion or interest in helping us. Maria took the situation somewhat calmer. It was the kind of disappointment we could have seen coming, she argued. We went back to the other neighbors and told them what happened with the police. Everybody agreed that this meant that we had to talk to "the guys."

Maria's reaction makes it clear that a fruitless outcome to their efforts was anticipated, but it nevertheless led to feelings of frustration, as expressed by Martha. When we joined the other women again, and told them about our conversation with the police, some words of disapproval were uttered, but as no one had had very high hopes that the police would act, we moved rapidly to consider the other option: notifying the gang members. These we could go and talk to right away, as they usually gathered on the very same street corner where the incident with *el alacrán* occurred, so it did not take long to get hold of one of them:

Panzas, one of the older gang members, came walking down the street. "He is the right guy to talk to," one of the women said to me. Martha called Panzas over, and said that we needed his help. He walked over, and she told him what happened this afternoon. "You know this guy right?" Martha asked, referring to *el alacrán*. "Yeah I do, I know who you are talking about." "So this time it is her," Martha said, pointing at me, "and what will happen next? We cannot tolerate this! He just a piece of dirt; he has been bothering us for a while hanging around in the street where our children play without us knowing what he is up to, looking all dirty and drugged up." "So what do you want me to do then? Should I hit him, or go talk to him first?" Panzas replied. "Well, maybe talk to him first," Martha said while she looked around to the other women who nodded in approval. "Ok, I will see what I can do, all right." Panzas then went off and we continued talking. We went in to Maria's house and spent the rest of the afternoon there.

The neighbors knew whom to approach among the gang members, they knew who was the right broker. Panzas could not be replaced by any other gang member. He was one of the "old" gang members, less active in the gang than previously, and trying to change his behavior patterns—although not always succeeding—since becoming involved in the local church and settling down with a girlfriend. He nevertheless still had a lot of influence on more active current gang members, and was known as someone not to mess with. He had been involved in violent crime and murder more than once, and it was clear that he would do so again if the situation warranted. As a result, Panzas had a lot of leverage and was the best person to turn to about the issue of *el alacrán*.

The option of asking the youth gang to solve the problem might suggest a good relationship between the gang members and the neighbors. Certainly, the neighbors who approached Panzas addressed him in a familiar tone. This however fails to underline the ambiguity of the relationship between neighborhood inhabitants and gang members. On the one hand, gangs were seen as a threat because of the violence that they were inherently associated with—as *Doña* Lupe's story underscored—and there was a generalized avoidance of conflict with the gangs precisely because they did not refrain from resorting to violence to sort matters out. Gang members were also considered especially dangerous when they were under the influence of drugs, as their behavior often became unpredictable. Certain drugs—crack cocaine, for example—make their users very violent or extremely anxious, to the extent that they can end up attacking their friends and neighbors (see also Rodgers 2006a: 280). On the other hand, the individual gang members are generally not considered inherently bad people, but rather victims of the circumstances in which they grew up: poverty, family abuse, broken homes, and so on. They were more often than not the kids whom local neighborhood inhabitants had seen growing up; indeed, they were often their own children or grandchildren, or the kids of a next-door neighbor or of a close friend or relative living around the corner. Most neighbors would greet the gang members in the street and vice versa, exemplifying a certain level of mutual respect and understanding. Gang members would also benefit from their good relations with the local community. If they got into trouble with the police, gang members could call upon help from the community or else a neighbor with some nursing skills might look after gang members wounded in fights and in need of medical care. Some neighbors also talked about the gang as "the boys" (*los muchachos*), implying a certain sense of affection.

At the same time, however, a significant part of the insecurity in the neighborhood was clearly caused by the very existence of violent youth gangs and the fighting between them. Although gang members were often part of the security solution for local residents, they were also frequently the cause of the violence problem. Even if each youth gang was likely to offer some protection to neighbors living on their turf, and protected them from the violence of rival gangs, as Volkov (2002) has pointed out, it is the violent competition between the—in this case—youth gangs that enhances the need for protection, while their actions are also limited and governed by other armed actors such as rival gangs, drug dealers, and the police. The gang is approached not because they systematically fulfill an order-keeping task in the community, but as members of the community that help out the neighbors who see no other effective solution to their problem. If the police have been able to take care of the situation in a satisfactory manner, there would have been no need to involve the youth gang. To this extent, the state is not absent in Colonia Jalisco, and the youth gang is not a local parallel power structure that makes the law. Rather, it is the ineffectiveness of the police that makes the neighbors turn to the gang.

This was something that was also clear from the way that the problem with *el alacrán* was dealt with through Panzas. Contrarily to the police, the gang members were considered accessible, the justice process was quick, and there was some "democratic" deliberation about a suitable punishment. Yet even this solution contained the seeds of a certain ambiguity, as became obvious a few hours later:

A few hours later when it was time for me to go home. Martha and Maria decided to walk up with me, just to be sure. We were on our way when Martha said somewhat alarmed: "Oh, Gosh, there he is..." *El alacrán* came walking towards us. Maria grabbed me tighter by the arm, as if that would protect me. *Alacrán* said he wanted to apologize to Martha and Maria. He was sorry he had caused trouble and told them he would never ever bother them or their children; he had no bad intentions and was really sorry that he upset them. As for me, he saw the whole affair a little differently: "Who did you think you are? You're not even from here, you stupid foreigner, you stupid American or Canadian or I don't care where you come from! I'm not finished with you yet, I'll get you, you're going to pay for this," he said angrily. The women looked at him angrily, took me each by an arm, and we quickly walked on: "Come on, let's go." They warned me: "You have to be careful Monique. Tomorrow if you come down, give us a call first, and we will come to pick you up, all right?" I agreed, and we said good-bye.

The next day I was picked up by Maria and her grown up daughter Lula. They told me what had happened after I left. Maria and Martha had been upset by the threats and had gone back to Panzas to tell him about what happened. The gang members consequently made clear to *el alacrán* that they were serious and warned him not to show his face again in the neighborhood. *El alacrán* clearly took the hint this time. Martha had also told her husband Antonio—who had a reputation for being a tough cookie—about the whole affair, and later that afternoon he told me how he had run into *el alacrán* in the street in the morning, and when he tried to approach him because of what had happened, *el alacrán* panicked and ran, shouting so that he would go away, that he knew they would kill him, and that he would not show his face again.

El alacrán stayed away for the rest of my stay, but I didn't have to worry anymore. Later that afternoon Pascual, one of the gang members, came up to me and told me that I did not need to be concerned about my safety around the neighborhood, because I was considered a friend of the people who live there. They were watching out for me, I was told, and they would be on top of things before anything would happen to me.

It was obvious that Panzas had acted on his word when *el alacrán* came to apologize to Maria and Martha. He was aware that he had crossed a line, but only in relation to them, however. From his point of view, I was an obvious outsider to the community and he therefore initially felt that the warning he had received only referred to the trouble he had caused the community, not me. However, the broader nature of the gang's warning became clear when both gang members and Antonio told him that he should leave me alone as well. *El alacran* knew then that he was in trouble and did not take the warning lightly this time.

Conclusion

This chapter has discussed the complexities of the local security market that arose in Colonia Jalisco in the face of high levels of violence and the absence of adequate policing. The chronic public insecurity has led to the need for autonomous local forms of security service provision. Different violence entrepreneurs compete with each other and the state in these spaces, and alternative power structures can arise in a space left empty by the lack of universally protective state structures. As Volkov (2002: 20) has pointed out, the provision of security as a commodity does not depend solely on the level of demand and available choices. The provision of security is sometimes also forced upon the "clients" with varying degrees of coercion, insofar as not obtaining security can expose clients to threats of violence by violence entrepreneurs.

What the more economic approach to the security market of Elwert (1999), Volkov (2002), and Bandiera (2003) fails to take into account, however, are the influences of contextual social relations. As I hope is clear from the case study presented, coercion is not the only factor that influences the processes of offer and demand. The example of the youth gang in Colonia Jalisco shows the multiple complex relations between the residents and violence entrepreneurs, which are not only economic in nature, but also social. The gang members originate from the community and are the children, siblings, friends, and partners of local residents. The gang as a whole might be despised as a cause of violence and insecurity, but the individual gang members are integrated into the social fabric of the community. This condition makes it much harder to tackle the perverse relationship the gang maintains with the wider community, and places residents in a vulnerable position.

The residents need to maneuver between the police as a legal state institution for security, but with often illegitimately acting policemen, and illegal social phenomena such as gangs that arguably constitute legitimate violence entrepreneurs within the context of the local security market. Within their territory, gangs can indeed enhance a sense of order by keeping out other youth gangs and individual criminals. However, at the same time their power is limited by the interaction of other armed actors, such as rival gangs, the police, and drug dealers. Moreover, there is no guarantee that the gang members will actually provide security to the residents. Certain economic interests can either have more importance, or become more important, than providing security services (see Rodgers 2006a), and the gang members are of course themselves sources of insecurity at a general level, even within their own territory. Such ambiguities make the relationship between local residents and local gangs extremely difficult and volatile.

To this extent, it can be argued that the alternative security strategies and services of violence entrepreneurs that emerge in low income neighborhoods tend to offer limited solutions for a real improvement in security and safer living conditions. This is perhaps the reason why citizens continue to hope for a state-based solution to their tragic predicament, even though the state institution of the police force has lost a considerable part of its legitimacy.

Notes

1. Despite the terminology, I want to stress that these structures intertwine and interact with the state and should therefore not be seen as completely separate from the state.
2. My research revolved around two contrasting case studies of two different communities in Guadalajara's Metropolitan Zone: a working-class *colonia popular* and a well-to-do gated community. I conducted extensive anthropological fieldwork in both during 2006 and 2007. The focus of this chapter is on the security strategies and the market of the urban poor in Colonia Jalisco, where I lived for eight months during my fieldwork in 2006. In 2007 my fieldwork had a stronger emphasis on the gated community, but I nevertheless frequently visited Colonia Jalisco.
3. According to Article 21 of the Mexican constitution, public security is a task of the state (Moloeznik 2003: 2). Public security is described by the Mexican Ministry of Public Security as the primary obligation of the state and as presently the most important resource of a society, claiming that with security, citizens have the possibility to develop their complete potential and to freely exercise their rights (Secretaría de Seguridad Pública 2005: 9).
4. The idea of the security market is derived from the model of "markets of violence" as presented by Elwert (1999) and the "market of protection" used by Volkov (2002) and Shah (2006). Volkov (2002) uses the market of protection in reference to his study of the proliferation of armed actors, especially extortion, in the context of market reforms and the emergence of private businesses in Russia.
5. Uncivil society consists of "agents or groups that force their interest upon the public domain on the basis of coercion and violence, in such a way that the legitimate aspirations of other groups or sectors in civil society are jeopardized and the rule of law is fragmented or shattered" (Koonings and Kruijt 2004: 7).

6. I use this notion after Koonings and Kruijt (1999; 2004). Governance voids can be defined as "spaces or domains in which the legitimate state is effectively absent in the face of armed actors that abide by the rule of force—but also in the internal erosion of the capacity and willingness of state agents themselves to abide the rule of law" (Koonings and Kruijt 2004: 2).

7. The *ejido* constitutes a form of land tenure that was established as a result of the Mexican Revolution (1910–1917) in which landless peasants demanded "land and liberty" from the state (Nuijten 2003: 4). Right holders in the *ejido* community could use the lands assigned to them for agriculture, but they were not the legal owners and as a result were not entitled to sell these lands.

8. This stigma is, for example, illustrated by the fact that residents of Colonia Jalisco see their chances of obtaining a job or a loan decrease steadily when they use their original address on an application form.

9. It has to be noted, though, that many residents stated that the current violence is a little less intense than a few years ago. Although it goes beyond the extent of this chapter to discuss why violence has become less intense, I want to point out there is no clear indication that there is a general, perceptible trend of the area becoming structurally safer over time, but the situation is somewhat calmer after an explosion of violence.

10. These were the ones that had the largest territories and had been around for a while.

11. Venkatesh (1997) has described similar practices and police responses in Chicago. The practice of residents hiding people from the police is, particularly with reference to youth gang members, something that is widely recognized among the local population, with neighbors, in fact, often criticizing each other for doing so. At the same time, however, it is a very understandable act, because gang members and neighborhood residents generally have close personal ties with each other. They are each others' relatives, friends, or friends' relatives.

12. The names of informants are pseudonyms.

13. On January 22, 2008, local radio announced that two policemen in Colonia Jalisco had been reported to the Procuraduría General de la República (PGR) for protecting a local drug dealer who had his business in a seedy bar called *El Desierto* in Colonia Jalisco. Such reports are rare, however, because the police usually deal with these kinds of affairs internally. A corrupt policeman will generally be transferred to another department rather than punished (interview with police officer Colonia Jalisco).

Bibliography

Bandiera, O. 2003. Land reform, the market for protection, and the origins of the Sicilian mafia: Theory and evidence, *The Journal of Law, Economics & Organization*, vol. 19, no. 1, pp. 218–244.

Caldeira, T. 2000. *City of Walls: Crime, Segregation and Citizenship in Sao Paulo*, Berkeley: University of California Press.

Denissen, M. 2008. *"Winning Small Battles, Losing the War": Police Violence, the Movimiento del Dolor, and Democracy in Post-authoritarian Argentina*, Amsterdam: Rozenberg Publishers.

Elwert, G. 1999. Markets of violence, in G. Elwert, S. Feuchtwang, and D. Neuberts (eds.), *Dynamics of Violence: Processes of Escalation and De-escalation in Violent Group Conflicts*, Berlin: Duncker and Humblot, pp. 85–102.

Gay, R. 2005. *Lucia: Testimonies of a Brazilian Drug Dealer's Woman*, Philadelphia: Temple University Press.

Goldstein, D. 2004. *The Spectacular City: Violence and Performance in Urban Bolivia*, Durham: Duke University Press.

Haber, P. 1994. The art and implications of political restructuring in Mexico: The case of urban popular movements, in L. Cook, K. Middlebrook, and J. Molinar (eds.), *The Politics of Economic Restructuring. State–Society Relations and Regime Change in Mexico*, San Diego: Centre for U.S.-Mexican Studies/University of California, pp. 277–302.

Koonings, K., and D. Kruijt. 2004. Armed actors, organized violence and state failure in Latin America: A survey of issues and arguments, in K. Koonings and D. Kruijt (eds.), *Armed Actors: Organized Violence and State failure in Latin America*, London: Zed Books, pp. 5–15.

Koonings, K., and D. Kruijt. 2007. Fractured cities, second-class citizenship and urban violence, in K. Koonings and D. Kruijt (eds.), *Fractured Cities, Social Exclusion, Urban Violence and Contested Spaces in Latin America*, London: Zed Books, pp. 7–22.

Kruijt, D. 2008. Violencia y pobreza en América Latina: Los actores armados, *Pensamiento Iberoamericano*, vol. 2, pp. 57–70.

Kruijt, D., and K. Koonings. 1999. Introduction: Violence and fear in Latin America, in K. Koonings and D. Kruijt (eds.), *Societies of Fear: The Legacy of Civil War, Violence and Terror in Latin America*, London: Zed Books, pp. 1–27.

Leach, E. 1977. *Custom, Law, and Terrorist Violence*, Edinburgh: Edinburgh University Press.

Leeds, E. 1996. Cocaine and the parallel polities in the Brazilian urban periphery: Constraints on local-level democratization, *Latin American Research Review*, vol. 31, no. 3, pp. 47–83.

Leeds, E. 2007. Rio de Janeiro, in K. Koonings and D. Kruijt (eds.), *Fractured Cities, Social Exclusion, Urban Violence and Contested Spaces in Latin America*, London: Zed Books, pp. 23–35.

Moloeznik, M. 2003. *Seguridad Pública, Justicia Penal y Derechos Humanos en el Estado de Jalisco (1995–2002)*, USMEX 2003–2004 Working Paper Series, originally prepared for the conference on "Reforming the Administration of Justice in Mexico" at the Center for U.S.-Mexican Studies, May 15–17, 2003, http://repositories.cdlib.org/cgi/viewcontent.cgi?article=1034&context=usmex [accessed June 6, 2009].

Moser, C., and C. McIlwaine. 2004. *Encounters with Violence in Latin America: Urban Poor Perceptions from Colombia and Guatemala*, London: Routledge.

Nuijten, M. 2003. *Power, Community and the State: The Political Anthropology of Organisation in Mexico*, London/Sterling: Pluto Press.

Ramírez Sáiz, J. M., and A. Chávez Sevilla. 1998. La seguridad pública, talón de Aquiles de los ayuntamientos panistas del AMG, in J. M. Ramírez Sáiz (ed.), *Cómo Gobiernan Guadalajara? Demandas Ciudadanas y Respuestas de los Ayuntamientos*, Guadalajara: Instituto de Investigaciones Sociales, UNAM Centro Universitario de Ciencias Sociales y Humanidades de la Universidad de Guadalajara, pp. 217–248.

Regalado Santillán, J. 2001. *Sociedad y Gobierno: La Seguridad Publica en Guadalajara*, Unpublished PhD thesis, inter-institutional programme of the University of Guadalajara and the Centro de Investigaciones y Estudios Superiores en Antropología Social (CIESAS) de Occidente, Guadalajara, Mexico.

Rodgers, D. 2006a. Living in the shadow of death: Gangs, violence and social order in urban Nicaragua, 1996–2002, *Journal of Latin American Studies*, vol. 38, no. 2, pp. 276–292.

Rodgers, D. 2006b. The state as a gang: Conceptualizing the governmentality of violence in contemporary Nicaragua, *Critique of Anthropology*, vol. 26, no. 3, pp. 315–330.

Rodgers, D. 2007. Joining the gang and becoming a *broder*: The violence of ethnography in contemporary Nicaragua, *Bulletin of Latin American Research*, vol. 27, no. 4, pp. 444–461.

Sánchez Jankowski, M. 1991. *Islands in the Street: Gangs and American Urban Society*, Berkeley: University of California Press.

Secretaría de Seguridad Pública. 2005. *Estado y Seguridad Pública*, Mexico City: Fondo de Cultura Económica/Secretaría de Seguridad Pública.

Shah, A. 2006. Markets of protection: The "Terrorist" Maoist movement and the state in Jharkhand, India, *Critique of Anthropology*, vol. 26, no. 3, pp. 297–314.

Sluka, J. 2000. *Death Squad: The Anthropology of State Terror*, Philadelphia: University of Pennsylvania Press.

Suárez de Garay, M. 2006. *Los Policías: Una Averiguación Antropológica*, Guadalajara: ITESO/Universidad de Guadalajara.

Tilly, C. 1985. War making and state making as organized crime, in P. Evans, D. Rueschemeyer, and T. Skocpol (eds.), *Bringing the State Back In*, Cambridge: Cambridge University Press, pp. 169–191.

Venkatesh, S. 1997. The social organization of street gang activity in an urban ghetto, *The American Journal of Sociology*, vol. 103, no. 1, pp. 82–111.

Volkov, V. 2002. *Violent Entrepreneurs: The Use of Force in the Making of Russian Capitalism*, Ithaca: Cornell University Press.

Weber, M. 1972. *Gezag en bureaucratie*, edited by A. van Braam, Universitaire Pers Rotterdam/Antwerp: Standaard Wetenschappelijke Uitgeverij.

Weber, M. 1995. *Political Writings*, edited by P. Lassman and R. Speirs, Cambridge: Cambridge University Press.

Zaluar, A. 2004. Urban violence and drug warfare in Brazil, in K. Koonings and D. Kruijt (eds.), *Armed Actors: Organized Violence and State failure in Latin America*, London: Zed Books, pp. 139–154.

Chapter 4

Good Times and Bad Blood: Violence, Solidarity, and Social Organization on Dominican Streets

Jon Wolseth

The Gómez and Independencia Crew

The corner of Gómez and Independencia is one of the Distrito Nacional's busiest yet manageable intersections. Everyone wants a piece of the traffic flow. The northwest corner is an ideal staging ground for all sorts of economic activities because a large tamarind tree gives off enough shade to keep most people out of the sun. Adjacent are a large *paletera*, or cigarette and candy stand, a fruit seller, and three middle-aged women who sell newspapers to passing motorists. These share their turf with the nine boys and young men who sit along the low stone wall waiting for the traffic light to change to red so that they can rush to wash the windows of the halted vehicles. When traffic stops, they have 90 to 120 seconds to make their transaction.

There is little overhead involved with window washing, which makes it more attractive than shining shoes. All one needs is a five gallon bucket, usually from a used can of cooking oil rummaged from the trash, a water source near the intersection that has been marked off as part of the group's territory, a sponge, and a squeegee fashioned from an old windshield wiper and attached to a metal or wooden handle. The squeegee is, of course, the precious tool of any self-respecting windshield washer, the item most treasured and guarded. Material goods come easy on the street, flowing and circulating among street kids via theft, damage, loss, and lending. Shoes may be stolen, clothes traded, but squeegees are cherished and kept on a person when not in use. The two Juans[1] have their squeegees by their sides, their hands occupied with a piece of coarse brown paper topped off with fried sausage bits and plantain slices. Their oversized t-shirts drape down their skinny bodies. The motion of their jaws as they chew fills out their normally gaunt cheeks. These two share more than first names. They share a crack habit whose cost ranges between 500 and 700 pesos a day, almost U.S.$ 25. Juancho and Juan Carlos have grown to look like each other over the months, despite Juancho's teased out afro and *café con leche* skin and Juan Carlos's shaved head and moreno coloring. Juancho has been on the streets for 5 years, slowly descending into each new depth of vice and danger with aplomb and apparent glee. Juan Carlos has been living on the streets for a little over a year. After meeting Juancho, his change in demeanor and physical appearance has been rapid. He went from marijuana to crack as his primary drug of choice. Juancho also started pimping Juan Carlos to foreign tourists and taught him the basics of pickpocketing and breaking and entering. Between remunerative sex, petty theft, and washing car windshields, they feed their habits and share most things between them. They are both 15 years old.

This paper is a preliminary investigation of the social organization of children and youth living full time on the streets of Santo Domingo, much like the Gómez and Independencia crew to which the two Juans belong. Street kids deserve special consideration as participants in local street cultures because they tend to confound easy classification based on their behaviors, self-proclaimed identities, and their appropriation of wider cultural practices. They live outside the home yet are rarely truly "homeless." They are children who have been exposed to and reared by local cultural practices yet are often viewed by the dominant cultural forces in which they are found as uncultured, wild, or deviant. They may exchange sexual favors for goods or money yet not identify as prostitutes. They may participate in theft without being part of a criminal network. And they may protect their territories in the city as groups (some quite large) without being characterized as territorial gangs. The ambiguity and range of practices that constitute the activities of street children can appear chaotic. However, this jumbled mix of economic survival strategies, appropriation of public space, and random violent clashes with each other and the authorities is a highly organized and structured cultural reality. Nowhere is this organization more visible than in the invocation of solidarity and cooperation among kids living in the same work zone.

Solidarity is not how we often characterize life on the streets. Indeed many researchers of street kids in Latin America deny that solidarity can exist, given the inherent violent nature of street-based relationships (see Kovats-Bernat 2006; Márquez 1999). Hecht (1998: 137–144), for example, argues that in-group violence is a major source of agency for street kids in Recife, Brazil, even while it is also more destructive than parastatal death squads targeting street youth. Members of the nongovernmental organization (NGO) where I worked doing street outreach while conducting research, however, continually asserted that solidarity among street youth was an important part of kids' lives. This simultaneous recognition of and call for *solidaridad* by outreach workers stuck with me during the 2 plus years I spent in the Dominican Republic. It would be easy to reject *solidaridad* as a projection of outreach workers and a way of placing an egalitarian ethic on street relationships that appear brutish and violent. Yet, kids who shared a similar territory did express affiliation, affinity, and trust, to limited degrees, among themselves. Under what conditions is solidarity expressed? I wondered. Further, does an ethic of trust and solidarity necessarily mean an absence of interpersonal violence? The majority of the young men and boys I knew consistently talked about stalwart friendships with individuals in their group while at the same time they decried group tensions and the daily outbreaks of violence. Could there be solidarity without a solid group identity?

Miranda, in her ethnography of Chicana gangs in Oakland, points to the embedded and shifting nature of trust between gang girls, a trust that is predicated on the "day-to-day work of maintaining and building solidarity" (2003: 92). Violence on the streets, even violence between members of the same peer group, is the phantom figure of forms of trust; a trust that, like Korbin (2003: 432) reminds us for the concept of violence, is socially and culturally constructed. It is tempting to read Juan Carlos and Juancho's relationship as one based primarily on exploitation, especially in the instances when Juancho pimps his buddy out. Yet, the relationship, like many of the exploitative and damaging relationships kids enter on the street, exists because of a history of shared experiences and sociability that conditions a limited trust between the two. It would be too easy to read such relationships as debilitating and inauthentic because they involve drug use and addiction. Rather, drugs are one medium through which kids express and display friendship and trust.

In what follows, I examine the tensions between group identity and individual friendship for Dominican street youth. Shared drug consumption is a source for a common identity and solidarity, an activity that also has the potential for being the cause of interpersonal violence and group discord. Drug consumption is a major arena in which Dominican street youth display values of friendship, cooperation, and trust. Friendship does not mean the absence of exploitative relationships or shared harmful behaviors, as we can see in the relationship between Juancho and Juan Carlos. Indeed, these anomalies can become the very bonds upon which friendships are based, as the two expressed an intimate bond based on their shared crack use. It does not mean that an ethic of care and trust does not exist; it means that such an ethic is conditioned by local contexts and expressed in locally meaningful ways—even if it includes violent behavior.

In order to examine this issue of solidarity on Dominican streets, I first provide a brief sketch of the types of social organization that can be found among street oriented groups of kids and youth. On one end of the spectrum are highly organized, neighborhood based gangs which demand sworn allegiance and a certain conformity among members. On the other end exists the lone street kid, alienated from dominant society and from his peers due to the exigencies of daily survival and nihilistic drug addiction. Kids who share similar work and sleep territories in Santo Domingo exist someplace in between these two extremes. Indeed, the ways in which kids consume and share drugs and defend breaches of respect with violent reprisals marks their social relationships to such a degree that it may make sense to label them as being part of a "proto-gang." The ambiguity in their position, somewhere between the isolated homeless and the barrio based gang, parallels the ambiguity of their own, often violent, social relationships.

Street Order and Social Organization

The large body of ethnographic gang research originating in the Chicago School offers an instructive point of comparison to the nascent and provisional support offered among Dominican street kids. From Thrasher (1927) on, a recurring theme from research on marginalized urban youth is that gangs offer a replacement for weakened families, schools, and other social institutions in slum and inner-city areas.[2] Vigil (1988, 2002, 2003), throughout his work, details the multiple forces that marginalize working poor youth, pushing them to seek refuge in gangs. Gangs position themselves as stronger and more reliable support networks than youths' families by creating affective ties among youth via shared signifying practices (Phillips 1999). Vigil (2002: 24) is most explicit on this point, affirming that the "family-like functions and new cultural customs" of gangs foster "friendship and mutual trust" and that "learning to back each other up during times of trouble cements the bonds between youths in a gang, a type of fictive kinship network." Mutual aid and collective action against outside threats define a gang's internal governance and group identity. Love for one's gang family, the intensity of feeling for the gang, and gang identity in and of itself primarily comes from social forces external to the gang—rival gangs who threaten the territorial integrity of the local gang. Indeed, Phillips (1999: 91) goes so far as to argue that a group of youth classify as a gang only in so far as they "struggle for existence" within the larger political landscape of the city and nation-state.

The degree of formal leadership structure in street kid groups, although varying across ethnographic contexts, rarely reaches those present in neighborhood gangs. Some street groups exhibit more self-conscious organizing principles such as rules, leaders, and affiliation and others appear to be more fluid and relational such as among the kids I knew in Santo Domingo. Early research in Colombia highlighted the well-organized tiers of bands of street boys and youth called *galladas*. Researchers describe the constellation of *galladas* throughout major cities like Bogotá and Cali as age graded, with significant contact, direction, and mutual aid between younger groups of boys and elder youth (Aptekar 1988; Goode 1987). Group members provide assistance in times of need to a *gallada* member with the expectation that the member in need has been an economic contributor to the group's wellbeing (see review in Ennew 1994). The literature paints a portrait of *galladas* as an approximation of American-style gangs mixed with an *Oliver Twist* ethos. Hierarchy, specialization, and territorial concerns exist for *galladas* but the evidence of pernicious violence and exploitation is downplayed.

Galladas are the exception in the street child literature, the only evidence of highly formalized social structure. Like in gangs, there is evidence that some street kids organize group relations through fictive street relationships. However, unlike in gangs, these groups self-consciously structure themselves into literal "street families" where the idiom of kinship and cooperation mediates and structures various survival strategies. With the development of a kin or household model for life on the streets, children and youth organize themselves into replicas of dominant society's primary institution for social life. Hansson (2003) describes how street youth in South Africa understand their stroller bands (as they are known) as mix-gendered households in which girls play a far more problematic domestic role than boys. In essence, girls recapitulate the domestic role they would have had if they had lived with their natal families, caring for the living site, in charge of food preparation, and monitoring the behaviors of younger members. Street families, however, tend to be just as dysfunctional and strife ridden as the natal families the kids left, offering weak support and constantly rotating allegiances which precludes any sense of hierarchy or authoritative decision making (see Hagan and McCarthy 1998). Furthermore, the use of a wide variety of spatial niches throughout the city for economic exploitation, a common survival strategy for many street kids, precludes deep-rooted territorial association found among neighborhood gangs (Van Blerk 2005). The absence of collective symbols and signifying practices such as graffiti, tattooing, and hand signs used to represent territory, group bonds, and/or membership also bespeaks of the loose affiliation among street youth.

In some cases, street kids may be peripherally involved in transnational gang activity yet their day-to-day survival strategies rely on their self-designated street families. Taylor and Hickey's (2001) extended case study of street kids living on the U.S.-Mexico border demonstrates that kids call upon gang identity and relationships as they move from the Mexican side of the border into Arizona and beyond, when they are incarcerated on the U.S. side of the border, and in the event that they may be able to tie into more lucrative illegal economic activities. Their immediate street family, however, provides affection, care, and concern, despite the fluidity of membership, especially while living at their home base in Nogales.

At the other end of the spectrum, some ethnographers have described only the most tenuous forms of sociability for kids on the street. Kovats-Bernat (2006) portrays the lives of young Haitian *timoun lari* in Port-au-Prince as a constant violent struggle to stake out and maintain access to coveted areas of income generation in a setting in which much of the city's population is straining to make ends meet. There is little cooperation evident in his description and even those boys and girls that may work or sleep together for protection do so more out of safety in numbers than affection or mutual care. Lucchini (1996) argues that the lack of defined territory and street children's high mobility in Rio de Janeiro precludes the formation of any sort of group identity and the formation of social roles. Cooperation is at a minimum except when glue is bought collectively and shared out based on each individual's contribution. The buying and allocation of the drug appears to be the only time that kids congregate in large groups.

The youth on the streets of Santo Domingo don't fit easily into any of these descriptions of social organization. Absent are any well-defined groups like the *galladas*. Absent as well are the formation of street families, perhaps due to the general scarcity and invisibility of street girls. Yet the group—in all its fluidity—does exist and is centered around more or less recognizable territorial spaces like parks and various street intersections, in a manner very similar to gangs. Geographic territory is however not fiercely protected nor does there tend to be oppositional groups competing for lucrative spots. Added to this are the evident affective bonds and cooperative relationships I witnessed daily among pairs of youth like Juancho and Juan Carlos who shared their work and sleeping territory with other youth. Unlike gangs, though, there was little evidence of any institutionalized forms of group stratification or clearly identifiable leaders. The absence of group mechanisms of hierarchy and leadership positions did not mean that a violence-free, egalitarian ethic existed—group life was far too unstable for this to be the case. Interpersonal violence was the way of mediating disagreement and conflict between youths, instead of being group-on-group violence as in the case of gang warfare. In other words, members of the same street clique turned on each other instead of raging against some external threat to group survival. Kids broached any slight or harassment from others with retaliatory violence.

Violence on the Streets

Julio César's eyes are shut and his hands rest on his abdomen. He has an IV drip and a bladder bag. I pity him for the bladder bag. The plastic tube, jammed into the head of the penis, causes immediate infection and burns a steady discomfort. It hurts being put in, hurts more being pulled out, and is a constant reminder of one's hospitalized state. I press my hand into his shoulder to let him know I am there. He opens his eyes to fine slits and smiles. "Jon! This is my brother!" He says "brother" in English, so it comes out in a strange guttural tongue that at first I do not recognize. Without my asking, 17-year-old Julio César—always the talkative sort—begins, moving his hand down his thorax and on the left side of the abdomen, saying, "Oh, Jon, I am in such pain. Here, all this down here hurts. I can hardly move or breathe because the pain is so great."

The medic on staff interrupts him. She is checking the pulse of a young lady on the farthest bed. "Says he was hit by a motorcycle. Must have been some motorcycle." She goes back to counting the heartbeats, and Julio César motions me to come closer. I kneel down so that my face is near and he whispers in his throaty tobacco voice. "I just told them it was a motorcycle so that they would attend me here and not send me to Dario Contreras Hospital. The truth is, it wasn't a motorcycle. Pretty Boy and his woman beat me up because they think I stole Janis' tennis shoes. I'm no thief…" He starts to get worked up and has to cough, which throws his body into pain. A grimace settles upon his features and his hands go to his left side, unconsciously cradling where the blows had been. "Can you imagine the shame I felt huddled on the beach? Pretty Boy with a machete in his hand while his woman kicks me. What could I do? I had to lay there and take it. How humiliating to be beaten up by a girl! And then Pretty Boy steps in to finish me off." He goes on. "The thing is, how could I have taken her shoes? Wasn't I held at the police station yesterday until afternoon? Then I went down to the beach front to bathe. I was there bathing, right? When along comes Rosy. You know who Rosy is, right?." I know who 14-year-old Rosy is, I think, knowing where this is going to lead. "There I am, bathing, naked, and she comes along and everything perks up, you know it. And she's interested too because she comes closer. And me without a condom! So we go into the ocean instead. And I thought my luck was changing, after three consecutive days being picked up by the police. Huh, some luck." Julio César continued: "I can't go to sleep in the abandoned mansion now because all of the others want to burn me up, light me on fire. They tried it once already—don't think they won't do it again. So after Rosy leaves, I find one of the little rooms along the beach to rest. There I am when in the morning Pretty Boy finds me and kicks the shit out of me. Goddamn! When is my luck gonna change?"

Peer group violence, like that experienced by Julio César from Pretty Boy, a member of his group, is a cross-cultural reality of street life, be it in youth gangs or groups of street youth. Indeed, interpersonal and sexual violence is something of a regulatory device for maintaining group structure, a device tied to propping up the self-esteem of group members through embodied, visceral reactions to breeches in an ethic of mutual respect. In the case related above, it was Pretty Boy who defended the honor of his girlfriend against the supposed theft of the tennis shoes. What Julio César did not bother to mention in his retelling of events was the long history of antagonism and hostility between himself and Pretty Boy. Both shared common territory along the boardwalk and had years of interacting with each other, but their friendship had soured over time. Both laid claims to the area and refused to vacate, although Julio César's position among the larger group was increasingly met with disfavor. Eventually he would leave the boardwalk area altogether amid fears of further violent backlash. He continually lost face among his peers. As Horowitz and Schwartz remind us, that those youths like Julio César, Pretty Boy, and Janis who have "a heightened concern with personal honor" simultaneously demand "deference from others and [are] sensitive to any act that suggests that one is not worthy of respect" (1974: 240). Violence in street oriented groups becomes "a strategy to achieve respect and to constitute a shared world" (McDonald 2003: 72; cf. Cintron 1997: 151). Kids must appear ready to act and intervene at all times when facing harassment. Their very bearing must bespeak of violence (Anderson 1999: 72). Pretty Boy's attack was preemptive and regulatory, sending a clear message to Julio César that he had become *persona non grata*. Julio César's inability to muster the resources and support of others in the group to defend himself meant he couldn't appropriately answer Pretty Boy's violence with equal force.

On the streets, young males are free to make their own decisions and live as they please without the restrictive, overbearing, and oftentimes violent authority found in their homes. Common refrains on the street among kids where phrases such as *nadie me controla* and *nadie me gobierna*, nobody controls or rules over me. In talking about his street cohort, 16-year-old Andres answered the following about whether there was a leader:

> It's better no one controls [the group]. Because if one guy controls [the group] there are many who are going to want to fight. Listen up! If one controls [the group] some of the guys are not going to want that this guy controls the group, they are going to want to control the group them-selves. They don't want the other guy to control them. So then, this being the way it is, there is going to be a lot of fighting because many of the guys aren't going to want the other guy to control the group.[3]

Andres' comment bespeaks of the internal problems of the group when one kid wants to be in charge. He knows from experience that whenever some-one feels he can be the leader, others in the group rebel, creating a sense of competition instead of cooperation. If there is going to be a leader, their logic follows, it's better that its me and not some other guy who thinks he can tell me what to do. Having a leader violates the sense of freedom from authority that led kids to leave their natal households for the street. Each kid is on his own to negotiate his relative position and status within the group, as long as there is no formal leader. The revolving positions of influence and pull to get fellow cohort members to do what you want maintains a volatile environment where violence against other members is one way of resolving conflict. If a strong-armed leader were to be present, perhaps a formal hier-archy would limit the continual violent posturing.

The irony is that while kids may have left a violent and controlling home, they subject themselves to violence on the streets, both by peers and adults. Often, when there is an irrevocable breach between group members, it can fester into outright hostility and violence, as occurred between Julio César and Pretty Boy. Julio César's beating was not solely concerning Janis's lost shoes, however. It was part of an ongoing push to remove Julio César from the general territory along the Malecón and edge him out of the clique. The clique may not have had a formal leader or even formalized organizational structure, but it did sometimes reach consensus concerning its actions, espe-cially if enough members were in agreement. This had happened with Julio César, whom others in the clique viewed as a liability. They believed that the increased number of raids of the Malecón by the local police force was due to Julio César's deteriorating relationship with the police. The group collec-tively decided to push him out of the territory. Within a week of being beaten up by Pretty Boy, Julio César began working the pedestrian mall as his new territory. Collective action by his old cohort led him to go it alone.

Drug Consumption and Group Relationships

Kids on the streets in Santo Domingo live and work in larger groups (of between 8 and 20 young people) primarily in tourist zones and around shopping centers and malls in the upscale sections of the city. In talking with street educators and street adults, it became clear that this is a change in geography and social grouping that occurred in the late 1990s to early 2000s. Their theory is that greater access to tourists has changed the types of drugs kids today use. Young adults in their early to mid twenties who had been on the street for 7 to 10 years were primarily glue and solvent sniffers, the drug they started with and continue to use at all times during the day. Glue use physically deteriorates the body and leaves the user with a sticky, dirty appearance. Glue users look haggard and disoriented. The odor of the solvent is unmistakable and sits like an aura around the user. Because of their appearance and violent and erratic behavior, kids and adults who are solvent sniffers are given wide berth, marginalized to aging, poor neighborhoods far from the tourist trade.

Young people who are relatively recent to street life utilize marijuana and, increasingly, crack. Marijuana is cheaper than beer and carries the same social possibilities associated with alcohol consumption. Crack offers intense highs at a more attainable cost than cocaine. Both crack and marijuana, especially in the quantities used by these younger street kids, are still expensive and require income-generating techniques that will keep them in their drug of choice. One surefire income source is through contact with tourists, either through begging, shining shoes, pickpocketing or the sex trade. Especially for those youth involved in remunerative sex, physical appearance and general cleanliness is an important marker for seeking clients. Regardless, to move with relative ease through tourist areas and relative freedom from police harassment, young people have developed a strategy of maintaining a physical appearance that does not mark them as different from the majority of Dominican society. Indeed, these kids would make disparaging remarks about other homeless youth who let their appearance go.

The difference between the drugs of choice—solvents versus marijuana and crack—represent not just differences in geography and work options, but also differences in how the drugs get consumed. Solvent use is a private affair done in public—users do not share (see Shaw 2007). Youth constantly sniff glue from plastic juice bottles or cardboard milk cartons, periodically lifting the vessel to the nose. Sniffing is an unconscious habit throughout the day. Glue sniffers position themselves in opposition to the mainstream through their defiant use of the drug in public; however, the drug is not used to mediate social relationships between users. By contrast, marijuana and crack use are social events. Not only do kids work together to earn the money for their habit, they also consume the drug as a group, in the case of marijuana, or in pairs or trios, with crack. Unlike solvent use these drugs are used away from the general public and are shared and passed among members. The drug becomes a method of marking who is part of the group, as all who are present share and participate in the consumption of the drug in a party-like atmosphere. The good times associated with marijuana, crack, and the rare occasions cocaine is acquired, are a form of sociability glossed over with the borrowed terms from mainstream Dominican slang for hanging out: *hacer coro, compartir, estar en la juntiña*. While these terms are a prevalent part of dominant society's lexicon, they carry an added meaning on the street. Normal linguistic use would indicate spending time with friends and perhaps the exchange of food, soda, and beer, but on the streets these terms become synonymous with drug consumption. It would be inconceivable to hang out in your street clique without consuming together.

Consider the following account of 18-year-old Manuel, who describes his first encounters with a mixed group of street adults and kids:

> When we headed for the Malecón, we made friends...we made friends. The very first guy we made friends with was Mamey and we stayed there hanging out with (*hacienda coro*) Mamey and we became part of the crew (*juntiña*), of the group (*coro*) and we stayed there in the Malecón...I don't know, but this *coro*, I don't know...everyone that comes here stays here hangin' out, I don't know if it is this that draws people, the guys, I don't know what it is, because, look, guys from over there in San Juan, from Los Cacaos, they come here and end up here in the Malecón. There came this guy from New York even...a professional type. He would travel, he had his visa and he sold his visa to do his shit.

Manuel signals to us the primary connection between one's group, or *coro*, and the mystique or pull that drug use has on creating a good vibe that keeps people on the street. Doing drugs and hanging out together go hand in hand to such a degree that consuming is what makes the mood so enjoyable. Manuel was 13 when he first headed to the *Malecón*, and although he would move between the streets and temporary shelter with foreign and Dominican lovers, he always kept coming back to the original *coro* on the *Malecón*. Manuel justifies the allure of drugs and good times by pointing to the urban legend that even a professional from New York found the *coro*'s pull too strong: he sold what he had to hang out with the group and "do his shit," to do his drugs of choice.

Sociability—the sharing of drugs to set the mood and atmosphere of the good times—delineates membership in the street group. Akin to Lockhart's (2002) example of gang rape, in order to be marked as a member of a street clique, a kid must partake in drug consumption. This is made clear in 11-year-old Wilson's description of his first impression of street life.

> I left [my grandmother's home] begging, just like that, until my brother entered there, entered the club.

I asked him what he meant by "the club," to which he answered the following:

> In the street kids' club...At first I was begging and they called my brother over and said to him, "Do you want to stay here with us?" And he said yes...So, he stayed there and he slept there and then I had to go back home and so I left and slept at home for two days and then he stayed there

[on the streets] for good and I wanted to be with him so...Then I entered [the club]...They showed me how to smoke [marijuana]...My brother was telling me, "Smoke, smoke" and so I smoked it.

Wilson posits the clique of boys he and his older brother became involved in as a *club*, clearly articulating the social aspects involved in being on the streets. It is no coincidence that he sees obvious benefits to hanging with this group of boys. In his narrative, Wilson moves from joining the club to describe not only what he learned—how to smoke marijuana—but we get the sense that to be a part of the clique, smoking is something he *must* do. The pressure is augmented by the fact that it was his older brother who induced him to use the first time.

If kids consume their drugs together and having access to drugs is a benefit of group membership, they also spend their time earning enough during the day to support their habits by working together, like the group of windshield washers of which Juancho and Juan Carlos are a part. Work and drug consumption are major group activities in their day. Take, for instance, 16-year-old Carlos's description of a typical day on the streets:

What do we do on the streets? We smoke, we eat, we walk around, we get cleaned up, we get fucked up. A lot of stuff, you get me? As if it were a home.

Seemingly incongruously, Carlos aligns his daily tasks and those of his clique with the domestic space of the home, metonymically linking his clique to the concept of family. His street residence is not the same as any Dominican household, however, as domestic activities such as cooking and cleaning are absent and individual roles are not aligned with such work. Absent too is the collective ethos common in Dominican households where money earned is turned over for use by the entire family. Rather, in Carlos's clique, everyone is responsible for his own food and drug purchases. But, once purchased, drugs are readily shared within the group. 13-year-old Antony for instance claims "I buy my [drug] and I give to those that I know well," while 19-year-old Diego, for his part, puts it in the following terms:

[The cost] depends on what you use. If you buy a rock [of crack] it's one hundred [pesos]. If you buy a joint, it's thirty. But I don't go to buy just one. I go and I buy five or six, sometimes up to ten. And when I've got a lot of money, I go...and I buy an ounce which is eight hundred and I get rid of this itch. I've got enough drug for a week. If the other guys share with me I have to share with them. If you give to me I have to give to you...If you, for example, if you one day have money and buy me a juice and one day I have money I can buy you a juice [in return].

The large quantities of marijuana and crack that Diego purchases are not just for personal use but to share within the group. Such sharing is not formalized to the extent that every day a different kid is in charge of buying for the group, but rather it is understood that whoever has money on any given day is expected to share his good fortune by buying drugs that will be consumed *as* a group. They buy, knowing that if they consume while others from their cohort are present, they must share. In this respect, drug consumption parallels Dominican etiquette involving food or drink. As Diego pointed out, it is rude not to offer when anyone sees you eating and drinking and rude not to accept that offer. If you don't want to share food or drugs you go somewhere where no one will see you, away from the *coro*. Included in this etiquette are periods when a windfall may be earned and kids go on group benders, consuming more than their usual amount, for it is best to share one's good fortune with others. 16-year-old Miguel explains this ethic of sharing in the following way:

> When we buy a hit of marijuana, what we are doing is…we smoke it, we all smoke it together because it's all the same. So when they have some, they give some to me. We're like that, see? Today it's my turn, tomorrow it's yours. That's just the way we are. We get along well that way.

Though the ethic of sharing acts as a leveling mechanism within the group (Stephenson 2006), it also leads to identification with one's clique because a kid's addiction is synonymous with being a part of the group. In fact, group members encourage and aid in each other's addiction by providing opportunities to work for the benefit of the group for those kids who don't have money on any given day to purchase drugs to consume. 18-year-old Pretty Boy tells us how this works in a conversation:

> Jon: Do you buy marijuana right here or do you have to go someplace else?
> Pretty Boy: I have to go someplace else to buy it or when I don't want to go I send another kid to go get it.
> Jon: How does that work?
> Pretty Boy: I send another kid that likes marijuana as much as I do, so that he can smoke my marijuana without him having the dough to buy it. And so he and I will smoke it together.
> Jon: And there are others that send you off to buy it, too?
> Pretty Boy: Sure, there are others who send me to buy it too, when I don't have money, I'll go and buy it so that I can smoke his marijuana, otherwise I don't get to smoke.

Such opportunities to consume drugs even when a kid doesn't have the money to buy his own reinforces a kid's desire to be part of the group as well as his loyalty to his clique. Good times, as manifested in the hanging out of the *coro*, combined with kids' assistance in locating and buying drugs and an ethic of sharing with those who are closest to them creates an environment where drug consumption, friendship, and identity intersect. This double identification of sociability with drug consumption makes leaving the street even more difficult. A kid is not just addicted to the substance, but to the environment and friendships woven around the use of drugs. In particular, it is a kid's primary drug buddy, like Juancho is to Juan Carlos, which cements the street's powerful allure and provides a modicum of protection from the volatility of the group, as the next section explores.

Dyadic Friendships

I paused as Fernando and I came out onto the street from the hospital, in order to get my bearings in the night, and put the pieces in sequence of what we needed most urgently for Eduardo, also known as "Shoeshine Boy": money, blood bank, call his grandmother. "Jon! Jon!" A voice called, coming from across the street. From the doorway of the building in front of the hospital emerged the figure of a man who had been crouched out of sight. I didn't recognize him from where I stood, but Fernando did. "Well, look who it is, but Luisito," he commented in a wry voice, somewhere between sarcasm and dry irony, "The hero himself." I didn't understand the reference that Fernando was making at that moment. I knew there was no amity between the two of them but was unsure why bad blood existed. It went beyond territorial rivalry and the usual animosity that Fernando elicited from most of the other kids, though. Luisito had slowly moved into new realms of delinquency over the past few months, finding himself part of a thieving ring with two older men, and my guess was that Fernando and Luisito's bad relationship had something to do with Luisito's new business relations.

Luisito's transformation over the year since we had first met had been near total. A helpful, bright-eyed 15-year-old who took to the streets because of unspecified "neighborhood problems," Luisito was now a 16 year old deeply enmeshed in the world of robbery and drugs. It had been painful to watch as Luisito kept drifting, moving from a peripheral position on the Malecón to being a central figure in the lives of the boardwalk's inhabitants. He had become moody and addicted to crack-laced marijuana cigarettes. He was violent, fighting his way to a dominant position within his cohort. When I had first met him, I thought the streets would devour him. Instead, Luisito fed off the streets not only surviving but managing to thrive.

He wore an oversized Yankees baseball cap, black, cocked to one side and pulled over the ears. His jean shorts and long grey polo shirt were dotted with dark stains. The shorts, in particular, had a dark velvety patch that extended over the right pocket and worked its way up under the shirt. He jerked his head in an upward motion in recognition of Fernando's presence, and took my hand as I extended it in greeting. The feel of his rough ice-cold hands told me that there was something not quite right.

Jon: What's up, Luisito?
Luisito: Jon, did you see Shoeshine Boy? Did you see him?

Jon: Yeah, I saw him. Fernando told me what happened. He's not too good.
They say it was a deep wound.

Luisito: I know. I saw it go in. The damn thing was shoved in to the hilt and
it was a big knife.

Jon: You saw it?

Luisito: Yeah. I saw it. I was sitting right next to Shoeshine Boy on that wall
there on the boardwalk, smoking a joint. Joaquin came by, exchanged
words with Shoeshine Boy. Nothing weird or angry. Then he comes back
five minutes later, comes behind us and drives this long blade, homemade,
you know the kind you make with a steel or copper shank. Shoves it all the
way in to where he grabbed a hold of it and then pulled it out and walked
away. Man, he was bleeding. Blood was everywhere, pooling around. I
took a t-shirt and held it on the wound, but the blood kept coming. I
carried him to where the taxis sit, picked him up and carried him all the
way there and paid a taxi 500 pesos to bring him here. They didn't want
to do it, but I said, "I got 500 pesos, who will go?" and then one I know
said he'd go, he'd do it. So I pulled Shoeshine Boy in the cab and we got
him here.

500 pesos would have been five times what that cab ride should have cost.
I couldn't help wonder where he'd gotten that kind of cash, what he did to
earn it. Then I remembered that Eduardo had started selling marijuana and
crack. It may not have been Luisito's cash—it might have been what Eduardo
had on him, or maybe it was Luisito's cut?

The events of that evening when Eduardo was stabbed sparked a chain
reaction that illustrates the tensions between a street ethic of sharing
to consume and the importance of dyadic relationships like the strong
bond between Eduardo and Luisito. Over the course of several conversations with Luisito, Eduardo, other kids on the Malecón, and with the
perpetrator himself, Joaquín, it became clearer that Eduardo had violated
the primary code of conduct of sharing drugs with his *coro*. I witnessed
time and again how violence leading to severe injury and even death of
kids on Santo Domingo's streets occurred when youth became involved in
not just consuming drugs but in trying to sell drugs to their own cohort.
Luisito, in his new work breaking and entering, decided to use his cash
to front his buddy, Eduardo, in selling marijuana and crack along the
Malecón, a move which put Eduardo in direct competition with Joaquín
who had also recently begun selling in the same area. It is unclear, as
Fernando insinuated by ironically calling Luisito "the hero himself," as
to whether or not Luisito had provided both Eduardo and Joaquín with
the start up cash or the connections to acquire the drugs. Later, when
I pressed him on this point and his wry way of referring to Luisito as
a hero, Fernando would only smile and reply "I don't know much, but
Luisito came out smelling clean, no?" He would not elaborate. Luisito and
Joaquín were known to be close and had worked together on a couple of
breaking and entering jobs, so further collaboration would not be exceptional. Joaquín, for his part, wouldn't let on as to the source of his cash,

only saying he was losing money when Eduardo started undercutting his prices.

What is clear, however, are the consequences of the sales competition. In a fit of anger, Joaquín struck out with the intention of removing Eduardo from the scene. Due to his actions and the ensuing involvement of Eduardo's father, a former military officer, Joaquín fled, creating a temporary fissure in the group as kids took sides in the conflict. The *coro* was disturbed, relationships became uneasy for a couple of months, and kids literally paired off or went it alone. Common work sites like the intersection of Gómez and Independencia became inactive for a few weeks until relationships harmonized. Pairs of youth, like Juancho and Juan Carlos, moved further down the Malecón to work. In times of crisis, kids rely on their closest friend and the group threatens to dissolve.

Dyadic relationships, as between Juancho and Juan Carlos or Eduardo and Luisito, involve coercion, self-destructive behavior, and a deepening of drug dependency. They are not "healthy" in any traditional sense. Yet, dyadic bonds are strong friendships that may ameliorate some of the harm done on the streets. Although street solidarity does not conform to the types of bonding we imagine, one based on trust and common support, drug consumption does ally kids into supportive cohorts. Affinity between street kids of the same cohort is no less authentic because it is characterized by harm to individual health and wellbeing. Likewise, dyadic friendships are lasting and demonstrate genuine affection, even as they are exploitative. Solidarity arises when behaviors and attitudes become collective. We must look beyond everyday forms of violence to analyze the affective bonds created among kids in spite of, because of, and as a result of that violence.

Habitual drug consumption configures the form which social solidarity takes for Dominican street kid populations. The cohort or group on the street is a revolving door that allows kids to move freely in and out of a shared work territory, yet kids themselves are not rootless. Instead, the emotional bonds caused by drug dependency and complicit criminal behavior between youths anchors them and provides them with support, affection, and, most importantly, someone to watch their back. But, as important as the *coro* is for the creation of a sense of belonging on the streets, youth also value dyadic friendships more than allegiance to the territorial group.

Bonds, such as between Juan Carlos and Juancho or Luisito and Eduardo, involved some shared illegal activities like drug use, thieving or pickpocketing. Sometimes these intense bonds turn exploitative, turning into unequal exchanges to fuel the consumption needs of the two youth. Although I hesitate to label these friendships as codependent, given the popularized self-help connotation of the word, it is hard to find an equivalent term that describes the ways in which the bonds between them could be anything but enabling. Juancho sends his best friend out to prostitute when they don't earn enough for their crack habit. Eduardo takes a knife in the back for his best friend Luisito who, Fernando intimated, may have set him up. Drug use and other complicit illegal activities make such bonds the strongest and most intense feelings for another person that a youth has had, stronger perhaps than any they may have had for their own families. Witness, for instance, 17-year-old Jorge Luis who, shook up at the recent murder of his best friend, recalls the importance of this friendship:

> We grew up together, since we were little kids…We raised each other, we would put on each other's clothes. I'd wear his, he'd wear mine. That's how we grew up. We held this habit, going around with each other up and down the streets, all over the place…I would tell him, don't do this, don't do that but he wouldn't listen to me. Because he was like my brother, when I found out that they murdered him, I didn't cry because I am a man and men don't cry, but his death hurt me deeply.

For Jorge Luis, the death of his friend was a painful event because of the intimate friendship the two had developed over the years they had been on the street together. Jorge Luis considered the youth his brother, sharing all things from clothes to food to drugs. For him, it is a matter of street relationships replacing failed family relationships, a similar process to that which Vigil (1988) describes for Chicano gangs in Los Angeles. In gangs in particular, intense pair-bonding and mentor relationships provide an inclusive sense of brotherhood and camaraderie for members (cf. Phillips 1999). In Chicano and Central American gangs, blood brother pair bonding uses the Spanish term *carnal* to express fictive ties, a term which connotes a direct link to flesh and blood. These bonds enhance but do not replace overall allegiance to the gang.

Vigil's description of Chicano gangs resonates with the lives of Dominican street kids insofar as family ties clearly become replaced with street ties. Similarly, pair bonds among Dominican street youth were almost always expressed in kinship or fictive kinship terms, though in this case ties of sanguinity were less metaphorical through the use of terms like *compadre, hermano, primo-hermano*, and the use of the English loan term *broter* (brother). Instead of the invention of a term to highlight flesh and blood connections between members, the Dominican street scene relies on importing terminology already in circulation in Dominican society. Jorge Luis calls his fallen friend his *hermano*, drawing him into the sphere of family. In explaining why he paid the 500 pesos for a taxi to take Eduardo to the hospital Luisito replied, "I couldn't let him lie their, bleeding like that, all that blood all over. Eduardo's my *broter.*" For Luisito and Jorge Luis, the invocation of the terms *hermano* and *broter* was all the evidence needed to explain the closeness of their relationships and their selfless, sharing behavior. Particularly acute in times of violence, intense dyadic friendships are what mitigate survival on the streets, even as they may place kids at deeper risks. This is where cohort affiliation among street youth and among gangs differs. Whereas *carnal* and blood-brother relationships enhance gang affiliation and loyalty, pair-bonding for Dominican street youth takes precedence over the *coro* or cohort. Intense friendship develops between youths at the expense of territorial and group affiliation.

Conclusion

What are we to make of the friendships that kids develop on the streets? Are they little more than inauthentic survival networks put to the test by petty bickering and low stakes posturing for economic success in an uncertain social environment? Despite the misgivings Fernando may have had concerning Luisito's complicity in Eduardo's stabbing, we must take into consideration that Luisito did not leave him there to die. In fact, he actively sought medical attention for his friend. He would not leave me that evening, accompanying me to the Red Cross blood bank. Whatever guilt he may have been feeling, Luisito was adamant to make amends, offering to donate the necessary blood so that we could make a withdrawal of the two liters needed for Eduardo's operation. When the nurse tactfully turned down his request due to his status as a minor, he earnestly repeated how he couldn't leave his friend in need. It left little doubt in my mind as to the depth and sincerity of his feelings, regardless of whether or not Fernando was right in his intimation of Luisito's behavior. On the day that Eduardo showed back up on the streets after months of recuperating and living with his grandmother, Luisito exclaimed to me in excitement: "This is my brother [*hermano*], the only one I trust!" If anything, the whole incident had cemented the bonds between the two teenagers and was offered as evidence of their friendship.

Pairs of youths, like Eduardo and Luisito or Juancho and Juan Carlos, do not stop being part of the larger street cohort, but they do ally themselves in such ways as to garner support for collective action. It is almost as if such pairs make up coalitions within the group which could lead to influencing critical decisions. The primary reference group for most kids was not the group or street territory, although this was important, but rather the close partnership formed with one other person in the group. In many ways pairs of friends constituted the larger group. The street group attracts kids despite its volatile nature because it is constituted by dyadic relationships. Indeed, due to the absence of collectivist ideology, it is doubtful that the street would have such pull as a living place if it were not for these deep-rooted friendships that kids develop.

If gangs are "a net that people have woven to keep themselves from falling any lower" (Phillips 1999: 65), they, too, are a net woven from primary relationships like those of the *carnal, broter,* or mentorships between peewees and veterans. What holds the dyadic relationships present in gangs in a constellation of hierarchical or more formal group organization is the inclusion of signifying practices that push for a seamless identification between one's gang brother, the gang, and the barrio they represent. These relationships condition trust across the different segments within a gang, so that younger members become allied with older members and enculturated in the process. Members, by learning to communicate with those in their gang, learn that they can trust those who share the same cultural language.

For the kids on the street of Santo Domingo, however, trust didn't go much beyond one's closest friends and didn't extend to others in the volatile group. It is not that solidarity is a basic building block for coordinated social organization. This is a truism. What focusing on street kids demonstrates for youth gangs and social groups in general is that solidarity requires certain features to be present for intricate social systems to form. Dominican street kids demonstrate solidarity by caring for their closest friends in times of need. Consuming marijuana and crack together also provides a limited sense of group identity, as this revolves around sharing in something they all enjoy. The group stays together so that its members have better access to the drug, not necessarily out of any great sense of loyalty to the larger group or even protection from harm. Consuming drugs together, however, is not enough to formulate more than a nascent sense of belonging. Even rituals of joking, smoking, and sharing food only foster fleeting good times but not sustained sociability. In all, the loose affiliation to the group but apparent trust among pairs of youths present in street kid populations points to the ways that solidarity may not be the best measure of group identity. Instead, solidarity and trust are necessary features of survival, however brittle that trust may be, and exists without a solid group identity.

Notes

Research for this paper was conducted between November of 2004 and November of 2006 while I served as a U.S. Peace Corps volunteer in the Dominican Republic with the NGO *Niños del Camino* in Santo Domingo. I give special thanks to Adele Williams and Estivaliz Ladrón de Guevara for the chance to serve. My Dominican coworkers Natividad Sosa, Epifanio de Jesús Castillo, Héctor Ramírez, Martha Alcántara, and Dorca Rojas were stalwart companions in the rough and tumble world of the NGO and street outreach. Fellow volunteers Eli Barbado, Núria Perelló, Roberto Palencia, Rúben Gallegos, Isabelle Deneyer, Laura Ibañez, Rachelle Olden, Emily Hoffman, and Mary Rolle offered much needed emotional and physical support. Most of all, to the hundreds of kids and youth working and living on the streets who let me into their world and their lives, I am indebted for the ways they enriched my life. *Pa'lante!*

1. All names are pseudonyms, and some identities and situations described are composites of actual people and events.
2. For reviews and critiques of the Chicago School literature, see the chapters in Kontos et al. (2003) and in Venkatesh (2003) especially.
3. Excerpts are from tape-recorded interviews gathered as part of the *InteRed/Comunidad de Madrid/Jóvenes del Tercer Mundo*–funded research project, *Porfiles Sociales de los Niños, Adolescentes y Jóvenes que Viven Fuera del Hogar en Santo Domingo, Santiago, y Barahona*. Interviews were conducted by the author with assistance from the staff at *Niños del Camino* in Santo Domingo, *Acción Callejera* in Santiago, and *Hogar Mamá Margarita* in Barahona. Translation and interpretation of the interviews are the sole responsibility of the author.

Bibliography

Anderson, E. 1999. *Code of the Street: Decency, Violence, and the Moral Life of the Inner City*, New York: N.W. Norton and Company.

Aptekar, L. 1988. *Street Children of Cali*, Durham: Duke University Press.

Cintron, R. 1997. *Angel's Town: Chero Ways, Gang Life, and Rhetorics of the Everyday*, Boston: Beacon Press.

Ennew, J. 1994. Parentless friends: A cross-cultural examination of networks among street children and street youth, in F. Nestman and K. Hurrelmann (eds.), *Social Networks and Social Support in Childhood and Adolescence*, New York: Aldine de Gruyter, pp. 409–426.

Goode, J. 1987. *Gaminismo: The Changing Nature of the Street Child Phenomenon in Colombia*, Latin America Report No. 28, Hanover, NH: Universities Field Staff International Reports.

Hagan, J., and Bill McCarthy, 1998. *Mean Streets: Youth Crime and Homelessness*, Cambridge: Cambridge University Press.

Hansson, D. 2003. "Strolling" as a gendered experience: A feminist analysis of young females in Cape Town, *Children, Youth and Environments*, vol. 13, no. 1, pp. 1–19, http://colorado.edu/journals/cye [accessed October 1, 2007].

Hecht, T. 1998. *At Home in the Street: Street Children of Northeast Brazil*, Cambridge: Cambridge University Press.

Horowitz, R., and G. Schwartz. 1974. Honor, normative ambiguity, and gang violence, *American Sociological Review*, vol. 39, no. 2, pp. 238–251.

Kontos, L., D. Brotherton, and L. Barrios (eds.). 2003. *Gangs and Society: Alternative Perspectives*, New York: Columbia University Press.

Korbin, J. E. 2003. Children, childhoods, and violence, *Annual Review of Anthropology*, vol. 32, pp. 431–446.

Kovats-Bernat, J. C. 2006. *Sleeping Rough in Port-au-Prince*, Tallahassee: University Press of Florida.

Lucchini, R. 1996. *Niños de la Calle: Identidad, Sociabilidad, Droga*, Barcelona: Los Libros de la Frontera.

Marquez, P. 1999. *The Street is My Home: Youth and Violence in Caracas*, Stanford: Stanford University Press.

McDonald, K. 2003. Marginal youth, personal identity, and the contemporary gang: Reconstructing the social world? in L. Kontos, D. Brotherton, and L. Barrios (eds.), *Gangs and Society: Alternative Perspectives*, New York: Columbia University Press, pp. 62–74.

Miranda, M. 2003. *Homegirls in the Public Sphere*, Austin: University of Texas Press.

Phillips, S. A. 1999. *"Wallbangin": Graffiti and Gangs in L.A.*, Chicago: University of Chicago Press.

Shaw, K. 2007. *Agony Street: A Reflection on Masochism and Politics on the Street*, Digital Edition, Santa Fe: Shine a Light, http://www.shinealight.org [accessed May 27, 2008].

Stephenson, S. 2006. *Crossing the Line: Vagrancy, Homelessness, and Social Displacement in Russia*, Basingstoke: Ashgate.

Taylor, L. J., and M. Hickey. 2001. *Tunnel Kids*, Tucson: University of Arizona Press.

Thrasher, F. M. 1927. *The Gang: A Study of 1,313 Gangs in Chicago*, Chicago: University of Chicago Press.

Van Blerk, L. 2005. Negotiating spatial identities: Mobile perspectives on street life in Uganda, *Children's Geographies*, vol. 3, no. 1, pp. 5–21.

Venkatesh, S. 2003. A note on social theory and the American street gang, in L. Kontos, D. Brotherton, and L. Barrios (eds.), *Gangs and Society: Alternative Perspectives*, New York: Columbia University Press, pp. 3–11.

Vigil, J. D. 1988. Group processes and street identity: Adolescent Chicano gang members, *Ethos*, vol. 16, no. 4, pp. 421–445.

Vigil, J. D. 2002. *A Rainbow of Gangs: Street Cultures in the Mega-City*, Austin: University of Texas Press.

Vigil, J. D. 2003. Urban violence and street gangs, *Annual Review of Anthropology*, vol. 32, pp. 225–242.

Chapter 5

"Gaining Respect": The Logic of Violence among Young Men in the Barrios of Caracas, Venezuela

Verónica Zubillaga

Introduction

In Latin American cities, such as Caracas, where luxurious shopping malls contrast with walled in neighborhoods and precarious *barrios*, violence has become a daily event. Although frequently linked to the ever-growing presence of criminal networks and organizations in Venezuelan society or to the abuse of force by police agents, violence is a phenomenon that is becoming increasingly embedded into particular types of social relationships that can be said to exhibit a lack of restraint, and are determined by a logic of revenge. This is perhaps especially true of young men living in poor urban barrios, whose daily lives involve confrontations with their peers and with the police, in which risking their own life, terminating the lives of others, and dying is a constant possibility. How are we to understand the violence both suffered and perpetrated by these young men? When asked, they keep repeating that what they do is a *demand for respect*, but what is the meaning of this "respect," and how does it play out in different situations and among diverse social interlocutors? How do meanings attached to violent actions relate to the construction of personal and social identity? Is it possible to redefine and rebuild "respect" in an alternative, nonviolent manner?

This chapter is organized in three parts. In the first, I provide a synthetic outline of the extent and basic characteristics of violence in Venezuela, and offer some tentative general explanations before outlining some key definitional issues. The second section proposes a framework for understanding young men's narratives about their search for respect, which I suggest needs to be understood as the subjective management of a threatened and negated identity, the consequence of a retreat to the barrio where the experience of respect is primordially forged. The connections between different types of demands for respect and their associated violence are specifically drawn out in order to show how the violence constitutes an attempt to obtain a form of personal recognition. Finally, the third section of this chapter presents a more diachronic vision of these subjective social processes through the biographical reconstruction of the life trajectories of young men who previously led violent lives but managed to forge new, nonviolent lifestyles.

Violent Deaths and Research Concerns

The most obvious, and perhaps the most shocking, indicator of violence in Venezuela is the homicide rate. According to official data, the rate doubled in the 1990s from 13 per 100,000 people in 1990 to 25 per 100,000 by 1999 (PROVEA 2006). In Caracas, recorded cases were three times greater: in 1990 the homicide rate was 44 per 100,000, increasing to 94 per 100,000 inhabitants by 1999. With the change of political regime in 1999 and the initiation of the *Bolivarian revolution*, a period of transformation and political conflict began, marked by a further increase in the number and rate of violent deaths. By 2003, the national homicide rate had risen to 44 per 100,000, although it fell slightly to 37 by 2005, while in Caracas the homicide rate rose to 119 homicides per 100,000 inhabitants in 2003 before registering a fall to 88 per 100,000 in 2005 (PROVEA 2005).

These data, however, need to be supplemented by two other indicators. The first are "deaths under investigation," as such killings that are not officially recorded as homicides. The number of deaths recorded in this category can be twice the figure for homicides: in 1991, while there were 2,502 registered homicides, there were 3,437 "deaths under investigation." Between 2001 and 2003, an average of 3,500 deaths under investigation were registered, with a significant increase in numbers thereafter to 4,031 in 2004 and 4,158 in 2005, partially correcting for the decline in the homicide rate over this period. The second category to also take into account is "deaths while resisting authority," usually a reference to somebody who is killed while resisting arrest or questioning by police. In 1990, 313 deaths were registered in this manner, almost doubling to 607 deaths in 1999 and increasing four-fold to 2,305 in 2003. Although numbers fell to 1,355 deaths by 2005, between 2000 and 2005 a total of 9,724 civilians were killed by police, equivalent to 39 civilians for each police officer killed in the period (PROVEA 2005).

Adding these different statistics together, 15,477 individuals died in violent circumstances in Venezuela in 2005. Obviously, the question to be asked is who is dying in such a way? On this point the data are fairly unequivocal. Overwhelmingly, the victims are young men from the barrios (PROVEA 2005). Studies show that 95 percent of the victims of homicides are men, 69 percent of whom are aged between 15 and 29 years, and homicide has become the primary cause of death for men between 15 and 34 years old in Venezuela (Sanjuán 1999, 2000).[1] Indeed, while the homicide rate per 100,000 inhabitants was 33 nationally in 2000, the rate for young men was 225 (PROVEA 2003). In Caracas, data reveal that victims have died near to their homes (83%), during fights in public areas (55%), in assaults (21%), especially between Friday and Sunday (55%), and usually from firearm use (92%) (Sanjuán 1999, 2000). Moreover, young men from the barrios are the preferred target of extrajudicial executions by police and military agents: men are the victims of choice (98%); with one half between the ages of 18 and 30, and 14 percent recorded as under 18 (PROVEA 2005).

There are many ways in which these data might be interpreted. At a general level, the violence must be seen as fundamentally linked to a double historical movement whereby global transformations have intersected with more traditional local-level structural tensions and evolutions over the past 30 years (Briceño-León and Zubillaga 2002). The former is linked to the world wide hegemony of a free market economy, the weakening of national states, the imposition of hyperconsumption as a form of social participation, and the expansion of an illegal trafficking economy in drugs and firearms. The latter is related to the increasingly precarious nature of the state, the devaluation of historically constituted social rights among the most vulnerable populations (housing, education, employment, health, personal security), and the economic recession of the 1980s and 1990s. The intensified penetration of the drug trade, the expansion of organized crime, and the spread of firearms, in the midst of a broader process of political and economic polarization, has contributed decisively to the deinstitutionalization of the already undermined Venezuelan justice system and state security agencies, which in turn has led to an increasing concern for personal security among the general public, as is regularly reflected in opinion polls (PROVEA 2006).

At the same time, however, violence invites us, when looking at its forms and meanings, as well as its actors, to try to understand that, beyond any instrumental orientation, there lies "an impossible and denied subjectivity" (Wieviorka 1998, 2004). This chapter focuses on understanding the multiplicity of meanings underlying the logic of violence undertaken by young men, and in particular how these youths construct identities in relation to a violent life. In so doing, the chapter employs the term "young men of a violent life" to refer to youth who are routinely involved in armed confrontations with peers, and who also participate in illegal trafficking networks and/ or organized crime. When speaking of a "violent life," we refer to a lifestyle that is related to both *doing* and *being*. It is important to note in this respect that I do not speak of "violent youth," that is, as if they were inherently violent individuals, and I do so explicitly in order to emphasize the possibility of transformation of lifestyles from violent lives to nonviolent ones. A specific element of the fieldwork that the material presented in this chapter draws on involved engaging with previously violent young men who had succeeded in forging nonviolent ways of life, something that drew attention to their different social conditions, personal options, and life projects.[2]

Identity and the Need to Become "Respected"

Different sociological theories have understood identity construction as a never-ending project, an activity in which the subject is permanently involved throughout their life, and that is at the core of all social relationships. It is a process in which the subject displays a multifaceted logic of action, and in which meaning is forged from the capacity to structure a life history into a biography. This is what allows a subject to relate to the boundaries and opportunities established by their social environment (Bajoit 1997), and negotiate the different identities attributed to them by the multiple social relationships they engage in, and through which they impose, submit to, or break with, definitions of themselves (Dubar 1991). By arranging always unstable orientations of meaning and logics of action, a subject constructs and creates their personal and social identity, that is to say, they actively mediate between different logics of action in a fundamentally relational manner (Dubet 1994). Certainly, a range of studies have revealed that the experience of exclusion, understood as a denial of social rights, integrity, or recognition, profoundly marks personal and social identity, in which strategies of retreat and individual resistance are observed (Paugam 1991). As Bourgois (1995) observes, for example, young men in a New York ghetto, unable to find stable jobs and blocked from gaining the material support to legitimate the traditional influence that they exercised over women and their children, took refuge in underground economies and reconstructed their masculinity and the corresponding respect through aggression and self-destruction.

Youth interviewed during the course of my own research in the barrios of Caracas revealed that they also defined themselves as men for whom "respect," a value inextricably linked to their masculine identity, was fundamental. This demand for respect constituted the mode through which a range of different threats to identity were managed: the *threat to physical integrity* (preservation) in a scenario marked by abandonment; the *humiliation of being poor* (economic participation) in a society marked by inequality and the obstruction of channels of social mobility; the *threat of disaffiliation* (affiliation) in a society where lacking personal social relationships represents the extreme of vulnerability; and, the *threat of not having good reasons to feel worthy of recognition and esteem* (ascendency). Violence clearly provided youth with an identity dividend; that is, the exercise of violence allowed them to obtain recognition and self-realization as a warrior and protector (demand for life preservation); as a gang member or avenger (demand for affiliation); as an economic agent, consumer, and provider (demand for economic participation); and as a show of masculinity identified with the exercise of power (demand for ascendancy).

This recurring demand for respect was the mode by which different threats to identity were managed; a mode that could however be understood from two points of view. First, at the level of *meaning*, respect is an ideal value that guided the action of youths, associated with particular notions of masculinity. This translated at the level of *social interactions* into active normative claims for recognition and ascendance. Whether these were met or not is what defined both the subject and those they related to. Acceptance of the demands of respect was viewed as a recognition of existence, whereas conversely the lack of respect—"anti-respect"—effectively constituted a denial of existence. Semantically important in this respect are the slang classificatory descriptors *culebras* and *chigüires*. A *culebra* is a snake in Spanish, and in the context of Caracan barrios is a term often applied to the *enemy* and *the situation of conflict that is settled with death*, and that is prolonged in a chain of revenge and of more deaths. A *chigüire* derives from the Venezuelan name given to the capybara, or water pig (a small, semiaquatic, rodent, herbivorous animal), and is a youth who robs and attacks his own community and companions; it is a term that designates an individual who needs to be subjected into submission, or even exterminated (also see Duque and Muñóz 1995; Márquez 1999). As we will describe in greater detail below, these are terms that constitute key markers of the politics of respect, as also came out clearly during an interview with a youth called "Jairo," who described the consequences of lacking respect:

> Jairo: A *chamo* (guy) has to be aware—when a woman is working and lives where you live, then why are you going to take away the money she lives on, if she is working? You see? Rob someone who has money instead. But then there are some who say "we're going to take away that woman's money, we're going to take away her things." There are some who do it out of bad habits, because I know *chigüires*. [...]. But they know very well that if they behave really bad, someone will come and execute them, kill them.
>
> Verónica: Who kills them?
>
> Jairo: As I say, the people who carry out justice with their own hands, so to speak. Like the group of guys who cover their faces, the hooded ones, [who say] "you came to rob my mother, or rob my friend, or rob my uncle"— then—"look! There's the *chigüire*!" They kill him, and the next day he's found dead and no one knows who killed him. You see?

The combination of different demands and transactions mean that young men prioritized different types of demands for respect at different moments of their life path and, concomitantly, were involved in changing forms of violence. This evolution is the key to understanding the sense underlying their violence, and distinguishing the mode of action of each different young man, as the next section outlines synthetically.

The Four Demands for Respect

The Demand for Preservation

A fundamental demand in the claim for respect is the *demand for preservation*. This demand is connected to the threat to physical integrity associated with the sense of helplessness that is pervasive in the barrios of Caracas, which in turn relates to a historical process of deinstitutionalization of security and justice. Many youth emphasized that they had felt a need to be respected from a very early age, particularly vis-à-vis the harassment of older and armed peers. In this sense, the demand for preservation is established against *others*, whom youth dehumanize by casting them as being "anti-respectful," and therefore in need of elimination. Freddy recalled a threatening experience from when he was 14 years old:

> It was a gang called *Los Cucos*, named after the sector where they came from. Every time they came, they razed everything, they started from the *barrio* there, taking shoes, caps, wallets, money, everything, and for those who resisted or reacted, they were given a whack with a *cachazo* (pistol butt). I was a victim of that about 3 or 4 times and I felt very angry from my impotence. Then one day I said: That's enough. Moreover, my father, since I was a kid, always tried to teach me that I don't have to be under anyone's control, and I always had that mentality and in fact, I have kept it and I have kept it until now. But at that time, what could I do if they had a gun and I had nothing! [...] Then I made the decision to do it, and well, when they came. Yeah! Look at this *papita* (situation)! When they went to see that *papita*, it backfired on them, because they never imagined... because everything reaches a limit and it was there that I stood up for myself, because my father and mother didn't have anywhere to move, I wasn't going to leave the barrio for that reason, I liked my barrio. It was after that when I withdrew from it, so to speak, and I retained an image of respect, a respect that no one would bother me.

Freddy in other words exercised violent action defensively and spectacularly, since only through the projection of one's own capacity for intimidation could humiliation be avoided. The demand for respect (and the violent action to obtain it) therefore seeks to erect a symbolic barrier vis-à-vis the anticipation and the aggression of others. This form of potential violence evidently pays a dividend in terms of identity: in a hostile environment, one of retreat and distrust, it becomes a source of personal esteem when youths can affirm that they are recognized for their capacity to offer protection. As another young man narrated about his relationship with his girlfriend: "They respect her because she is my girlfriend. 'No one bothers me,' she told me. She said to me: 'I feel good with you, because everyone respects me, everyone.' Do you understand?"

The Demand for Affiliation

The *demand for affiliation* is related with the need to be accepted and recognized by others as part of a peer group, gang, or member of the community. This demand is intimately linked to processes of urban segregation, whereby youth in the barrios find themselves expelled from both metropolitan institutions and the city more generally. This generates a withdrawal into the barrio, and the search for localized collective forms providing a sense of "us." This fragmentation of the city reduces routine sociability and intensifies the affiliation of the few existing connections, normally the most intimate and localized, while the more spread-out and diffuse become more foreign and increasingly the object of contempt, that is to say, of "anti-respect." The need for affiliation and recognition, for example, lies at the heart of the gang's *raison-d'être*, with their group identity inevitably defined against a "them," insofar as the demand for respect is accompanied by the concession and recognition of symmetry, of equal conditions between comrades, of "*you respect me and I'll respect you.*"

This sense of the demand for respect emerges particularly clearly in the expressions of the youths, when they speak of the principles that govern the relationships in the gangs where there is a strong affective commitment among members. As one young man related:

"We were raised in the same way, in good and bad times. The problems of our mates, we never turned our back on them, instead we helped them. [...] I saw how they killed a friend here, the police...we saw things that made us stronger...and that was the respect, the dignity that one has to have, to be loyal to his companions."

I asked in reply to this, "what does respect mean?"

He answered: "Look, respect means a lot, for us it is like loyalty, I am actively loyal, we are companions, you respect me and I respect you, you're loyal and I'm loyal. Respect is when you're in that corner and I'm here, and I'm calm, because this is a guy that will get it done, and he is going to *echar plomo* (shoot lead)...that's respect for us..."

This expectation of a *quid pro quo* can be rapidly transformed, however, especially in groups of youths who are connected by economic interests such as illegal drug trafficking. A young man narrated an armed confrontation that he had with old "drug friends":

That was a friendship of drugs, pam-pam-pam, everything fine with the guys being together and stuff like that. But like I say, everything went downhill, little by little, until the friendship was broken. Then the guys began to hang out with other people who hated us and then one day we were here talking, drinking *curda* (alcohol), and the *chamos* burst in [shooting]...

Demonstrating that one possesses respect through confrontation with others is one of the ways that group affiliation is reinforced—insofar as violence consolidates belonging to the group (for similarities with U.S. gangs see Horowitz 1983; Sánchez Jankowski 1991). To belong to a gang and obtain the respect of friends, a youth has to show his willingness to exercise violence, to kill the enemy, and also to die. The stories of the young men highlighted a remarkable capacity to associate with their gangs until death; disaffiliation was perceived as the ultimate vulnerability. In this respect, it is not by chance that the figure of the *chigüire* emerges, as a symbol of absolute rejection and degradation that implicitly justifies the need to maintain the respect granted by friends. Consider Rony's response when we spoke of collective violence and I asked him if the possibility of death distressed him. He explained,

> Rony: Of course, I am distressed about it, but if I make peace with all my ene-mies, then, where do I stand with my *panas* (mates)? I'll be like a *chigüire*. Then, for instance, I do become distressed, because anyone gets distressed by the idea of dying, but as long as I can kill him first, well...
> Verónica: Why is it so important to be in the good graces of your *panas*? Isn't it maybe better to look like a *chigüire* in front of your *panas* but at least not be killed?
> Rony: The truth is that I don't see it that way. I prefer to stay with my *panas* instead of being a *chigüire*. No one accepts a *chigüire*. A *chigüire* is a *chigüire* wherever, and where he goes he will continue being a *chigüire*. So, if from the beginning I got people to respect me, that I wasn't anyone's *chigüire*, now after so many years I'm not going to become a *chigüire*. I already earned my respect...

Although this type of violence is customarily viewed quite functionally in relation to the constitution of the gang group, it is clear from the life stories of these youths that even for the youngest, involvement in daily armed confrontations and violent action can become a source of personal esteem. A young man's willingness to use violence provides confirmation of his membership, while a gang's affective solidarity reinforces his levels of confidence, as does the fact that his peers are ready to risk their own lives for him.

At the same time, this logic can also lead to significant sources of disso-nance. Violence in order to obtain the respect of a gang peer group almost inevitably places young men in open tension with their sense of affilia-tion with their local communities, insofar as they precipitate a dynamic of violence that affects all within the community. This tension manifests itself in two forms. First, because affiliation with the gang is often asserted through a violent demonstration of power over local neighborhood inhab-itants, although this may also take the form of indifference, that is where youths are indifferent to community neighbors who may be caught up in the crossfire of their conflicts with other youth. This approaches in many ways a logic of "anti-respect" against the community; as an interviewee recalled,

> We were really bad, we were terrible at that time, we shot all over the place. We killed a boy in the barrio, all of us were the ugliest, a nightmare! [He laughs]. And that's how they considered us, they wanted our heads...
> Verónica: Who thought that way, the neighbors or other guys?
> The neighbors from the other sectors, the mothers of children, their jew-els. When they saw us and aaaah! They called the police, and we had to jump out the window. That was really crazy!

In these circumstances, the young men often take over the space of the barrio, deny free movement to neighbors, ignore their criticisms and revel in the
environment of fear.

The second form that the tension can take is more semantic in nature, as
is well illustrated by the way that youth appropriated the negative identities
ascribed to them by the wider community:

> Among my friends, among my group, they know that one is a *malandro*
> [armed thug]. Jokingly, I always say; "I'm a *malandro*" in front of them,
> the people I trust. But the less people know who you are, the better. For
> my reputation, the less they know that one is a *malandro*, the better,
> because, listen, then you don't get singled out. But the people know, they
> know who you are. There are others who make one look like an ogre, like
> a guy who gets involved in what he wants to 'cause he wants to, but you
> know...

A possible resolution here can be found in the also semantic emphasis in
youth gang members' discourse of the need to "be serious" and to restrain
their violence vis-à-vis the local neighborhood community. Once again this
can be associated with the notion of respect, insofar as a positive relationship with neighbors can be built around a common suspicion of the police,
and recognition of the youths' vigilante role as guarantors of community
protection.[3]

It was clear that many youths sought to avert the stigma of being *malandro*
with the adoption of a persona of community vigilante or "avenger," either
protecting local inhabitants or else conducting the most brutal "punishments" attacks, especially on those who invaded the neighborhood, or on
those whom they perceived as *chigüire*, that is to say, incarnating "anti-
respect" (this often included drug addicts or street kids). One of the interviewees said the following:

> Well, everyone knows me here, outside as well, but I mean, as a serious
> person—You see? You try to avoid problems. You know that the fight
> that is won is the fight that is avoided. Not shooting at each other here
> and there. Because some times, many times when you go through that,
> there are innocent people who are shot. You know what is good and what
> is bad, what you don't like or what you like, at least, for example: I don't
> like people robbing in the neighborhood, as I was saying, that people act
> like *chigüires*, I don't like that. And *a la hora del té* (at the right moment),
> I arrive and punish the *chamos*. "No man, this *chamo* is robbing." "You
> know that they're gonna get you, *huevón*." You see? Then one, as one accu-
> mulates more respect, becomes more of a leader. Do you understand?

Young people therefore had to both limit their violence, in deference to neighbors, and exercise spectacular violence in order to maintain credibility, which was
a balance that was especially difficult for younger gang members. Ultimately,

youth managed their disrepute, as Goffman (1963) would put it, by emphasizing their capacity for protective violence against the *chigüire* or other youth
gangs, while simultaneously adopting strategies that minimized the visibility of
their more violent public identity acting, especially vis-à-vis local neighborhood
inhabitants, in order to avoid being considered a scourge by the community.

The Demand for Economic Participation

The demand for respect associated with *economic participation* needs to be
understood against a society in which social mobility is perceived as an empty
promise and is associated only with illegal economic activity. In the drugs
economy or organized crime, which are characterized by intense rivalry
and deregulated competition, violent action is principally *instrumental*. For
Pedro, however, the instrumental exercise of violence inevitably merged with
its expressive and affiliative dimension, particularly when what was at stake
was obtaining the necessary respect to be accepted in a gang:

> There are *chamos* that, for instance, think: "to be able to be with them,
> to get a *cartel*,[4] I have to do something so they pay attention to me."
> For instance, this guy brought in some money, and others responded:
> "*Firmaste*[5] the *chamo*?" "Listen, the *chamo* is making an effort." Then,
> already, they respect him a little: "look, the *chamo* is serious, the *chamo*
> isn't like that *chigüireo*"... and that's how one is allowed to get into the
> group. The chamo is serious, let's let him remain with us...

Violence is understood here as capacity, the possibility of vanquishing or
eliminating competitors. It represents a routine form of exchange, with
antagonist "others" simply reduced to obstacles that have to be handled
through overwhelming force.

At the same time, however, the exercise of violence allows for the forging
of an identity dividend, in the form of the capacity to become both *providers*
(breadwinners) and *consumers*, as well as obtaining the recognition of partners and colleagues for a certain *professional expertise*. Thus, youths claimed
recognition as economically viable subjects, able to generate resources for
living from an early age, in order to attain consumption patterns in line with
certain consumerist self-images, including, for example, becoming providers
in their homes (the material base of respect within barrio culture). Among
the older and most "respected" youth, the exercise of violence can often
become a service, even a potential monopoly, for which they may be con-
tacted by outsiders needing protection in the barrio. To this extent, the exercise of violence constituted a source of personal esteem, but it was also a skill
and an ability, that could "open the doors" to more earnings, as one interviewee put it. Similarly, another 26-year-old interviewee described how:

> I have earned the respect so that no one quarrels with me and now I have
> a salary. Because there is a [construction] company that has been robbed.

They saw the alternative to prevent those things as giving me a job as a guard. [...] Then the rumor spreads that I work as a guard and then no one thought of wanting to rob anything else. Because they said: listen Fredo doesn't want us to rob [them] ... I let people know, I appeal to people's consciences regarding how things should be done.

The exercise of instrumental violence associated with economic participation thus constructs a reputation that is a form of respect. It is a two-way process, however, which also evolves according to the age of the young men. The youngest are engaged in a period of construction and expansion of their reputation, and speak of the need to demonstrate courage and engage in spectacular violence in order to show what they are capable of. Older youths speak of being "serious," of the importance of keeping one's word, and judge violent actions as an issue of management: among youth considered partners, violence is about granting respect and recognizing the symmetry of the association; toward opponents it is about eliminating competitors.

The Demand for Ascendance

The demand for ascendance is linked to the recovery of a traditional model of masculine respect (Ramírez 1993). Interviewee discourses highlighted a desire to be recognized for their masculine identity and exhibited strong performative elements, including, for example, seeking distinction by acquiring fashionable brands on the one hand, but also emphasizing the need to be able to give and impose orders in a way that is traditionally deemed "male" (although it should be noted that men exercise and rework their masculinity according to a hegemonic ideal associated with domination and control in terms of available resources and scenarios—see Connell 1987; Messerschmidt 1993).

The demand for respect is stressed in everyday speech by the preeminence of a notion of "ordering" through a wide range of verbs—*firmar* and *malandrear*—that underline the performative content of this identity drama.[6] One interviewee outlined how respect is earned individually, but is linked with ordering others outside the gang:

"A *chigüire* is a *chamo* who practically isn't worth anything, who has no life, who doesn't *firma*..."

"Firma?" I repeated.

"That is, for instance, another tells me: 'You *firmas* as a *malandro* because of me, because I'm the one who is recommending you.' No! that crap no! I get angry. I *firmo* because I make myself respected, not because another comes and says: 'You're going to respect that one.' No. What I am I earned on my own."

"What does *firmar* mean" I asked.

"That is, for instance that I command more than someone, someone who is not in our group. For instance a *chamo* who doesn't get into trouble, who is *sano*,[7] one treats him like a *chigüire* because one knows that they are never going to be *firmando* any one other than themselves."

"Why is it so important to command and not to be commanded?" I said.

"The truth is that, at least there, that was the custom, I don't know why, those *chamos* [his older peers in the gang] got me used to it, because if I hadn't become accustomed to it I would be a *chigüire* to them."

The demand for respect related to ascendance is displayed through command over others. Violent action here acquires an *expressive sense*, as a rite of domination providing the reason to look up to an actor. The logic of "anti-respect"—that youths have toward a *chigüire*—implies that respect ceases to be intersubjective, there is a loss of the capacity of recognition that reduces the other into someone who is subjugated.

Synthesis

I have argued that young men construct their identities through the daily management of different demands linked to respect—for preservation, affiliation, economic participation and ascendance—and that each of these underpin different logics of violence that lead to different identity dividends, as well as forms of ascriptions of "anti-respect." The demand for respect through preservation involves a logic of defensive violence; the dividend is a sense of self-identity as a warrior or protector. Affiliation provides a sense of identity through gang membership, and also casts a sense of "anti-respect" for the enemy. In terms of the wider community, however, its logic of violence is delicately balanced between intimidation and containment, with youth drawing ambiguously on being either feared community members or supported vigilantes. Their "anti-respect" alter egos are outsiders and those that feel no sense of obligation to the local community, as epitomized in the figure of the *chigüire*. The demand for economic participation draws on an instrumental logic of violence, but which spills over into a bifurcated sense of identity that sees subjects regarding themselves both as consumer/providers, as well as antagonistic competitors. Finally, the need for ascendance draws on a highly performative logic of violence, including in particular in relation to enacting particular constructions of masculinity related to being able to command others about, in relation to which violence constitutes both a valued capacity as well as a source of personal esteem.

The various accounts provided by interviewees highlight how particular demands for respect become more relevant than others over time. We can understand this in relation to violent actions being part and parcel of a diachronic life trajectory, whereby demands for respect are cyclical in nature, and linked to the specific circumstances of each youth. Youths belonging to a gang, for example, emphasized the need for respect deriving from their affiliation with their gang as their principal driving force, while others involved in illegal drug trafficking pointed to the need for economic participation not only as their most important concern, but one that actively operated in tension with the demands of gang affiliation. More specifically, the notion that youth gang members needed to gain some sense of respect from the local community was frequently seen as fundamentally contradictory of drug trafficking. One drug-dealing youth, for example, emphasized the contradictions between the respect he derived from being a provider for his siblings with the contempt he faced from his neighbors for his frequent resort to intimidation and violence in order to protect his drug trafficking. Similarly, one youth involved in drug trafficking belonged to a gang where there were close friendship ties (affective solidarity), whereas another youth also involved in the drug trade was a member of a gang where the fundamental tie was financial (contractual solidarity). To be a gang member was particularly relevant in the narrations of the former, whereas the latter tended to put special emphasis on defining himself as an economic agent. What these different cases show is that identities based on violence often intermix different logics that clearly make renouncing violence difficult. Yet, youth have managed to define and construct alternative identities. In the final section of this chapter, what I want to outline is how the search for respect among youths who successfully manage to renounce violence involves a critical management of the Self, understood here as a process of permanent socialization that allows for the conversion of social interactions marked by negation and death into interactions marked by consensual and reciprocal recognition, and therefore the possibility of change (Dubar 1991).

Biographies of Reconversion to Nonviolent Lifestyles

Forging the possibility of life paths different from those of the youths that we have just described would imply the unfolding of integrated substantive actions and policies that "will neutralize" the different threats experienced by them. Thus, it would demand fundamental structural and cultural transformations. It would demand in the first place, from the political point of view, a public policy of human life preservation that might be translated into a plan of disarmament and control of weapons as well as the cleaning up of the police and the justice system (in the face of threats to physical integrity). It would demand, from a social and economic perspective, the reduction of social gaps between the population through the strengthening of the institutional systems of social solidarity—health, education, housing—as well as the stimulation and creation of worthwhile jobs in which youths may invest their personal passions and build a "respected" identity.

From a social perspective, it would demand the promotion of social networks and projects of community and youth participation from which the people of the communities can repossess their spaces, their city, and perceive the "other" as a possible interlocutor—and not as a fatal enemy—(vis-à-vis the threat to disaffiliation). Finally, from a cultural perspective, it would require the establishment of a platform of meaningful activities through which youth can build the recognition sought from identities different from the masculinity linked to power and domination. We refer here mainly to

expressive activities such as music, dance, sport; that is, spaces to drama-
tize identities liable to be recognized and appreciated by their performance
being linked to a particular sensibility—musical, for example. This would
demand, finally, installing a capacity for discussion as a critical vehicle to
appeal, demand, request, and question the realities lived as threats.

In this section I want to consider what I am terming the *biographical
reconversion of male youths of violent life* as an experience of redefinition of
self-identity and of substantial modification of the routines of daily life. I
speak of *reconversion* because it is a process that involves a second phase of
transformation of identity and lifestyle. The first process was the initiation
into the violent lifestyle or, as expressed by interviewees, the "entry into
another world," from having a "healthy mind" to having a "sick mind." It
involves an experience of rupture in the biography of the subject (Berger and
Luckmann 1979: 200; Dubar 1991: 117), from a *before* marked by evalua-
tions of the Self based on virility and fearlessness, to an *after* characterized
by the definition of the Self on the basis of an alternative lifestyle and a projection into the future. In many ways, this experience of reconversion can be
seen as a process of *resistance*, insofar as there are few incentives to abandon
violent lifestyles. The biographies of the youths interviewed highlight that
the process of reconversion can be analyzed at two levels: the "subjective
plane of the Self," and the "subjective plane of Others" (i.e., of social relationships). Both planes are however intimately linked and discussed here
separately for heuristic purposes.

The Subjective Plane of the Self

There exists a range of subjective processes involved in the reconversion of
youths of violent lifestyles that are intimately experienced by their individual
Self. In many ways, these can be seen as fundamental milestones in individual life biographies, and can be divided into three basic categories. The
first involves the assimilation of *protective elements* that limit the subjective
influence of activities linked to violent lifestyles. These, for example, include
encountering new tastes, practices, or skills that may potentially allow for the
construction of an alternative identity, including an alternative conception
of masculinity, based on different forms of vindication than those sought
by armed young men (see also Barker 2005). This is something that is often
associated with the world of work, for example, which can become for youths
an alternative nonviolent repertoire of activities, interests, resources, and
opportunities that can be incorporated in the subjective workings of the Self,
particularly at difficult moments in time. Other concrete examples include
developing a passion for a particular form of music and/or dance, as well as
conversion to Evangelical Christianity.

The second process that can intervene in reconversion is the *possibility
of destruction of the Self*. Young men of violent life frequently witness the
death of close friends and gang partners, and have to confront the fact that
"I could have been in his place," because they shared the same routines and

enemies. Awareness of the potentially high cost of continuing with lifestyles involving violence brings a capacity to question themselves, that the youths describe as a sort of "existential crossroads." This is a fundamental moment because youths become aware that they have options with definitive consequences: redemption or perdition. The existential crossroads may be the result of a personal reflexive process or the outcome of a configuration of events in which they are implicated, such as, for example, being detained by the police. The youths of violent life may well know that life can be ephemeral, but it is frequently necessary for them to stark confront this fact in order for them to think of choosing an alternative path.

This impulse often becomes materialized into new life projects, whereby the Self itself is seen as something transformable, and therefore able to intervene in changing one's own history. The emergence of such existential projects allows for the redefinition of the meaning of respect or self-esteem, that is to say, the sense of personal accomplishment and social recognition to which one aspires (Bajoit 2003). It involves, as one youth put it, establishing a new "life goal." For some youths, this goal was expressed in a dedication to a particular type of music, while for others, the life goal was related to having children, being a provider for the family, and also looking after one's mother.[8] Many youths defined work as a means to attain a nonviolent respected identity. They distinguished, however, between self-employed, low productivity, and humiliating jobs, and those that provided status and recognition, thereby allowing investment in one's own creativity; activities with meaning for the Self and opportunities for recognition (Llorens 2005: 181).

The Subjective Plane of Others

While the subjective plane of the Self clearly constituted a critical space in which reconversion processes occurred, youths also recognized in their biographical accounts the importance of social bonds, and more specifically the notion that there needed to be an awareness of personal change that went beyond the Self. As one youth implicitly suggested in an interview, a meaningful redefinition of a negative public image and the viable emergence of a revitalized notion of respect necessarily implied a public awareness of this transformation:

> Now it's different, they respect us because they know that we have changed, and we now want improvements; they respect us for what we do, for what you are doing and not because you have a gun, you're going to threaten them, you're going to rob them, or you're going to kill them.

I thus refer in this section to the importance of the "subjective plane of Others" in order to describe processes linked to the collective aspects of youths' identity modification and the materialization of individual existential projects, or in other word, to the important role played by the existence of a network of alternative social relationships in the definition and confirmation of a new self-identity and changed routines of daily life. Because of the prominent role these social relations play, I identify them as *allies*, of which there are two types.

The first type are family allies, generally the mother, female partner or girlfriend, and children. Although the masculine identities of youth with violent lifestyles tend to be built around domination, women have also been recognized as key originators and (re)enforcers of change (Barker 2005: 150). Certainly, many ethnographic studies of violent male youth have pointed out that the Mother is frequently one of their most significant social attachments (Assis 1999; Márquez 1999; Salazar 1998), and a powerful reason to desist from violence that emerged from youths' discourses was to prevent painful gossip about them reaching their mothers. Furthermore, mothers were seen as offering unconditional emotional support and companionship in the processes of redefinition of the young men's routines. Female partners and girlfriends also opened up possibilities for personal reconversion, although it should be noted that life as a couple was also seen as inherently involving certain tensions such as the pressure to be monogamous, and renouncing friends for family. In many cases, however, the partner of young men initiated them into Evangelical Churches, which provided an institutional structure that allowed them to extricate themselves (generally progressively) from the routines associated with a violent life, as I will discuss further below.[9]

The second type of ally can be subdivided into two categories: individuals external to the family, and institutions. Both could open new horizons of meanings, and provided opportunities and resources for change, with their affective commitment often fundamental to the reconversion process or biographical rupture (following Berger and Luckmann 1979: 197–202). Individual allies included the work bosses and music producers who encouraged the projects of youth, for example. The efficacy of these allies in the reconversion process depended on their capacity to offer possibilities to realize life projects but also the existence of a strong affective connection with the youth; they were their companions or guides in the process of biographical reconversion, models of what they could become. In this sense, the individual ally also represents an affective figure with whom a youth can chat and discuss life; a type of paternal figure with whom a reflexive dialogue can be maintained (Llorens 2005: 178). This dialogue is what enables a youth to distance himself from his violent Self and question the attributes of the particular masculine identities he has (see Barker 2005: 148). The permanence of this dialogue confirms—through verbalization and exteriorization—the parameters of a new identity and helps commit youths to alternative models of conflict resolution through nonviolent means such as dialogue, forgiveness, and the capacity to negotiate (see Dowdney 2005).

Institutional allies, such as Evangelical Churches, are probably the most holistic route for identity modification, because they are totalizing in nature, and provide a readymade set of activities, metaphors, and narratives of massive life transformation, as well as the networks and resources through which to achieve it. Indeed, such religious communities often explicitly offer youths programs for the total transformation of their Self and their daily routines (be it through seminars, study, prayer groups, or vacations with a purpose). More generally, though, they also allow youths to identify with and feel members of a community, of an "Us" with whom past experiences and common goals are shared. The notion of an existential crossroads is important here, insofar as joining a religious community takes on meaning as a new horizon to reconstruct one's identity and life routines. A fundamental experience is the modification of self-identity through events or acts of mysticism that have symbolic weight, where youths publicly renounce their previous lives, and embrace new structures that will actively seek to sustain their new identities and associated routines by providing a range of opportunities, for example, for studies or work, both of which are especially powerful for youths without family networks (Smilde 2005).[10]

The individually and collectively fostered subjective reconversion process not only translated into a redefinition of identity and a change of routines, but also a modification of the appreciation of time. Youth talked about the past in terms of a "lost time," and new projects as being connected to an emerging future. At the same time, however, a number of tensions and potential threats to successful reconversion were also evident in youths' testimonies. In abandoning a violent life and consolidating an alternative identity, they often transited via a condition of *defenselessness*, and many consequently argued that they could not entirely give up their guns as they needed these for personal and family defense, for example. Many also noted the continued *persistence of deadly conflicts* within their new lives, albeit more often than not affecting others, even if past feuds could also resurface at any moment. Similarly, many also talked about the fact that *commitments acquired while in the gang* could not necessarily be dropped so easily, and some feared retaliation or revenge from their erstwhile peers. Some also expressed *nostalgia* for their previous violent lifestyles, which clearly continued to exert a certain "seduction," with a number of interviewees commenting that few activities could match their past ones for strong emotions and excitement. Certain individuals also referred nostalgically to the easy money that their illegal activities had provided them with, particularly those without regular and sufficient income.

Conclusion

This chapter set out to understand the different modes through which, in circumstances of adversity, young men of violent lifestyles actively construct their personal and social identities, and manage to become subjects of their own lives. It traced four different meanings to their demand for respect, linking them generally to a state of threatened subjectivity and helplessness precipitated by broader structural and institutional factors such as the regression of the State, especially with regards to public urban security, and the liberalization of the economy. Youth violence from this perspective is a clamor for a subjectivity that is denied its potential by structural processes of exclusion and a concomitant atrophication of the very sense of recognition of the "Other."

I have discussed how for these youths to become subjects implies a daily search for respect against a range of different threats to their subjectivity. Two threats in particular, emerge as affecting their sense of personal identity: the threat to physical integrity, and the threat of feeling worthless and lacking self-esteem. Social identity is threatened by the humiliation of being poor and the limits of a society marked by inequality and obstructed social mobility, with the threat of disaffiliation and the concomitant lack of social relationships representing the culmination of vulnerability. Youths focus their efforts at preserving their subjectivity in relation to four distinct demands for respect: for *life preservation, ascendance, economic participation*, and *affiliation*. Each of these demands is associated with different forms of violence that can respectively deny, submit, or annihilate a predatory or nihilistic "Other," tighten the bonds of a violent collective unit such as a gang either by brutally establishing their own or their community's boundaries in opposition to an enemy, subjugate a group or context for instrumental reasons relating to economic rationale, or dramatically express a sense of being and belonging.

Although all of these different forms of youth violence can likely be seen as excessive, and sometimes even cruel, I do not want to condemn them as such. In a society where the right to life and physical integrity are not guaranteed, violence becomes a skilled practice on the basis of which one can construct a sense of respect—sometimes even the only viable one. Violence provides an "identity dividend" to youth, who may be variously recognized as *warriors-protectors, gang members*, or *vigilantes*, for example. They can also be recognized as *consumers* and *providers*, with a certain professional expertise for their conduct of illegal activities, and finally, they can also be acknowledged as *men of power*. Even if I have shown that some youth are able to turn away from lives of violent action, in the final analysis violence remains a primordial identity practice that proliferates in hostile environments where it becomes simultaneously the best guarantee for protection, a requisite of group affiliation, an instrument to obtain resources, and a source of personal recognition, a situation which will unfortunately likely very much remain the case in the barrios of Caracas, Venezuela for the foreseeable future.

Notes

This chapter benefited from the advice of Guy Bajoit, Magaly Sánchez R., Olga Avila, Roberto Briceño-León, and Manuel Llorens. Fieldwork involved Marifé Fernández, Sandra Zuñiga, and Rafel Quiñones and was conducted with financial support from the *Cooperation Universitaire au Developpement* and the *Comité National d'Acccueil* in Belgium; the *Fundación Gran Mariscal de Ayacucho* in Venezuela; and the *Consejo de Desarrollo Científico Humanístico y Tecnológico* and the *Centro de Investigaciones Jurídicas* of the *Universidad Católica Andrés Bello* in Venezuela. The chapter was translated thanks to the *Decanato de Investigación y Desarrollo* of *Universidad Simón Bolívar*, Caracas, Venezuela.

1. According to data from the *Anuarios de Mortalidad del Ministerio de Salud*, for 15–34 year olds, homicide and injuries (with or without use of firearms) constituted the first and the second causes of death in 2004. For men, in 1997 homicide was the fifth cause of death and in 2004 it was the third (CISOR-CESAP 2006).

2. A range of life stories were collected between 2000 and 2006 with a range of young people: with nine 17–27 year olds in Caracas barrios; with fourteen 17–18 year olds who were detained in *Centros de Tratamiento y Diagnostico para Menores Transgresores* in 2000; and with ten 22–30 year olds who had extricated themselves from violent lives. I use the term "life story," in contrast to "life history," to emphasize the fact that the narrative is a response to the demand of the researcher and is not a history experienced by the person being interviewed.

3. This type of management was evident in the discourses of youths who had family networks in their barrio, especially older youths dedicated to criminal activity who sought to avoid being captured by the police.

4. In slang, cartel and its adjectival derivatives, *cartelúo/a*, mean prestige, much derived from the reputation earned through drug trafficking and/or an act of fearlessness (Duque and Muñoz 1995).

5. *Firmaste* in this context means noting the presence or action of another.

6. *Firmar* (to sign) alludes to the public image that is dramatized in a situation: "*él firma una de malandro*," means a display of gestures associated with the social identity of the *malandro*, such as to show off. *Malandrear* as a verb refers to the interactions associated to the demonstration of power and of being able to dominate the will of the other.

7. Someone who does not consume drugs or does not get involved in illegal activities.

8. Many studies point to the importance Venezuelans attach to the mother and the family group in the construction of their identity (Hurtado 1998; Moreno 1995; Smilde 2005).

9. Furthermore, children were often perceived as representing a form of Self projected into the future; they were considered the reflection of one's being. For males committed to an identity of respect by being providers, the fear of what might befall their children in the event of their death also provided a powerful rationale to abandon routines of violence, possession of weapons, or consumption of drugs or alcohol.

10. I am not suggesting that Evangelical Churches will intrinsically support reconversion; indeed, some studies have shown them to be highly intolerant of difference, sexist, dogmatic, and very arbitrary (Smilde 2007). At the same time, processes of reconversion should not be confused with processes of *normalization*; we are not dealing with deviants on the one hand and normal youth on the other; rather, youth violence is simply one possible logic of actions of that age-category's general lifecycle in context with very harsh conditions of existence.

Bibliography

Assis, S. G. de. 1999. *Traçando Caminhos em uma Sociedade Violenta: A Vida de Jovens Infratores e de sus Irmaos nao Infratores*, Río de Janeiro: Editora FIOCRUZ.

Bajoit, G. 1997. Qu'est-ce que le sujet, in G. Bajoit and E. Belin (eds.), *Contributions à une Sociologie du Sujet*, Paris: Editions L'Harmattan, pp. 112–130.

Bajoit, G. 2003. *Todo Cambia, Análisis Sociológico del Cambio Social y Cultural en las Sociedades Contemporáneas*, Santiago de Chile: Ediciones LOM.

Barker, G. 2005. *Dying to Be Men: Youth Masculinity and Social Exclusion*, London: Routledge.

Berger, M., and T. Luckmann. 1979. *La Construcción Social de la Realidad*, Buenos Aires: Amorrortu Ediciones [Orig. 1967].

Bourgois, P. 1995. *In Search of Respect: Selling Crack in El Barrio*, New York: Cambridge University Press.

Briceño-Leon, R., and V. Zubillaga. 2002. Violence and globalisation in Latin America, *Current Sociology*, vol. 50, no. 1, pp. 19–37.

CISOR-CESAP. 2006. *Venescopio*, Reporte Mensual No. 17, http://www.venescopio. org.ve/docs/reporte_agosto-septiembre06.pdf [accessed December 14, 2008].

Connell, R. 1987. *Gender and Power*, Cambridge: Polity Press.

Dowdney, L. 2005. *Ni Guerra Ni Paz. Comparaciones Internacionales de Niños y Jóvenes en la Violencia Armada Organizada*, Rio de Janeiro: COAV, http:// www.coav.org.br/ [accessed December 14, 2008].

Dubar, C. 1991. *La Socialisation*, Paris: Armand Colin.

Dubet, F. 1994. *Sociologie de l'Expérience*, Paris: Du Seuil.

Duque, J. R., and B. Muñoz. 1995. *La Ley de la Calle: Testimonios de Jóvenes Protagonistas de la Violencia en Caracas*, Caracas: Fundarte, Alcaldía de Caracas.

Goffman, E. 1963. *Stigma: Notes on the Management of Spoiled Identity*, New Jersey: Prentice-Hall.

Horowitz, R. 1983. *Honor and the American Dream: Culture and Identity in a Chicano Community*, New Brunswick: Rutgers University Press.

Hurtado, S. 1998. *Matrisocialidad. Exploración en la Estructura Psicodinámica Básica de la Familia Venezolana*, Caracas: Ediciones FACES.

Llorens, M. 2005. *Niños con Experiencia de Vida en la Calle*, Buenos Aires: Editorial Paidós.

Márquez, P. 1999. *The Street is My Home*, Stanford: Stanford University Press.

Messerschmidt, J. 1993. *Masculinities and Crime*, Lanham: Rowman and Littlefield Publishers.

Moreno, A. 1995. *La Familia Popular Venezolana*, Cursos de Formación Sociopolítica No. 15, Caracas: Fundación Centro Gumilla y Centro de Investigaciones Populares.

Paugam, S. 1991. *La Disqualification Sociale*, Paris: Presses Universitaires de France.

PROVEA (Programa Venezolano de Educación-Acción en Derechos Humanos). 2004. *Situación de los Derechos Humanos*, Informe Anual, Caracas: PROVEA.

PROVEA. 2005. *Situación de los Derechos Humanos*, Informe Anual, Caracas: PROVEA.

PROVEA. 2006. *Situación de los Derechos Humanos*, Informe Anual, Caracas: PROVEA.

Ramírez, R. 1993. *What It Means to Be a Man*, New Brunswick: Rutgers University Press.

Salazar, A. 1998. Violencias juveniles: ¿Contraculturas o hegemonía de la cultura emergente? in H. J. Cubides, M. C. Laverde Toscano, and C. E. Valderrama (eds.), *"Viviendo a Toda": Jóvenes, Territorios Culturales y Nuevas Sensibilidades*, Santa Fe de Bogotá: Siglo del Hombre Editores, pp. 110–128.

Sanjuán, A. M. 1999. *Estudio Sobre los Indicadores de la Criminalidad y la Delincuencia en Venezuela*, Unpublished Mimeograph, Programa Seguridad y Convivencia Ciudadana.

Sanjuán, A. M. 2000. Violencia y criminalidad en Venezuela, *SIC*, vol. 63, no. 627, pp. 292–294.

Sánchez-Jankowsky, M. 1991. *Islands in the Street: Gangs and American Urban Society*, Berkeley: University of California Press.

Smilde, D. 2005. A qualitative comparative analysis of conversion to Venezuelan Evangelicalism: How networks matter, *American Journal of Sociology*, vol. 111, no. 3, pp. 757–796.

Smilde, D. 2007. Notas sobre el estudio de la conversión Evangélica en Caracas: Historia de vida, historia de evento y muestreo, *Ensayos en Homenaje a Alberto Gruson*, Caracas: Universidad Católica Andrés Bello.

Wieviorka, M. 2004. *La Violence*, Paris: Editions Balland.

Wieviorka, M. 1998. Le nouveau paradigme de la violence, *Cultures et Conflits*, vol. 29/30, http://www.conflits.org/Numeros/30WIEVIO.html [accessed December 14, 2008].

Zubillaga, V. 2003. *Entre Hombres y Culebras: Hacerse Hombre de Respeto en una Ciudad Latinoamericana*, Unité d'anthropologie et de sociologie, Louvain-la-Neuve: Université Catholique de Louvain.

Chapter 6

Piloting Experimental Methods in Youth Gang Research: A Camping Expedition with Rival *Manchas* in Ayacucho, Peru

Cordula Strocka

Social scientists have used a variety of research methods to investigate youth gangs and youth violence, including, for example, participant observation, surveys, and interviews. But regardless of what methods have been applied, the principle has generally been the same: to observe and record incidents of youth gang violence but not to intervene. Contrary to academic practice, the study presented in this chapter aimed to *change* the behavior and attitudes of research participants and to *reduce* intergang conflict by means of a quasi-field experiment.[1] The study was undertaken as part of a long-term participatory field research in Ayacucho, a region in the southern-central Andes of Peru (Strocka 2006). Throughout the 1980s and early 1990s, Ayacucho was seriously affected by a protracted armed conflict that was triggered by the violent insurgency of the guerrilla group *Sendero Luminoso* (Shining Path) and subsequent military reprisals.[2] With the gradual decline in political violence over the course of the 1990s, rates of petty crime and criminal violence rose in Ayacucho and particularly in the region's capital Huamanga. This increase in criminal violence has been largely attributed to the parallel increase in territory-based youth groups, the so-called *manchas*,[3] which are commonly blamed for the bulk of violence and crime occurring in the city.

The research was carried out in Huamanga City from September 2003 to December 2004 and aimed to explore the characteristics and social functions of the local *manchas*. A further goal was to examine whether, and how, the recent rise in *mancha* activity was linked to the previous political violence. Approximately 100, predominantly male, members of six *manchas* from different parts of Huamanga participated in the study. A combination of quantitative and qualitative methods was applied, including participant observation, participatory techniques, semistructured interviews, a survey, and a quasi-field experiment in the form of a camp with rival *mancha* members, which will be presented here. Before describing the design of the camp study, however, I will give a brief summary of the major characteristics and activities of Huamanga's *manchas*.

Manchas in Huamanga

In 2003–2004, there existed approximately 35 active *manchas* in Huamanga City.[4] The number of members per group varied between 20 and 150. Roughly speaking, about 1,000 youths were involved in *manchas*, that is, approximately 3.5 percent of the 15 to 24 year olds and 0.7 percent of the total population of Huamanga. Thus, only a small minority of the city's youths were *mancha* members. Nevertheless, the local and national media generally portray the *manchas* and their members in an extremely negative fashion. They are considered to be criminal and violent by nature and are, therefore, routinely blamed for the perceived rise in common crime in the region since the demise of *Sendero Luminoso*. Moreover, a survey I conducted in July 2004 showed that inhabitants of Huamanga City perceive the *manchas* as a serious and constant threat to public security and tend to scapegoat them for whatever kind of violence and crime occurs. Yet reliable crime statistics that could corroborate, or refute, such claims do not exist. *Mancha* members generally are well aware of their extremely negative image. My research participants regularly emphasized that they felt discriminated against by people in their neighborhoods and the wider society. *Mancheros* generally claimed that their bad reputation derived from people's prejudice about rural migrants and their ignorance of the manifold hardships migrant youths faced.

The majority of *mancheros* I met in 2003–2004 were children of rural migrants and therefore spoke *Quechua* and Spanish. Many of their families had migrated to Huamanga as a consequence of the internal armed conflict, which particularly affected the rural areas of Ayacucho. A considerable number of *mancha* members' families, however, had settled down in the city before the conflict erupted. Most of the youths had been infants or young children when the internal war reached its climax, and had therefore not actively taken part in combat. Due to their migrant background, most *mancheros* lived in the marginal suburbs of Huamanga. Recently established squatter settlements often lack even the most basic services of drinking water, electricity, and sewers. And even suburbs that were built over two decades ago are still largely devoid of schools, health centers, and recreational areas. The majority of migrant families live in conditions of chronic poverty and receive no, or only very limited, assistance from the State or nongovernmental organizations (NGOs). For rural migrants, the only possibility to earn a living is to work in the tertiary and informal sectors, for the city lacks industry. Most *mancheros* I knew had dropped out of secondary school and sporadically worked in agriculture or informal, low-skilled jobs such as street vendors, shoeshine boys, or as temporary assistants to carpenters and builders.[5] The age of *mancheros* ranged from 8 to 30 years, the majority being 15–20 years old. The vast majority of *mancha* members were male. Female members, usually the male members' girlfriends, tended to be only loosely attached to the group. Over the course of my research, I did not come across any active all-female *mancha*. However, I met several young women who claimed having been members of female *manchas* in the late 1990s.

The *manchas* I encountered in 2003–2004 were not characterized by clear-cut and stable hierarchical structures. Instead, both positions within the *mancha* and group composition were highly variable and volatile. None of the six *manchas* I met regularly seemed to have a stable internal hierarchy; and leadership was sometimes assumed by a group rather than a single person. There were no internal subdivisions according to age groups, but older members tended to be more influential than younger ones. Moreover, the *manchas* were, in general, territory-bound, but some of the older groups operated, and recruited their members, in different parts of the city. Rivalries were strongest between *manchas* with adjacent territories and between the oldest and most prestigious ones. In street battles between rival groups, *mancheros* usually threw stones at each other and used knives and other stabbing weapons. Very few possessed firearms. Despite the limited weaponry, however, fights between rivals often resulted in the death, or serious injury, of *mancha* members. Occasionally, *mancheros* also engaged in pickpocketing, mugging, and burglary, mostly to obtain small change for drinks and acquire desired consumer goods such as branded clothes or mobile phones.

Manchas are not the only form of youth organizations in Huamanga City. There exist a number of sports clubs, faith-based youth groups, youth organizations of political parties, and associations of university students. However, most of these youth groups are based in the city center, charge fees, and hence are joined primarily by middle-class youth. Poor migrant youths from the marginal suburbs, in turn, do not have much choice as far as the availability of peer groups is concerned. For some of them, the *mancha* therefore appears to be the only attractive youth group available in their neighborhood. There are a number of characteristics that differentiate a *mancha* from other youth groups, including the attachment to a territory that is defended against the intrusion of rival groups, *mancha* members' strong sense of unity and strict adherence to a code of honor, and the occasional collective involvement in petty and violent crime.

Mancha membership is a transitory life phase. My research participants generally claimed that they had joined the *mancha* voluntarily and were also free to leave at any time. Female members usually left the *mancha* when they became pregnant, while male members tended to mature out once they had found a stable job. Both male and female members usually left the *mancha* by "fading out," that is, by gradually withdrawing from group activities.

However, leaving the *mancha* did not necessarily imply a complete severing of friendships with its members.

Objectives and Design of the Camp Study

Rationale

Rivalry and violent conflict between youth gangs represent a major obstacle for policies and programs aimed at improving educational and employment opportunities of youths involved in gangs. In Huamanga, several attempts to organize vocational trainings and cultural activities for *mancha* members have failed. This has been due, in part, to lack of commitment on the part of the authorities responsible for the projects but also because members of different rival *manchas* refused to participate in the same program. As a consequence, these projects were either cancelled after a short time, or the organizers ended up recruiting the bulk of participants among non-*mancha* youths. Moreover, the violent street battles between rival *manchas* were a major reason why many organizations and institutions in Huamanga that worked with adolescents and youths shied away from including *mancha* members in their programs.

In view of this situation, I designed the camp study with a view to finding a way to break the vicious circle of violent intergroup conflict. In particular, the study aimed to test whether enmity and violent conflict between *manchas* could be reduced by bringing them in contact with each other under nonviolent and noncompetitive conditions. The idea of organizing a camp for rival *manchas* was inspired by social psychological research on the so-called contact hypothesis (Allport 1954; Brown and Hewstone 2005; Pettigrew and Tropp 2006) and by the classic *Robbers Cave Experiment* (Sherif et al. 1961).

The contact hypothesis was originally formulated by the social psychologist Gordon Allport (1954). He proposed that contact with members of a disliked group, under appropriate conditions, would lead to the growth of liking for, and to decreased prejudice toward, this group. The contact hypothesis does not assume that simply bringing opposing groups together will be sufficient to improve intergroup relations. Rather, Allport specified four features of the contact situation that would maximize the potential for contact to reduce prejudice and promote positive intergroup relations: equal status of the groups, the pursuit of common goals, intergroup cooperation, and institutional support. Over the past 50 years, the contact hypothesis has instigated a vast array of research and has undergone important theoretical developments (cf. Brown and Hewstone 2005). A recent meta-analysis of over 500 studies on intergroup contact has shown that intergroup contact per se typically reduces intergroup prejudice. But this effect is substantially stronger in those contexts in which Allport's four situational conditions apply (Pettigrew and Tropp 2006).

Overall, empirical research has largely supported the hypothesis that intergroup contact is related to more positive intergroup perceptions, attitudes, and emotions. However, there is little direct evidence that contact actually changes intergroup *behavior*. Changes in attitudes and feelings do not automatically lead to changes in behavior, for behaviors are constrained and facilitated by many factors, including, for example, social norms, habits, and power relations (Ajzen 1991). Moreover, a considerable proportion of the research on the contact hypothesis consists of laboratory studies, sometimes using artificial groups. Studies in settings of actual intergroup conflict, on the other hand, are often confined to survey methods. Finally, most studies on the effect of contact on prejudice are cross-sectional and therefore do not allow for making strong statements about the direction of causal influence. Longitudinal studies are better at examining causal relationships, yet such studies are rare in intergroup research. A famous exception is the classic Robbers Cave Experiment (Sherif et al. 1961), which strongly inspired the present study and therefore requires a summary.

In the early 1950s, the social psychologists Muzafer and Carolyn Sherif and their colleagues conducted a series of experimental studies on intergroup relations among boys at summer camps (Sherif et al. 1961; Sherif and Sherif 1953). The aim of this study series was to analyze the development of intergroup relations under experimentally controlled yet lifelike conditions. The 1954 camp study, which was carried out in an area adjacent to Robbers Cave State Park in Oklahoma (United States) and, therefore, became known as the Robbers Cave Experiment, was aimed at identifying the conditions under which intergroup contact can effectively improve intergroup relations. In this study, 24 eleven-year-old boys from stable, white, middle-class families participated in a summer camp. The study consisted of three successive stages of approximately one week each. At the first stage, the boys were randomly assigned to two groups, which were subsequently kept separate from one another. Each group engaged in activities that required the group members' concerted action or coordinated division of tasks. Stage two brought the two groups together in a series of competitive activities, which generated overt intergroup conflict. During stage three, the groups first came into contact under neutral, noncompetitive conditions. Such intergroup contact, however, did not prove effective in reducing intergroup conflict, but rather exacerbated hostility between the two groups. Only after introducing superordinate goals did the relations between the two groups become more harmonious. These superordinate goals had a compelling appeal for both groups and could not be achieved by the efforts of one group alone. However, both groups had to be repeatedly brought together under cooperative conditions in order to substantially improve intergroup relations.

The present study does not aim to replicate the Robbers Cave Experiment. Rather, as will be shown below, its design combines central features of the Robbers Cave study, such as the longitudinal design and the introduction of cooperative tasks, with elements of more recent elaborations of the contact hypothesis, which have stressed the important role of intergroup friendships

(Pettigrew 1998), salience of group membership (Brown and Hewstone 2005), and intergroup emotions in intergroup contact (Islam and Hewstone 1993; Pettigrew and Tropp 2000). Perhaps the most fundamental difference between the camping expedition described here and the summer camp organized by Sherif and colleagues (1961) is that the latter experimentally created intergroup conflict between randomly formed groups, whereas the participants of the present study belonged to natural groups that already had a history of intergroup conflict. In other words, my camping expedition with rival *mancheros* aimed to reduce already existing intergroup conflict between groups that had formed spontaneously prior to the study, while the summer camps by Sherif and his colleagues both created and later reduced conflicts between groups that had been formed through random assignment of participants.

Preparations

Over the course of my field research, I organized several day trips to the countryside near Huamanga with members of the six *manchas* I was meeting regularly. The youths thoroughly enjoyed these hikes, which proved to be ideal opportunities for the use of participatory research methods such as sociodrama and focus group discussions. Due to the rivalries between the six *manchas*, these outings were carried out with each group separately. After about 1 year of fieldwork, however, I felt that my relationship with each of the six *manchas* was sufficiently close and strong to make an attempt at bringing them together. I introduced the idea of a joint camping expedition at my informal street corner meetings with the groups. Their first reaction to my proposal was general skepticism about its feasibility. The *mancheros* generally expected that going on a joint camping expedition would inevitably end in a violent clash between the participating rival *manchas*. However, many youths found the idea of going camping for several days intriguing, for they had never done it before. I therefore asked them if they could imagine spending a couple of days together with their rivals without attacking one another, and what could be done to prevent violent conflict. *Mancha* members unanimously identified stabbing weapons and alcohol as the key factors that would increase the risk of violent fights to occur and escalate. Thus, after repeated conversations about the camping proposal, each of the six *manchas* independently came to the conclusion that a joint camping expedition could possibly work out without major incidents of violence, if all participating *manchas* committed themselves to abstain from alcohol and drug consumption and not to carry knives or other stabbing weapons.

Once the six groups had expressed general interest in participating in a joint camping excursion, I started having regular meetings with each of them to discuss the plan and purpose of the camp in more detail. These meetings served to explain the aim and program of the camp and to introduce the two fundamental conditions of participation (no alcohol or drugs and no weapons). Yet the only ones who could make sure that *mancha* members abided by these rules were the respective *mancha* leaders, and it was therefore crucial to win their support and encourage them to participate in the camp. Furthermore, considering the internal power hierarchies within the *manchas*, it seemed unlikely that, without the participation of the leaders and core members, potentially positive effects of the camping experience on intergroup relations would be sustainable and generalize to other *mancha* members who did not take part in the camp. Participation in the camping expedition was free of charge, but the *mancheros* were expected to participate in the activities and comply with the rules that were going to be set up by all the participants on the first day of the camp. After explaining the purpose of the camp and the conditions of participation, a list of those who volunteered to participate was drawn up for each *mancha*. Permission was obtained from the parents or guardians of *mancheros* under 18 years of age, and from schools for those who were studying. The activity was announced as a "youth camp," without disclosing the *mancha* membership of the participants.

Moreover, an organizing committee was formed, consisting of a group of local social work students who had been assisting me throughout my fieldwork and were familiar with the *manchas*. The committee was divided into four subcommittees responsible for (1) the program of the camp, (2) logistics, (3) security, and (4) catering. The program committee comprised six social work students (five females, one male[6]) with extensive experience in working with youths in general and *mancheros* in particular. They were involved in the elaboration of the camp activities and trained in the different participatory techniques to be applied during the camp. Their role in the camping expedition was that of facilitators, and each of them was assigned to one of the participating groups as a reference person. During the preparatory meetings with the *manchas*, the facilitators introduced themselves to the group they had been assigned to and explained their role, namely that the future camp participants could turn to them in case of questions and problems, both before and during the camping expedition.

Camping Site

The site for the camp was chosen according to a number of criteria. On the one hand, the site should not be too far away from Huamanga so that, in an emergency, it was possible to get help or return to the city within a few hours time. On the other hand, the camping site should not be too close to settlements or popular picnic spots. This was necessary both to ensure that camping activities were not being observed or disrupted by residents or picnickers and to reduce the opportunities for *mancheros* to obtain alcohol. The surroundings of Huamanga are characterized by arid mountains and steep, narrow river valleys. Fertile plains are scarce and tend to be densely populated or frequently visited during weekends and holidays. Thus, the place finally selected for the camp was a relatively narrow and arid valley, intersected by a small creek. Being the end of the dry season, vegetation was scarce, but a number of eucalyptus trees provided shade, and dry shrubs that could serve as firewood were abundant. The site was located about a 45-minute drive away from Huamanga and approximately half-an-hour's walk from the next village. Permission for camping was obtained from the local district administration, and the district police station as well as the mayor of the neighboring village were informed. Again, the activity was announced as a youth camp in general terms, without revealing the *mancha* membership of its participants.

Selection of Participants

A selection had to be made among the large number of *mancheros* who showed interest in participating in the camp. Participants were chosen on the basis of two criteria: gender and position within the *mancha*. They had to be both male and leaders, or core members, of their respective groups. Female *mancha* members were not included for several reasons. First of all, I had established rapport with only a small number of female members. Second, most of the girls and young women I knew were either working or studying, or had small children to look after. Third, I feared that the camping arrangement, which included sleeping in the same tent, might encourage sexual relations or even expose the girls to the risk of being sexually abused. And last but not the least, most female *mancheras* did not participate in violent intergroup conflict. The reasons for choosing leaders and core members, that is, those youths who regularly participated in *mancha* activities and occupied a superior position in the internal hierarchy, were twofold. First, they exercised more influence and power over their fellow *mancha* members than did peripheral members. And second, leaders and core members were also more likely to be perceived as prototypical *mancheros*. Experimental studies have shown that intergroup contact changes negative stereotypes more effectively if participants in the contact situation are perceived as typical members of their respective groups (see Brown and Hewstone 2005 for a review). Consequently, I assumed that the participation of leaders and core members would facilitate the generalization of positive contact effects from the camp participants to the other members of their respective *manchas*. Furthermore, the overall number of camp participants was limited to approximately 40 for safety reasons and because, due to budget restraints, the duration of the camp was limited to four days. Within that short time, a larger group would not have the chance to get to know each other individually. Moreover, most of the participatory methods that were going to be applied during the camp required relatively small groups. In addition, I tried to ensure the participation of an equal number of participants from each *mancha* in order to avoid major power differences between the groups due to minority or majority status.

However, this sampling strategy was only partly successful. A number of those *mancheros* who had registered for participation did not turn up at the agreed meeting point and time. In fact, only four out of the six *manchas* who had expressed their interest in participating eventually took part in the camp. One *mancha* dropped out at the last minute because a number of its members had been arrested by the police the night before; the other one decided not to participate because its leader and some of the core members had gone to Lima or to rural areas in search of temporary jobs. Thus, the final sample of camp participants was far smaller than originally planned. It consisted of 25 male members of the following *manchas*: La Sombra (6), Los Sangrientos (9), Los Túneles (5), Los Ruglats[7] (5). Participants were between 15 and 29 years old, with an average age of 20.4 years.[8]

Originally, the field experiment was designed to include a control group of *mancheros* who fulfilled the selection criteria but did not register for participation. Such a control group was formed during the preparatory stage of the camp, and questionnaire data were obtained prior to the camp. However, the control group design had to be given up, as attempts to gather this group again for the second measurement after the end of the camp failed.

Contact Situation

The setting and activities of the camp were planned with a view to maximizing potential positive effects of contact on intergroup relations. The aim was to create the four optimal situational conditions identified by Allport (1954). In addition, two more situational factors were included, namely salience of group membership and cross-group friendship potential. These factors have proved to be crucial for the positive effects of intergroup contact to be sustainable and to generalize from individual outgroup members to the outgroup as a whole (Brown and Hewstone 2005; Pettigrew 1998; Pettigrew and Tropp 2000). The situational conditions are briefly summarized below and will be described in more detail in later sections of this chapter.

Equal status and egalitarian norms: On the first day of the camp, participants jointly drew up a set of norms and rules. Each *mancha* had the same rights and obligations, and decisions were always made by the group as a whole. However, this procedure did not abolish preexisting status differences between the *manchas*, which had a considerable influence on intergroup processes.

Common goals and cooperative interdependence: The activities carried out during the camp required the cooperation of the rival groups in pursuit of a joint goal. For example, all *manchas* jointly set up the camp, collected firewood, and washed the dishes after meals.

Institutional support: The mayor of one of the districts of Huamanga City and a local NGO sponsored t-shirts with the logo of the camping expedition.

The t-shirts were later handed out in person to each participant on the final day of the camp.

Salience of group membership: In some of the joint activities, a clear differentiation between the *manchas* was maintained and emphasized, with each group taking a separate task toward the joint goal. For some activities the *manchas* formed separate teams that performed the activity alongside, but not in competition with, one another. However, for a number of other activities, particularly toward the end of the camp, mixed teams were formed that cut across group boundaries.

Cross-group friendships: The program of the camp provided ample opportunities for participants to interact on an interpersonal level and to get to know individual members of the other *manchas*. Games and activities were aimed at encouraging self-disclosure and perspective-taking, engendering mutual trust, and establishing friendships across group boundaries.

Hypotheses and Measures

According to the contact hypothesis, it was expected that contact between members of rival *manchas* at the camp, under the conditions described above, would lead to the following:

1. an improvement of perceived intergroup relations,
2. a reduction of reported negative intergroup emotions,
3. an increase in reported positive intergroup emotions,
4. a decrease in violent intergroup conflict, and
5. the development of friendships between members of rival *manchas*.

To test these hypotheses, a questionnaire was developed, which all the study participants filled in at two time points: a few days before the camp (t1) and at the end of the camp (t2). In this questionnaire, participants rated their relationship and identification with their own *mancha*, their relation to the rival groups present at the camp, and their emotions during an imagined encounter with members of the rival *manchas*. The t2 version of the questionnaire also included a measure of friendship with members of rival *manchas* and a qualitative evaluation of the camping experience.

Relations between and within the *Manchas* Prior to the Camp

Over the course of 1 year prior to the camping expedition, I had been observing numerous encounters between rival *manchas*, and *mancheros* had frequently told me about their enmities, alliances, and friendships with other *manchas*. From these observations and narratives, I reconstructed a general picture of the relations between the four participating groups prior to the camp.

Among the four groups, *Sombra* occupied the highest status, being the oldest, largest, and most feared *mancha* in Huamanga. Relations between *Sombra* and *Sangrientos* tended to be fairly positive due to the fact that the current leader of the *Sangrientos* was a former member of *Sombra* who, despite having formed a new *mancha*, continued to be friends with his ex-fellow *mancheros*. The *Túneles*, in turn, had a long history of violent conflict with both *Sombra* and *Sangrientos*. The *Túneles* were divided into two subgroups, a group of senior members who operated in a central area of the city adjacent to the *Sombra* territory, and the junior members, whose turf was located in one of the suburbs of Huamanga that neighbored the territory of the *Sangrientos*. The *Ruglats* were a more recent group compared to the other three. They were less well known and did not have deep-rooted enmities with any of the other three *manchas*. However, they engaged in occasional fights, particularly with the *Túneles* and a subgroup of the *Sombra*.

The results of the t1-version of the questionnaire, administered to the participants a couple of days before the camping expedition, support this picture of intergroup relations (see figure 1). The mean scores of perceived relations between the four *manchas* show that both *Sombra* and *Sangrientos* reported getting along fairly well with one another. In contrast, there were strong mutual hostilities between the *Túneles* on the one hand, and *Sombra* and *Sangrientos* on the other hand. Relations between the *Ruglats* and the three other groups were somewhat mixed and heterogeneous.

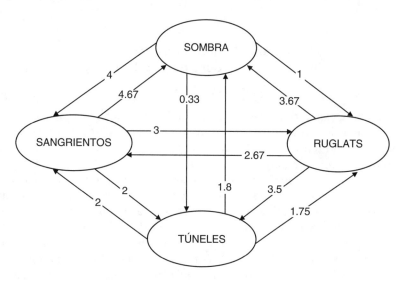

Figure 1 Intergroup relations before the camp

Note: The figure displays the mean scores of responses to the following question: "How do you get along with…(*name of rival mancha*)?" Responses were given on a seven-point-Likert scale (0 = "very badly" to 6 = "very well"). Arrows do *not* imply causal relations, but rather symbolize the direction of assessment (e.g., the arrow from *Ruglats* to *Túneles* indicates how the *Ruglats*, on average, perceived their relation to the *Túneles*).

Relations within each of the four *manchas* were generally positive. That is, the vast majority of participants reported getting along well, or very well, with members of their own *mancha* (see table 1). Overall, *mancheros* also tended to strongly identify with their particular group and felt proud of being a member of it (see table 2).

Table 1 Intragroup relations before the camp

Mancha	Mean	Std. deviation	N
Sombra	5.00	0.00	4
Túneles	5.40	1.34	5
Ruglats	5.25	0.50	5
Sangrientos	4.71	1.38	8

Note: The figures represent the responses to the question "how do you get along with your fellow mancha members?" Responses were given on a seven-point-Likert scale (0= "very badly" to 6 = "very well").

Table 2 Identification with the mancha before the camp

Item	Mean	Std. deviation	N
"I am a member of the [*name of respondent's mancha*]."	4.48	1.63	21
"I am proud of being a member of the [*name of respondent's mancha*]."	4.14	1.59	21

Note: Responses were given on a seven-point-Likert scale (0 = "absolutely wrong" to 6 = "absolutely correct").

Development of Intragroup Processes and Intergroup Relations during the Camp

Day One

The camping expedition began with a joint bus ride of all the participants to the camping site. At first, the encounter between the four *manchas* resulted in a hostile and tense atmosphere, with members of different groups avoiding physical proximity, eye contact, and verbal interactions. Upon arrival at the camp site, the *mancheros* only reluctantly got off the buses and started unloading the camping equipment. When carrying the baggage from the road down to the camping site, members of rival *manchas* mostly avoided direct interactions and eye contact with each other. Each of the four *manchas* pitched their own tent, which they shared with one of the facilitators. The tents had to be built fairly close to one another, for the camping site comprised only a relatively small area of plain surface. Each mancha was free to choose a place for its tent. The final arrangement was a semicircle, with the *Ruglats* on one end, the *Túneles* on the other, and *Sombra* and *Sangrientos* in between and next to each other. Over lunch, the four groups sat down separately, keeping a clear distance from one another. The distance was greatest between the *Túneles* and the other three *manchas*. Afterwards, all the camp participants jointly drew up a set of ground rules of conduct as a means to overcome distrust and prevent conflicts between the rival groups (see box 1). Following this exercise and a joint treasure hunt in the afternoon, the youths appeared to be more relaxed but remained in their respective groups and largely refused to interact or intermingle with their rivals. Shortly after dinner, the *manchas* left the campfire and separately retreated into their chosen tents.

In sum, during the first day of the camp, the four participating *manchas* showed a high degree of mutual distrust and avoided physical closeness, verbal interaction, and even eye contact with one another. Moreover, the particular configuration of intergroup relations the *manchas* had brought into the contact situation clearly influenced their behavior. The arrangement of the tents and the seating order during meals, for instance, reflected the alliance between *Sombra* and *Sangrientos* and the general enmity toward the *Túneles*. Although the cooperative tasks and joint activities contributed to a more relaxed atmosphere, they were not sufficient to overcome the mutual suspicion between the groups, which prevented them from approaching and interacting with one another.

Box 1   Group contract

The four *manchas* gathered separately in groups. The facilitators enquired about their expectations and worries about the camp and encouraged each group to come up with a number of rules that could help make the camp a pleasant experience for everyone. Once each *mancha* had drawn up its set of rules, the four groups gathered in a large circle and presented their rules to one another. In fact, all four manchas had come to similar results and it was therefore easy to summarize them and formulate a common set of ground rules, which read as follows:

- We will respect one another.
- We will help one another.
- We will all participate in the programmed activities.
- We will take care of our stuff and respect the possessions of others so that nothing gets lost.
- We will maintain the tents clean and tidy.
- We will not fight.
- Let's all be united and show solidarity with one another.
- We all commit ourselves to conclude the camp together.
- We will abide by the rules of conduct.

Moreover, the four *manchas* unanimously agreed on the suggestion that, in case somebody broke any of these rules, the whole group would come together and decide about possible sanctions. The rules were written on a blackboard, which was put up at a clearly visible spot for the duration of the camp.

Day Two

The morning after the first night in the camp, the *mancheros* showed clear signs of unease and distress. Many claimed that they had experienced night-mares or been kept awake by their fear of ghosts. Over breakfast, *mancha* members talked about their eerie experiences during the night, with the result that the whole group became increasingly convinced that the camp site was haunted by ghosts. To raise participants' spirits, the morning program started with a number of icebreakers that were aimed at encouraging mem-bers of different *manchas* to interact with, and get to know, each other (see box 2 for an example). These games were very popular among all four groups and helped dispel their worries and fears.

Box 2   Quick names

Participants were randomly divided into two teams of equal size. Between the teams, a large blanket was stretched out and held by two facilitators in a way that the groups could not see each other. Then each team silently selected one of its members, who had to squat down in front of the group, facing the blan-ket. On the count of three, the facilitators dropped the blanket, and each of the two selected team members had to call out the other's name as quickly as possible. Whoever was faster won, and the loser had to join the other team. The game was then repeated several times so that everybody had a chance to participate.

Afterwards, the *manchas* formed separate teams, each of which prepared a sociodrama about a typical situation of their lives and presented it to the other teams. The performances revealed striking similarities across the four groups in terms of their everyday life experiences. For example, excessive alcohol consumption was a central theme in all the drama performances and was presented as a strategy to cope with unemployment and domestic vio-lence (see box 3).

At the general assembly the day before, participants had expressed their wish to play football. Since the camp site was too rocky and uneven, it was decided to walk to the nearby village which had a football pitch. Thus, after the sociodrama, all participants left the camp and headed for Pacaycasa Village.[9] On the way, however, an unexpected encounter with members of the *mancha Tuxis* occurred. The *Tuxis* were supposed to participate in the camp but had failed to turn up at the agreed meeting point the day before. Now, three of their members had come all the way from Huamanga in order to join the camp. However, they were received with suspicion and open hos-tility by the rest of the camp participants who refused to let them participate in the football match. The three *Tuxis* therefore finally decided to return to Huamanga.

Box 3   Sociodrama

Each *mancha* was asked to elaborate a brief drama presentation that represented a typical situation of their lives about which they were worried, sad, fearful, or angry. The groups were free to choose the themes to be presented and to decide on the distribution of roles. Once all four *manchas* had elaborated their stories, they presented them to each other. After each performance, the audience was invited to reflect on what they had seen: What was the story about? Had they experienced similar situations? What could be done to solve the problems presented? In a second round, the *manchas* were asked to elaborate a second scene, which presented a potential solution to the problems portrayed in the first scene. Again, each group presented their sociodramas, followed by a joint reflection.

Example: Sociodrama of the *Ruglats*

Scene 1

A group of *mancheros* is hanging out at the street corner. They decide to go for drinks to their local. After having a couple of drinks there, they run out of money. The group leaves the bar and roams around the neighborhood looking for an opportunity to obtain some small change by stealing or robbing a passerby. Suddenly they are confronted by a security guard, who starts beating up one of the *mancheros*. The rest of the group comes to their friend's rescue. They collectively attack the security guard and stab him to death. Fearful of being discovered, they "disappear" the body by throwing it into a ravine at the outskirts of the city.

Scene 2

A group of *mancheros* is hanging out together, planning their next theft or assault. An old friend who has retired from the group joins them. They invite him to go for drinks, but the ex-*mancha* member declines, telling them that he has changed and doesn't like drinking anymore. He tells the group that his uncle, who is a building contractor, is looking for a couple of young men to work for him. First, the *mancheros* are not interested, assuming that, because of their bad reputation, they will not get the job anyway. But the ex-*manchero* finally manages to convince them to accompany him and meet his uncle.

By the early afternoon, the four *manchas* made their way back to the camp site, where they arrived very hungry and thirsty. Unluckily, the lunch prepared by the facilitators went wrong and turned out to be almost inedible. As a result, the atmosphere froze, and it took a great deal of effort to motivate participants to take part in the afternoon program. Yet a number of dynamic and inspiring games such as the "knotty problem" and the "talk show" (see box 4) lifted their spirits again and provided an opportunity for the rival *manchas* to familiarize with each other.

Box 4   Games I

Knotty problem

Participants formed a tight circle and closed their eyes. Everybody raised his or her right arm and grabbed the hand of one of the participants in front of him or her. Then, while holding on to each others' hands, they did the same with their left arms. Afterwards, the group opened their eyes and tried to disentangle the knot and form a circle again, but without letting the hands go. Surprisingly, the *mancheros* showed no signs of impatience and kept holding each others' hands, although it took over 10 minutes to disentangle the knot. Most likely, it was the first time they had been in physical, but nonviolent, contact with their rivals.

Talk show

This activity was developed specifically for the camp with rival *manchas*. Each *mancha* received a letter of invitation to a fictitious TV talk show that is well known in Peru. In the letter, each group was asked to appoint a representative who would be a "special guest" at the show. The rest of the *mancha* members made up the audience, together with my research assistants who took on different roles in the show, for instance, the role of authorities and people affected by *mancha* violence. My own role was that of the talk-show presenter. As a starting point, I asked the representatives of each *mancha* to come to the "stage" and join me as my special guests. I then involved them in a conversation about their lives as *mancheros*, their motives for joining the group, their daily activities, etc. The *mancha* youths in the audience were encouraged to ask questions to the "special guests," make comments, or correct the statements given by their representatives. In addition, the task of my research assistants was to make the debate more controversial by bringing in alternative view points, for example, that of a police officer or a mother whose son was killed by *mancha* members. The debate lasted about an hour and was filmed and tape-recorded. The youths were familiar with the structure of the talk show. They participated actively in the debate and apparently enjoyed it.

After dinner, a general assembly was held at the request of the *Sombra*. At this meeting, the leaders of the four *manchas* made the surprising announcement that all participants had agreed to move to a different camp site, because they regarded the present one as unsafe. Not only was the place haunted by ghosts, the leaders explained, but there was also no escape from the narrow valley in the dark. And since they were unarmed they would not be able to defend themselves against possible attacks by *Sendero Luminoso* or the *ronderos*[10] of the nearby village. Since the mid 1990s, Shining Path had no longer launched major attacks in the area. Thus *mancheros'* concerns about their safety were largely unjustified and seemed to reflect traumatic memories of the past rather than a real threat at present. The facilitators nevertheless took these concerns seriously and did not brush them aside, because one of the ground rules of the camp was that all decisions had to be taken unanimously by the entire group of participants. After jointly discussing the pros and cons of moving, all four *manchas* finally came to the conclusion that a change of location required too much effort and unanimously decided to stay at the camp site for the remaining two days and nights. Following this joint decision, everybody appeared visibly relieved and much more relaxed than the night before.

To sum up, over the course of the second day, a common group identity began to emerge among the camp participants. Two unforeseen incidents, in particular, brought the rival *manchas* closer together: the sleepless first night and the encounter with the *Tuxis*. Both their collective fear of ghosts and the perceived common threat by *ronderos* and guerrillas enhanced group cohesiveness among participants, by making rival *mancheros* realize that they shared a common fate. Moreover, as a reaction to the unexpected encounter with the *Tuxis*, the four *manchas* closed ranks and treated the newcomers as an unwanted outgroup,[11] which eventually led to the retreat of the *Tuxis*. The exchange of personal information during the talk show and the experience of joint decision making in the general assembly may have further contributed to the formation of a common ingroup among the camp participants.

Within this emerging inclusive ingroup, however, an internal hierarchy developed, which reproduced the status and power differences that characterized the relations between the four *manchas* prior to the camp. The *Sombra*, whose members were more senior than those of the other three groups, clearly assumed a leading role, closely followed by the *Sangrientos*, who traditionally had a fairly positive relationship with the *Sombra*. Moreover, the *Sangrientos* outnumbered each of the other three *manchas* at the camp, and together with the *Sombra*, represented a clear majority. As a consequence, leaders of the *Sombra* and *Sangrientos* tended to dominate conversations and activities and speak on behalf of the whole group. The *Ruglats* and *Túneles*, on the other hand, occupied a lower position in the camp hierarchy and tended to form an alliance with one another in order to counter the dominance of the *Sombra* and *Sangrientos*. For example, at the general assembly, the *Ruglats* and *Túneles* jointly voiced complaints about repeated verbal abuses by members of the *Sombra* and *Sangrientos*.

Day Three

The second night of the camp passed off without any incident. Next morning, the participants appeared to be well rested and cheerful, and nobody complained about nightmares. Over breakfast, jokes about ghosts went around. The morning program started with a number of games aimed at facilitating both self-disclosure and cooperation (e.g., see box 5). Then the four *manchas* gathered separately to conclude the sociodrama they had prepared and performed the day before. The groups were asked to reconsider their presentations of the previous day and to replace violent scenes by nonviolent alternatives of conflict resolution. All four *manchas* mastered this task without difficulties and came to very similar results. For example, all four presentations suggested that the creation of employment opportunities for young people could break the vicious circle of violence. The *mancheros* argued that their violent behavior was often triggered off by excessive alcohol consumption and that they often got drunk with their friends because they had no jobs and there was nothing else to do.

Box 5 Games II

Tug-of-war in a circle

Unlike the classic tug-of-war, this game is noncompetitive and requires the cooperation of the group as a whole. Participants formed a circle and held onto a rope, both ends of which were tied together. Holding tightly onto the rope with both hands, they extended the circle as much as possible. Then participants tried to sit down and stand up again altogether at the same time, yet without losing balance or letting the rope go.

Statues (adapted from Boal 1979)

The activity started with a brainstorming exercise, which consisted of participants naming as quickly as possible as many different emotions they could think of. Afterwards participants were divided into pairs or groups of three. Each group then secretly agreed on one emotion they wanted to enact. One person of each pair or group was appointed "the statue"; the other person(s) became "the sculptor." The sculptor's task then was to "form" the statue in a way that it expressed the emotion the group had agreed on. Verbal instructions were forbidden; the sculptor had to "mould" the postures, gestures, and mimics through gently touching and moving the statue's body. (Prior to the exercise, the group had agreed on certain "taboo zones" that were not allowed to be touched.) The completed statues were then presented to the other groups, which were asked to interpret them and find out which emotion they represented. The sculptors were allowed to group statues together or change their postures, and this was repeated until the whole group was satisfied with the way the different emotions were expressed. Then the whole exercise was repeated with swapped roles. Finally, participants were arranged in a circle for a joint reflection on their experiences during the exercise and the meaning and importance of different emotions in everyday life.

Subsequently, all participants left the camp site for a joint visit to Quinua, a major village located about 15 kilometers away from the camp.[12] During this visit, however, the internal power relations and status differences between the *manchas* again became evident and threatened the cohesiveness of the common ingroup. When selecting their teams for the football match, the members of *Sombra* and *Sangrientos* insisted that every player pay a small amount of money. The *Túneles* and *Ruglats*, however, did not have enough cash on them and were therefore excluded from the match, which caused considerable frustration among them. Back in the camp, the crisis reached its climax. Suspicion about the alleged intentions behind the camping expedition arose. Participants accused each other of unfair treatment and complained about the bad quality of the food at the camp. When two participants, belonging to the *Túneles* and *Sangrientos*, respectively, suddenly announced their return to Huamanga, the group threatened to break up, and several other participants made a move to fetch their belongings and leave the camp. Fortunately, the facilitators managed to calm this explosive situation through the convening of a general assembly, in which participants were given the opportunity to voice their complaints, clarify doubts, and reaffirm group norms and rules. The meeting had a cathartic effect and greatly improved relations among the four *manchas* as well as between *mancheros* and facilitators.

The third day ended with a "cultural night," a special program to celebrate the last evening spent together at the camp site. Each *mancha* contributed with a brief improvised presentation, such as telling a story, singing a song, or giving a dance performance. The cultural night was the crowning highlight of the camp, with participants surpassing each other in creativity and humor. For a while, the *mancheros* seemed to forget the tensions and rivalries between them. In sum, the third day of the camp was characterized by an internal power struggle between and within the four *manchas*. In particular, the *Sombra* and *Sangrientos* affirmed their dominance over the *Túneles* and *Ruglats*. Moreover, amongst the *Sangrientos* and *Sombra*, a core group formed, made up of the most senior members, which assumed overall leadership of the entire group of camp participants. However, their claim to leadership was contested not only by the *Ruglats* and *Túneles* but also by junior members of the *Sombra* and *Sangrientos*. This threatened the common group identity that had been gradually developing over the course of the past two days. The group was at the brink of breaking apart when two *mancha* members announced their return to Huamanga. This impending "desertion" was a clear breach of the camp rules and represented a crucial turning point in group dynamics, for it reminded camp participants of the basic norms and rules they had jointly committed themselves to. A general assembly in which these group norms were again confirmed helped restore and strengthen group cohesiveness and mitigate internal rivalries among the participants.

Day Four

The last night at the camp site passed quietly and without incidents. The following morning, participants gave the impression of being well rested and in a good mood. For breakfast, everyone spontaneously sat down in mixed groups consisting of members of different *manchas*. Conversations were dominated by jokes and anecdotes about the performances during the cultural night. The morning program elaborated on the sociodramas of the previous two days. These drama performances of typical scenes in *mancha* members' lives had revealed, among other things, that members of all four groups shared ambivalent feelings about their group identities. On the one hand, they were proud of their *mancha* membership, which helped them "make themselves respected" in their neighborhoods. But on the other hand, *mancheros* were also ashamed about their negative public image and felt offended when people labeled them killers and criminals. Moreover, *mancha* members were well aware of the fact that their bad reputation further reduced their chances of finding paid employment in the city.

In the group discussions following the sociodrama presentations, several *mancheros* expressed their desire to demonstrate that they were not as bad and violent as people in their neighborhood and society in general thought. Taking up this desire, the facilitators introduced the following exercise: First, participants were asked to think about what they could do to show people that the negative stereotype of the *mancha* was wrong; then, each *mancha* elaborated a plan of a small project or activity aimed at improving relations between the *mancha* and its neighborhood. The *mancheros* were free to develop whatever activity they liked, on condition that it did not require major material and financial resources and could be carried out within two or three months following the camp. The four groups discussed their ideas with zest and designed their projects quickly and without requiring much assistance by the facilitators. The results were then presented to the whole group. The project proposal of the *Sombras* was to decorate the forecourt and entrance of the chapel in their neighborhood. The *Ruglats* planned to organize a football tournament between children and youths from different neighborhoods. The *Túneles* intended to carry out a joint cleaning-up operation in their neighborhood. And the *Sangrientos* came up with the idea of transforming their *mancha* into a formal youth organization.

The morning program concluded with each of the four *manchas* meeting separately with their facilitators for a qualitative evaluation of the camping experience. Afterwards, all the participants individually filled in the t2 version of the questionnaire. After lunch, camp participants jointly dismantled the tents, cleaned the camp site, and packed their belongings. Then everybody left the camp site and headed for Pacaycasa Village, where the closing activity of the camping expedition—a football match between the camp participants and the village football team—was held. Without prior consultation with the facilitators, the *mancheros* lined up a mixed team, consisting of members of all four *manchas*. The team put up a brave fight, cheered on by the rest of the camp participants in the audience, but finally lost against the stronger village team. In a closing ceremony, all the *mancha* members were officially congratulated for their successful participation in the camp and received t-shirts with the camp logo.

To summarize, the fourth and last day of the camping expedition was characterized by a further harmonization of relations between the four *manchas* and the strengthening of a common ingroup identity. Members of different *manchas* spontaneously mingled and cooperated with one another during joint activities and meals. Moreover, the spontaneous selection of a mixed football team indicated a remarkable increase in group cohesiveness, given the fact that, the day before, attempts at including members of all four groups in a joint football team had failed. The *Sombra* and *Sangrientos* continued to hold a leadership position amongst the camp participants, but no longer used their power to exclude the other two *manchas* from activities. As a consequence, the *Ruglats* and *Túneles* no longer openly contested the *Sangrientos'* and *Sombra's* claim to leadership but seemed to accept the internal power hierarchy.

Intra and Intergroup Relations after the Camp

Qualitative Evaluation of the Camp Experience

The qualitative evaluation that was carried out with each *mancha* separately on the last day of the camp produced very similar results across the four groups. The positive experiences most frequently mentioned included: "making friends with members of other *manchas*"; "that we got along with each other and there were no fights"; "sharing the same tent with my mates"; and "the happiness, the jokes, and the fun we had during the games and the cultural night." Among the negative experiences most often reported were the inhospitable location of the camp site, the bad quality of the food, and breaches of the group norms by camp participants. The *Ruglats* did their evaluation in the form of a written group statement, which is cited here, for it summarizes the major points made by all four *manchas*:

> The nicest experience we will take home with us is the trust of the facilitators who were not afraid of us and stayed with us. We are leaving satisfied and are taking with us the jokes of the mates from the other tents, the songs of the cultural night, and the dance performance of the *Sombra* guys. We also think it was good to draw up the camp rules. Otherwise, how would we have managed to get along with each other?

> Bad experiences that we don't want to take home with us: Well, the location was not nice, it was very desolate and dry; there was no lawn etc. We also don't want to take with us the moment when all of us were feeling fearful of the *sirenas* and the guerrillas. We don't want to take with us neither the bad manners of some of the other guys nor the food, which was awful...Nor will we take with us the moment when the two guys left the camp, because, by doing that, they did not comply with the camp rules.

Quantitative Results

The quantitative data of the questionnaire filled in by camp participants before and at the end of the camp were analyzed statistically with a view to assessing the effectiveness of the camping expedition in improving relations between the participating *manchas*. A one-way repeated measures analysis of variance was conducted to compare relations between the four rival *manchas* at Time 1 (prior to the camp) and Time 2 (at the end of the camp).[13] The means and standard deviations are presented in table 3. There

Table 3 Relations between rival manchas before and after the camp

	Mean	Std. deviation	N
Time 1 (prior to the camp)	2.55	1.19	18
Time 2 (at the end of the camp)	4.46	.67	18

Note: Table presents responses to the item: "How do you get along with...(name of rival *mancha*)?" Responses were given on a seven-point-Likert scale (0 = "very badly" to 6 = "very well").

was a statistically significant improvement of intergroup relations over time (F(1, 17) = 33.82, p < .001), which corresponds to an effect size of Partial Eta Squared = .67.

Moreover, an inspection of the descriptive statistics revealed that intergroup relations improved not only on average, but also for all possible ingroup-outgroup pairs. In other words, at the end of the camp, the reported relations of each of the four *manchas* with each of the other three rival groups was more positive than prior to the camp (see figure 2).[14]

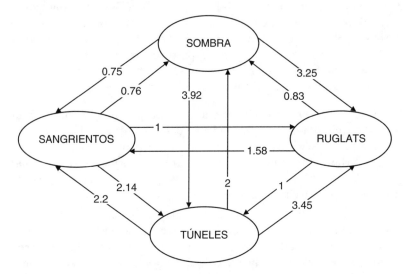

Figure 2   Intergroup relations at the end of the camp

Note: The figure displays the *average improvement* of intergroup relations, computed as the *difference* of the mean scores of intergroup relations prior to the camp versus at the end of the camp. Intergroup relations were measured through the following question: "How do you get along with…(*name of rival mancha*)?" Responses were given on a seven-point-Likert scale (0 = "very badly" to 6 = "very well"). Arrows do *not* imply causal relations, but rather symbolize the direction of assessment (e.g., the arrow from *Ruglats* to *Túneles* indicates how the *Ruglats* on average perceive their relation with the *Túneles*).

There were no statistically significant changes of intragroup relations and identification with the *mancha* over the course of the camping expedition. Both the reported identification with one's *mancha* and the perceived relations with members of one's own group remained at a high level (see table 4).

Three separate scales of intergroup emotion were computed on the basis of the correlation matrix of the intergroup emotion variables.[15]

1. Intergroup anxiety (Example: "I would feel anxious.");
2. Negative intergroup emotions (Examples: "I would feel furious." "I would feel hateful.");
3. Positive intergroup emotions (Example: "I would feel happy.").

The three scales moderately correlated with one another, but intercorrelations did not reach statistical significance. Internal consistency was high for

Table 4 Intragroup relations and identification with the mancha before and after the camp

	Mean	Std. deviation	N
Identification with one's mancha*			
Time 1 (prior to the camp)	4.31	1.54	21
Time 2 (at the end of the camp)	4.33	1.23	21
Intragroup relations**			
Time 1 (prior to the camp)	4.95	1.12	21
Time 2 (at the end of the camp)	4.76	1.22	21

* Items: "I am a member of the...(*name of respondent's mancha*)." "I am proud of being a member of..." Responses were given on a seven-point Likert scale (0 = "absolutely wrong" to 6 = "absolutely correct").
** Question: "How do you get along with your mates from...(*name of respondent's mancha*)?" Responses were given on a seven-point-Likert scale (0 = "very badly" to 6 = "very well").

the scales of intergroup anxiety (Cronbach's α = .81) and negative intergroup emotions (Cronbach's α = .82), and close to the conventional cutoff point of .7 in the case of the positive intergroup emotions scale (Cronbach's α = .59).

To compare intergroup emotions at Time 1 and Time 2, a one-way repeated measures analysis of variance was conducted. The means and standard deviations are presented in table 5. There were statistically significant reductions over time of both intergroup anxiety ($F(1, 19)$ = 12.27, $p < .005$) and negative intergroup emotions ($F(1, 19)$ = 41.72, $p < .001$), as well as a significant increase in positive intergroup emotions ($F(1, 20)$ = 60.04, $p < .001$). In other words, at the end of the camp, *mancha* members reported feeling less fearful, furious, and hateful, and more happy and cheerful than prior to the camp, when asked to imagine a future encounter with the rival *manchas* that had participated in the camping expedition. The Partial Eta Squared values were .39 (intergroup anxiety), .75 (positive intergroup emotions) and .69 (negative intergroup emotions).

Table 5 Intergroup emotions before and after the camp

	Mean	Std. deviation	N
Intergroup anxiety			
Time 1 (prior to the camp)	1.38	1.27	20
Time 2 (at the end of the camp)	0.43	0.89	20
Negative intergroup emotions			
Time 1 (prior to the camp)	2.93	1.62	20
Time 2 (at the end of the camp)	0.47	0.75	20
Positive intergroup emotions			
Time 1 (prior to the camp)	1.36	0.94	21
Time 2 (at the end of the camp)	3.43	0.87	21

Note: Responses were given on a seven-point-Likert scale (0 = "not at all" to 6 = "extremely").

Furthermore, the camping expedition also resulted in the development of new friendships between members of different *manchas*. Only one out of 21 participants reported not having made friends with any member of any other *mancha* during the camp. Eight participants (38.1%) said they had made friends with one or several members of one of the three other *manchas*. And 12 camp participants (57.1%) reported having made friends with members of more than one of the three rival groups.

Follow-Up

Over a period of three months following the camping expedition, I continued to meet the *Túneles, Sangrientos, Ruglats,* and *Sombra* at least once a week until the end of my fieldwork in December 2004. Participant observation and conversations with *mancheros* revealed that, during this period, the positive change of intergroup relations persisted. The *Túneles* and the *Sangrientos,* who lived in adjacent neighborhoods, even visited one another. Before the camp, such an intrusion into foreign territory would inevitably have led to violent conflict, whereas now the crossing of territory boundaries tended to be interpreted as a harmless "visit" without hostile intentions and was therefore tolerated.

Overall, during the 3-month follow-up, I neither witnessed nor heard about any incidence of violence between the four *manchas* that had participated in the camp. The only exception was a minor row between some members of the *Sangrientos* and a subgroup of the *Túneles,* which had not taken part in the camp. However, this incident did not strain the relationship between those members of the *Sangrientos* and *Túneles* that had participated in the camping expedition. This is not to say that camp participants had given up violence as a means of conflict resolution. Each of the four *manchas* continued to fight violent street battles, but only against other *manchas* that had not been involved in the camp.

Within three months following the camp, two of the four participating *manchas* managed to realize their planned activities and projects: The *Túneles* successfully carried out a cleaning-up operation in their neighborhood. Neighbors and authorities were invited, and a number of them joined in the cleanup. Obviously, they were very surprised to see a group of youths who were infamous for being troublemakers work for the benefit of their neighborhood. Even the mayor of the district turned up and lent a helping hand. The *Sangrientos,* on the other hand, constituted themselves as a formal youth association and changed its group name to "Association of Youth in Solidarity." With the collaboration of local authorities, NGOs, and the Catholic Church, they were able to establish a small youth center in an abandoned school building in their neighborhood. The new youth center was solemnly inaugurated, and by the time I left Huamanga, a group of senior members of the *Sangrientos* were busy planning a weaving workshop for youths from the neighborhood, which was going to be held in the new premises. However, a couple of months after I left Huamanga, the leader of the *Sangrientos* was erroneously accused of murder and imprisoned for several months. As a consequence, the newly formed youth organization disintegrated and the activities and meetings at the youth center came to an abrupt end. Moreover, an ex-*Sombra* leader, who had been a driving force behind the *Sombra*'s plan to embellish the chapel in their neighborhood, found a stable job and withdrew from group activities. Consequently, the plan was never carried out. Finally, at the time of writing, the four *manchas* that participated in the camp are again fiercely fighting each other, as members of the *Sombra* and the *Ruglats* have told me in my occasional email conversations with them. One of the camp participants, a *Sombra* member, was stabbed to death in a street fight in July 2006.

Conclusion

Given the apparent short-term success of the camping expedition in reducing enmity and violent conflict between the participating *manchas*, one may be tempted to recommend similar interventions to be integrated in programs targeting youths involved in *manchas*. For instance, a program offering vocational training to *mancheros* could start with a workshop in which rival *mancha* members are brought together under nonviolent, cooperative, and egalitarian conditions for a duration of several consecutive days. This may help reduce tensions and conflicts between program participants and thereby increase the program's effectiveness.

As effective as intergroup contact interventions might be in an individual case, however, they are certainly not a panacea for dealing with *manchas*. There are at least two major reasons for this: First, *manchas* tend to undergo rapid transformations due to the temporary nature of *mancha* membership and, hence, constant fluctuation of members. Accordingly, both internal power hierarchies and relations between different groups can change fundamentally within relatively short periods of time. As a consequence, improvements in intergroup relations achieved through intergroup contact interventions are unlikely to survive in the long run. This is because the participants involved in such interventions will sooner or later cease to belong to their respective *manchas*, because they either "mature out," are imprisoned, or even killed.

Second, attempts to reduce intergroup violence by improving relations between individual *mancheros* fail to tackle the structural root causes of the *mancha* phenomenon. One of the major reasons why *manchas* fight each other is that, by presenting themselves as tough and aggressive and by taking control over a territory, *mancheros* acquire a certain degree of respect and status, which they feel unable to achieve by nonviolent means such as education or employment. Thus, in order to effectively curb and prevent youth violence and *mancha* activity, policy makers need to make serious efforts to reduce inequality and social exclusion. In particular, disadvantaged migrant youth must be given opportunities to fulfill their material and social needs without having to resort to violence and crime.

Notwithstanding the limitations of the intergroup contact intervention described in this chapter, the major lessons learnt are highly relevant for policy and programming, for the present study disproves widespread deterministic and individualist conceptions of *mancha* violence. The results of the camping expedition clearly refute widespread assumptions such as that *manchas* exist "for the sake of violence" or that their individual members are violent "by nature." Instead, the present study gives ample evidence for the capability of youths involved in *manchas* to break the vicious circle of violence.

Notes

1. The term "quasi-experiment" (Cook and Campbell 1979) indicates that the study did not have a strictly experimental design. In particular, the camp study did not include a control group, and participants were not selected at random.

2. In the course of the prolonged armed conflict, other actors joined in, such as the Túpac Amaru Revolutionary Movement (MRTA), paramilitary groups, and peasant self-defense committees. Shining Path, however, commonly has been regarded as the principal perpetrator of violence. Between 1980 and 2000, approximately 69,000 people were killed and 600,000 displaced (Comisión de la Verdad y Reconciliación 2003). The majority of the victims hailed from peasant communities of the Andean and Amazonian regions (Comisión de la Verdad y Reconciliación 2003). Ayacucho was the birthplace of *Sendero Luminoso* and the epicenter of the armed conflict. More than 40 percent of the victims reported to be killed or disappeared during the war were from Ayacucho (Comisión de la Verdad y Reconciliación 2003), which also produced the largest number of internally displaced persons (PAR 2002). The capital Huamanga, alone, accommodated 30 percent of all Peru's internally displaced (United Nations Commission on Human Rights 1995).

3. Young people in Huamanga who join youth gangs generally avoid using the Spanish terms for youth gang (*pandilla*) and gang member (*pandillero*) because of their strongly negative connotations. Instead, they refer to their peer group as *mancha* (group, crowd) and prefer calling themselves *mancheros* (group members). I have adopted their usage of terms for two reasons. First, one of the main arguments of my research is that the negative stereotype of the youth gang or *pandilla* does not apply to youth in Huamanga; and second, I believe that the experiences of youths are best understood from their own point of view.

4. This estimate is based on a mapping of *mancha* territories, carried out in the course of my fieldwork. Local authorities and the media assumed a far larger number of more than 100 *manchas* in the city.

5. At the time of my fieldwork, the *manchas* were not systematically involved in the drug trade, but individual members occasionally worked in *coca* farming and the production of raw cocaine in the Río Apurímac Valley, the subtropical north of Ayacucho.

6. The high proportion of female facilitators was intentional. The excursions with the *manchas* prior to the camp had shown that male *mancheros* were much more willing to cooperate with female research assistants than with male ones. *Mancha* boys generally treated the female social work students in a gentlemanlike manner, whereas male students tended to be considered as potential rivals.

7. The name "Ruglats" derives from a comic strip called "The Rugrats."

8. The high dropout rate immediately before the start of the camp did not, however, lead to systematic bias in the final sample, at least with respect to the variables measured in the questionnaire that was administered prior to the camp. The only statistically significant difference between camp participants and those *mancheros* who had registered for participation but had dropped out before the start of the camp was that the latter reported, on average, more positive emotions toward the participating rival groups. This finding refutes the assumption that participants may have dropped out because of a particularly negative relationship with members of the other three *manchas*.

9. The visit to the village somewhat defeated the purpose of choosing an isolated camp site. However, over the course of the first day it became clear that the *mancheros* were not willing to spend four days at the camp without having the opportunity to play football, which is their favorite sport.

10. *Ronderos* are members of peasant self-defense committees (*rondas*), which were formed during the armed conflict to protect village communities from guerrilla attacks (Degregori 1998; Degregori et al. 1996).

11. Outgroup refers to a group one does not belong to, whereas ingroup is a group of which one is a member.

12. At the general assembly the previous night, participants had made a request for more time to play football. Accordingly, the assembly had decided to change next day's program and include a visit to Quinua Village, which possessed a proper football pitch, larger than that of Pacaycasa.

13. Intergroup relations were measured at the individual level. Camp participants rated their relations to their own *mancha* as well as to each of the other three *manchas*. From these individual measures, mean scores of intra and intergroup relations were computed.

14. Due to the small sample size, the mean differences reported here could not be tested for statistical significance and are, therefore, to be interpreted as trends only.

15. Due to the small sample size, the data could not be analyzed using factor analysis.

Bibliography

Ajzen, I. 1991. The theory of planned behavior, *Organizational Behavior and Human Decision Processes*, vol. 50, no. 2, pp. 179–211.

Allport, G. W. 1954. *The Nature of Prejudice*, Cambridge: Addison-Wesley.

Boal, A. 1979. *Theatre of the Oppressed*, London: Pluto Press.

Brown, R., and M. Hewstone. 2005. An integrative theory of intergroup contact, *Advances in Experimental Social Psychology*, vol. 37, pp. 255–343.

Comisión de la Verdad y Reconciliación (CVR). 2003. *Informe Final*, Lima: CVR.

Cook, T. D., and D. T. Campbell. 1979. *Quasi-experimentation: Design and Analysis Issues for Field Settings*, Chicago: Rand McNally College.

Covey, H., S. Menard, and R. Franzese. 1992. *Juvenile Gangs*, Springfield: Charles C. Thomas Publications.

Degregori, C. I. 1998. Harvesting storms: Peasant rondas and the defeat of Sendero Luminoso in Ayacucho, in S. J. Stern (ed.), *Shining and Other Paths: War and Society in Peru, 1980–1995*, Durham: Duke University Press, pp. 131–140.

Degregori, C. I., J. Coronel Aguirre, P. del Pino, and O. Starn. 1996. *Las Rondas Campesinas y la Derrota de Sendero Luminoso*, 2nd edition, Lima: IEP Ediciones.

Islam, R., and M. Hewstone. 1993. Dimensions of contact as predictors of intergroup anxiety, perceived out-group variability, and out-group attitude: An integrative model, *Personality and Social Psychology Bulletin*, vol. 19, no. 6, pp. 700–710.

Programa de Apoyo al Repoblamiento (PAR). 2002. *Censo por la Paz. Comunidades Campesinas y Natives Afectadas por la Violencia Politica 1980–2000*, Lima: Ministerio de la Mujer y Desarrollo Social (MIMDES).

Pettigrew, T. F. 1998. Intergroup contact theory, *Annual Review of Psychology*, vol. 49, pp. 65–85.

Pettigrew, T. F., and L. R. Tropp. 2000. Does intergroup contact reduce prejudice? Recent meta-analytic findings, in S. Oskamp (ed.), *Reducing Prejudice and Discrimination: The Claremont Symposium on Applied Social Psychology*, Mahwah: Erlbaum, pp. 93–114.

Pettigrew, T. F., and L. R. Tropp. 2006. A meta-analytic test of intergroup contact theory, *Journal of Personality and Social Psychology*, vol. 90, no. 5, pp. 751–783.

Sherif, M., O. J. Harvey, B. J. White, W. R. Hood, and C.W. Sherif. 1961. *Intergroup Contact and Cooperation: The Robbers Cave Experiment*, Norman: University of Oklahoma Book Exchange.

Sherif, M., and C. W. Sherif. 1953. *Groups in Harmony and Tension: An Integration of Studies on Intergroup Relations*, New York: Harper.

Strocka, C. 2006. *Growing up in the "Corner of the Dead": Youth Gangs, Identity and Violence in the Peruvian Andes*, unpublished doctoral thesis, Department of International Development, University of Oxford, United Kingdom.

United Nations Commission on Human Rights (UNCHR). 1995. *Core Document Forming Part of the Reports of States Parties: Peru* (No. HRI/CORE/1/Add.43/Rev.1), Geneva: UNCHR.

Chapter 7

The Dilemmas of Politically Sensitive Medicalized Approaches to Reducing Youth Violence in Pelotas, Brazil

Dominique P. Béhague

Introduction

Despite over two decades of a democratic government, contemporary Brazil is well known for its extremely high levels of everyday urban violence (Caldeira 2000; Costa 1998; Scheper-Hughes 1996; Zaluar 1995). Numerous social and economic indicators associated with violence—such as unemployment, social and economic inequality, and lack of housing—have clearly not improved in Brazil since the transition from military dictatorship to democracy in 1984, and many have in fact worsened (Alvarez 1997; Bacchus 1990; Caldeira 2000; Pinheiro 1997). The demographic group that is considered to be most widely engaged in violence, whether as victims or perpetrators, is youth, defined as the segment of the population between the ages of 15 to 24 (Cardia et al. 2003). Brazil is by no means unique in this regard. Youth violence is a growing international concern, with reports of high levels emerging from countries including the United States, large regions of Africa, and parts of Southeast Asia. Indeed, since the middle of the 1990s, many international organizations and national governments have made youth violence a top policy priority, developing programs geared specifically to tackling the issue (Sawyer and Bowes 1999; WHO 2000, 2003).

Although levels of international funding and institutionalized attention have increased significantly, programmatic initiatives are far from straightforward and can be best described as comprising contradictory ways of conceptualizing the causes and nature of youth violence, particularly when it pertains to young "perpetrators" of violence. In numerous countries, sociologists have documented an increase in vilifying attitudes toward youth violence, resulting from the growth of repressive juvenile justice and police enforcement systems. Backed by a growing body of scientific research in the field of youth criminology, these approaches tend to understand youth violence almost exclusively through a lens of denouncement and punishment

(Caldeira 2000). The circulation of vilifying conceptualization not only support simplistic responses to violence based on assigning blame and imposing legal responsibility; they also readily denigrate a large segment of the youth population, often leading the nonviolent to become violent (Ferrándiz 2004; Spencer 2005; Watts and Erevelles 2004).

Concurrently, medicalized approaches to violence have gained considerable prominence, in part as a response to the critique of vilification. Historians of medicine have shown that the creation of psychiatric diagnoses associated with violence, such as posttraumatic stress disorder, have at times enabled medical experts to rationalize the "irrationality" of violence, and thus, to respond to it in a more conciliatory way (Jones 1999; Fassin 2002; O'Shaughnessy 2004; Thomas and Penn 2002; Young 2002). In many ways, this historical trend continues today. Several international organizations and national governments have developed programmatic approaches that encourage empathetic responses to youth violence as a way of avoiding the forms of victimization and vilification that are often associated with criminalization. In these instances, attempts to reduce youth violence are based on psychiatric and medical models of adolescent mental pathology and providing youth with socially sensitive psychosocial support and psychiatric therapy (Cooper and Singh 2000; Grunbaum et al. 2002; Sawyer and Bowes 1999; WHO 2000, 2003).

At the same time that medicalization has taken hold, a substantial popular and academic literature-base argues that medicalization has more often than not negated the social, political, and moral dimensions of violence, reducing the problem to one of clinical pathology only. Furthermore, the creation of psychiatric categories such as "antisocial behavior" and "conduct disorder" have emerged from conceptual frameworks that generally attribute cause directly to individual-level attributes (see, e.g., Edwards et al. 2007; Fryer et al. 2007; Nigg and Breslau 2007). Critics argue that by pathologizing violence in this way, solutions are in the best of situations relegated to the realm of psychological support, and in the worst of situations to the even more reductionistic pharmacological treatment of violence (Gilligan and Lee 2004).

In recent years, a group of Brazilian "psi" professionals—as the psychological, psychiatric, social work, and pedagogic complex is frequently referred to (Russo 1993)—have developed responses to youth violence that are highly sensitive to both the critique of vilification and the critique of medicalization. Given the recent transition to democracy, psi experts have an added impetus to avoid repressive criminalizing measures. As such, the medicalization of violence in some parts of Brazil has partially developed as a counterpoint to the increase in repressive state-sponsored attitudes to youth violence. For example, a commonly ascribed-to view amongst members of the medical community in Brazil argues that the average practitioner must critically understand how youth violence is produced by the wider sociopolitical climate in order to avoid promulgating inappropriate gang-imbued stereotypes (Levisky 2001).

At the same time that overly vilifying approaches to violence are potentially being avoided, a medicalized response to youth violence based on a purely biological and psychological view of "pathological" behavior has also not developed in Brazil. While it is true that investigations into psychiatric disorders associated with violent behaviors such as "conduct disorder" have grown rapidly (Rohde et al. 2001; Silva et al. 1998), this has not led to widespread reductionistic approaches to youth violence. Instead, many intellectual and social service professionals—including physicians, psychiatrists, school directors, social workers, and teachers—view everyday violence committed by young people to be a political issue, a reaction to political class-based oppression, and a vehicle for the expression of political consciousness (Amann and Baer 2002; Schraiber et al. 2006; Zaluar 2000). These professionals have added a potentially useful dimension to the treatment of mental disorders amongst youth, focusing on raising awareness of the historical and sociopolitical reasons underlying youth violence and linking their work with community-based popular movements. Therefore, for all its potential trappings, medicalization has not been discarded but modified. If implemented in a politically sensitive way, it is believed to harbor not only improved therapeutic power, but great progressive political power as well (Béhague 2004).

My objective in this chapter is to understand how Brazilian professionals use and make reference to this politically sensitive medicalized framework when working with young perpetrators of violence. I do not aim to explore the effects of their particular approach on youth violence per se. Rather, I seek to understand how a politically sensitive medicalizing platform functions as an epistemological framework, including how it may or may not enable professionals to conceptualize and address youth violence in both a nonpathologizing and noncriminalizing way. The benefits—and limitations—of specific conceptual frameworks cannot be better explored than through empirical observations of their use in action. An empirical approach such as this one underscores the contingent nature of the various meanings attributed to youth violence, providing insight into the ways such meanings gain currency and agency within a particular set of social and political circumstances (Goldstein 2003; Korbin 2003; Riviere 2004).

The fieldwork upon which this analysis is based was conducted over a period of approximately 36 months, at different intervals over 7 years, between 1997 and 2004, in Pelotas, a town of 350,000 inhabitants in the southernmost state of the country with a relatively well-developed institutional network. Because I was interested in understanding the experiences of both professionals and youth, I conducted participant observation in the working arenas of a range of professionals, including clinicians, psychiatrists and psychologists, epidemiologists, teachers, government officials, and community leaders from nongovernmental organizations and informal neighborhood groups. Approximately 65 formal interviews were conducted with a selection of the professionals I came to know. In addition, four field assistants, an anthropologist based in Pelotas called Helen Gonçalves and I also explored the everyday life of a subsample of 96 young participants of a population-based 1982 birth cohort (Victora et al. 2003), selected to be roughly representative of the general population. Fieldwork focused specifically on urbanization, violence, medicalization, and the knowledge and values youth acquired through interactions with professionals in schools and health care institutions. We were fortunate in that the 7-year duration of this study enabled us to follow these young informants from age 15 to 22 years.

Tackling Youth Violence:
Ideologies of Democratic Change

One of the key features of democratization in postdictatorship Brazil has been the emergence of a new generation of urban social movements and community-based organizations that have effectively advocated for improvements in health, education, and living conditions (Cardoso 1989). This new sociopolitical context has transformed the nature of popular democratic representation and encouraged the development of numerous innovative health and development initiatives centered around decentralization of health services and schools, the implementation of participatory governance structures, and the political empowerment of the poor (Myers and Dietz 2002). With regards to youth in particular, this progressive era gave birth to the creation of the *Estatuto da Crianca e do Adolescente* (ECA, the Statute for the Child and Adolescent), a set of national-level decrees for the protection of children and adolescents that makes a clear and consistent case for protecting young people's rights, including their physical and mental health (Gomes et al. 2008; Morelli et al. 2000). Compared to other countries where legislation on children's rights has been mostly nominal, the ECA in Brazil has become a tool for social criticism, providing an official platform from which activists and researchers can publicly denounce a series of social problems affecting children and youth (Gregori and Silva 2000; Passetti 1999). It is within this broader context that innovative and politically sensitive forms of psi practice for children and youth, relying on the intermixing of influences from psychoanalysis, Marxist-inspired medicine and, more recently, the antipsychiatry movement, have flourished in some parts of Brazil, including Pelotas (Duarte 1999–2000; Lessa 1997; Souza 2000; Tenorio 2002).

The role of the expert service-sector professional in this new postdictatorial social context is by no means unproblematic, however, not least because of the tremendous class-based inequities that typify Brazilian society and that make direct interaction between professionals, most of whom are from the upper and middle classes, and shantytown dwellers a rarity. The rapid growth of shantytown neighborhood associations throughout the 1990s have helped shape what is today a clearly unified grass-roots, politicized and working class urban-based identity (Alves 1985; Ammann 1991; Cardoso 1983; Jacobi 1987; Scheper-Hughes 1992). As the lower classes have gained political prominence, so have denouncements of the upper classes' role in safeguarding entrenched economic inequities and political representational disparities (Alvarez 1997). Perhaps not so coincidentally, the growth of

class-based consciousness has been coupled with increased class-based conflicts and segregation (Caldeira 1996, 2000; Sheriff 2001). As a result, for
many psi experts, dealing directly with lower-class youth is not only a new
professional experience; it is also filled with tension.

In Pelotas, the first consistent initiative that encouraged professionals to
work directly with youth in shantytown contexts emerged from a multidisci-
plinary and specialized health program for young people, particularly those
of the lower classes, that began in 1989 within the Department of Mental
Health of the Federal University. This public health program was originally
designed to reduce drug and alcohol abuse among adolescents by working
directly in the public school system, although it rapidly came to serve as an
entryway into a number of problems associated with youth, including violence. The initiative relies on the expansive network of primary health care
clinics dispersed throughout the city's shantytowns, as well as two preexisting structures within the decentralized schooling system, the *Serviço de
Orientação ao Educando* (SOE, Orientation Service for the Student) and
the *Centro de Atendimento ao Educando* (CAE, Center of Assistance for the
Student), within which psychologists, social workers, and, at times, psychiatrists can provide direct medical assistance, act as an intermediary referral
entity, and gain access to other institutional entities situated within shantytowns, such as churches and neighborhood associations.

It is certainly no coincidence that the program was conceived by a relatively atypical group of psychodynamic "psi" professionals who had extensive
experience in the public sector and who were among some of the first to
seek ways of working directly in schools and clinics situated in shantytowns.
The philosophy of the program is very much based on providing as much
socially sensitive therapy and support within the school context as possible.
According to those who developed the program, teachers' observations of
youth in the school environment should ideally be given utmost attention, as
the school is deemed the best place to catch potential cases of child or adolescent problems that might otherwise go undetected. Educating teachers
regarding early signs of substance abuse and antisocial behavior are also considered preventive activities, and thereby comply with the primary healthcare philosophy. In some schools, resident medical students in psychiatry
visit the pedagogical advisor on a regular basis to discuss the progress of
different cases and give specialized assistance. Teachers with specific "problem youth" in their classrooms are encouraged to seek assistance from the
SOE first and, together with the in-house pedagogical specialist, attempt to
solve the problem within the school context. If this fails, the CAE structure
gives schools ready access to medical professionals who are brought in to
resolve the problem; this too should ideally occur in the school setting, since
referring youth to psychologists, psychiatrists, or paediatricians—the more
"artificial" setting of the clinic—should be used only as a last resort.

In addition to the practical implications of creating collaborative links
between clinics and schools, the program has expanded the concept of politically sensitive medicalization to include pedagogic knowledge. School staff

have become, once again, influenced by the works of critical theorists such as Paulo Freire, for whom "critical consciousness" constitutes the cornerstone of an empathetic, psychologically sensitive and, nondisciplinarian, pedagogical philosophy (Silva et al. 1998). This philosophy has been posited by pedagogic specialists as a much-needed response to the damaging "authoritarian" pedagogical practices that emerged during the dictatorship and thus, to what can readily become institutionally dictated conformism and adaptation on the part of students (de Oliveira 2007; Zaluar 1994). These newfound pedagogic ideologies are infusing psi knowledge with the hypothesis that violence is due to young people's social and political alienation and to the effects of a society destroyed by dictatorship and poor economic policies.

For many of my informants, youth alienation—and by extension, youth violence—can be tackled by creating a supportive, nurturing, and democratically organized school environment. To provide youth with a healthier, more rounded form of development, the school has become the main platform for the teaching of democratic values, egalitarianism, and "critical thinking." As one informant stated, by providing supportive social space, the school has the potential to "repair the scars of Brazil's history" by giving young people a sense of social belonging and opportunity to participate in political representation and democratic processes. Through these mechanisms, school youth are being encouraged to "stand up for their rights," voice their concerns, and develop their own modes of self-expression. As several informants asserted, the desire to empower youth by teaching them to "think critically" about the social and economic causes of their distress, even if this risks emotive and explosive frustration on the part of youth, should always be paramount.

According to some psi informants, working within these progressive school environments is also central to avoiding the adopting of reductionistic biologically oriented medicalization, which, if allowed to expand, would risk suppressing political consciousness and the successes achieved by popular political movements. Not surprisingly, within this ideological and institutional context, "antisocial behavior," "conduct disorder," and youth violence are often interpreted as semi-legitimate expressions of political and economic oppression. Politically sensitive medical experts therefore view local empowerment and representation, together with the politicized expression embedded in these diagnostic categories, as central to providing young people with opportunities for political action and analysis. As a result, the potential therapeutic approach adopted by some psi professionals seeks to treat not the diagnostic entities "antisocial behavior" or "conduct disorder" per se—even if these are initial objects of the professional's focus and intervention—but the quality and nature of school-based social relationships.

Ideologies in Practice: Underlying Ambiguities Regarding Democratic Change

It is clear from the description above that psi and non-psi professionals are at least partially swayed by a politically sensitive medicalized framework. Such an approach allegedly increases professionals' ability to contextualize the reasons for youth violence, and thus, to empathize with, rather than further alienate, perpetrators of violence. Many informants claimed that such a framework is useful for maintaining a constant critical vigilance on their own views and attitudes, thereby avoiding both vilifying and pathologizing understandings of youth violence.

However, ideology and reality are often at odds with one another, a social fact that only becomes apparent when considering actual practices. To explore the ways in which professionals' current ideological framework breaks down when it is implemented, informants were asked to relay specific instances when they interacted directly with violent youth in their professional roles. Where possible, these accounts were supplemented with insights derived from participant observation in schools, at local professional meetings, and in one main secondary level mental health clinic.

A review of actual case studies showed that professionals who directly engaged with young perpetrators of violence were faced, quite explicitly, with what they experienced as hostile, confrontational, and conflict-ridden aspects of youth violence. Not only did this unsettle them on an emotional level, it led them to openly grapple with accepting views of youth violence as either the rightful exercise of healthy politicized youthful resistance or the consequences of an ailing adolescent psychology produced by socioeconomic inequities and political injustices. Rather than fully embrace either of these conceptualizations, professionals voiced their concern with the cognitive and emotional "irrationality" of violence. Many, for example, focused on young perpetrators' lack of empathy for their victims and inability to control their actions, linking violent acts to "self-aggrandizing power" and emotions such as anger. As summarized by one psych-pedagogical advisor,

> It seems as though there is no longer respect, things have gone to another extreme [from excessive authoritarianism to excessive freedom], if the kids [we see here at the school] have to argue with you, they will, if they want to use foul language, they will, there is no more basic education, parents are so overwhelmed, they hope the school will provide this sort of basic education, but the school is not the place for this, it does not have the tools for it. This growing violence, this is something we have seen change quite a bit, young people no longer have that social solidarity created by strong friendships, any differences that emerge with their schoolmates, they immediately turn to aggression to resolve the problem. Even amongst girls, it is something that is frightening us. It is as though these young people are becoming devoid of human sentiment.

It was telling that when reflecting on specific instances of violence, professionals often ceased to refer to "youth violence" and "resistance," and instead, focused on psychiatric diagnostic categories such as aggression, conduct problems, and antisocial behaviors. This way of psychologizing violence was more likely to develop when professionals reported feeling vulnerable,

bewildered, and even frightened, by the difficult situations and confrontations violent youth posed. As one school director argued, to ensure a certain
degree of safety for staff and fellow students, the ideal of caring for youth
with violent tendencies within the school cannot always be maintained, and
"cases of aggressive behaviors that begin in the school but escalate once
outside the school [simply] have to be referred for psychiatric treatment."
The inclination to view violence as a consequence of irrational emotions
and mental illness was tempting for these professionals in large part because
youth violence, when experienced up close, came to represent not a legitimate reaction to social injustices, but one in a series of unreasonable and
inappropriate behaviors that disrupt the scholastic environment. One school
director demonstrated this attitude quite clearly as she shifted her focus from
a generalized discussion of youth violence to a description of specific students she knew:

> Youth violence is a societal problem, linked to inequities and poverty . . . But
> it is true that here at the school, there is always a certain percentage of
> students that have some sort of more serious difficulty, some behavioral
> problem, aggression, often relating to their family relationships, or to the
> communities in which they live. These are cases that we have to refer to
> the psychologist at the clinic.

Rather than help avoid vilification, then, the psychologization of violence also appears to support the adoption of stereotyping attitudes. Several
professionals, for example, used derogatory and maligning language, alongside psychologization, when describing the nature of youth violence. Young
perpetrators' use of "foul" language, the concurrence of various sorts of
"excesses," including drug and alcohol abuse, the demonstration of a litany
of associated antisocial behaviors, such as graffiti, and the lack of social integration and strong social bonds, were some of the characteristics that these
professionals cited as being typical of young perpetrators of violence.

Identifying Causes: Rapid Political Change and a "Backward" Population

This form of psychologizing youth violence was frequently underpinned
by conservative interpretive explanations of the causes of youth violence,
many of which also encouraged maligning, blaming—and even classist
attitudes toward young perpetrators of violence. Several informants repeatedly referred to factors such as inadequate parenting, young people's "lack
of basic education" and a generalized "loss of respect" to explain young
perpetrators' actions. In effect, these represented explanations that focus on
individual character flaws, weaknesses, and culpability. When asked about
the root causes of such individual weaknesses, informants reverted back to
a socially contextualized discussion, often focused on high levels of poverty. In doing so, however, their conservative inclinations readily emerged, as

they proceeded to center their attention not on social inequities and political injustices, but on the existence of a stagnated and impenetrable underclass that has failed to respond effectively to democratic changes.

Indeed, while most informants were hard-pressed to admit to anything but praising views of Brazil's new-found democracy, several informants, when discussing real cases of youth violence, spontaneously questioned assumption often made regarding the positive merits of Brazil's recent political transition. One government official, for example, whose main responsibility was the promotion and protection of children's and young people's rights, argued that the notion of youth rights was not a straightforward one to disseminate in Brazil, particularly amongst lower class youth. For him, behaviors and attitudes which may at first glance appear to be linked to the exercising of youth rights are in fact an antagonistic infringement on fundamental societal values and norms. He further argued that the creation of democratic processes is not "foolproof." in countries with a dictatorial and violent history where a large and "uneducated underclass" predominates. In such contexts, he stated, democratic empowerment cannot be assumed to automatically lead to healthy responses on the part of youth:

> Now, one thing everyone says is that to break this mess, you need more popular participation, put more power into the hands of the people. But I don't think the populace is ready for this...my opinion! Democracy is not foolproof, I think people, unfortunately, are not yet well educated enough to take on this kind of role.

For informants such as these, everyday urban street violence and associated rises in "youth aggression" are linked to the poorly managed implementation of democracy, where the vast majority are not ready to embrace the full tenets of popular participation and political awareness. Several informants explained quite specifically that the democratic changes and ensuing opportunities students now have to practice and voice "critical thinking" in schools have readily become a temptation for some youth to abuse the system and adopt violent attitudes themselves. As one psych-pedagogic advisor explained,

> It's difficult sometimes to find the right balance...Just because we have implemented a democratic process here in the school, doesn't mean a student has the right to get up and hit another student. This generates a certain degree of discomfort [for us].

For several informants, the fact that youth frequently demonstrated difficulties in distinguishing between empowerment and violence fomented intense skepticism and "discomfort" regarding what several informants termed "rapid" or "irresponsible liberalization." On the surface, "liberalization" was most commonly used in a neutral way to refer to political democratization, economic privatization, or the infiltration of democratic ideals into local and basic institutions such as schools. For informants concerned with the negative effects of unbridled democratic change, however, liberalization also took on a series of negative connotations relating to the lack of proper moral regulation. These included, most notably, the relaxation of social policies and laws governing issues such as education, sexuality, and child rearing.

Informants concerned with rapid liberalization also focused on the underlying causes of "poor parenting," and explained that the current generation of youth is the first in around 40 years to be socialized within the new postdictatorial philosophy and way of being—one in which the most readily found and popular definition of "democracy" focuses almost exclusively on near-total freedom of expression and choice. This generic definition of democracy has, according to some informants, influenced changing parenting styles. Informants routinely postulated, for example, that the current generation of parents, having experienced the excessively autocratic socialization techniques of their parents, as well as a long dictatorship, reject what they consider to be excessively rigid forms of child rearing. While psi professionals tend to agree with these parents that extreme authoritarian disciplinary techniques are repressive and potentially traumatizing to youth, they also explicitly claimed that the opposite—extreme freedom—can easily result in the widespread growth of violence.

"Placing Limits," or Reinstating Institutionalized Control

Psi and pedagogic professionals willing to voice opinions such as the ones highlighted above not only cautioned against the rampant and uncritical acceptance of new political ideologies; they also felt partially implicated in contributing to an institutional environment which may in fact be doing more harm than good. Such informants argued that by actively instating mechanisms to raise consciousness and support youth to become politically active, particularly within an uncontrolled sociopolitical context, professionals themselves could be held responsible for fomenting a form of violence that masquerades as "social resistance" but that in fact inappropriately justifies societal disruption and degradation. These informants felt it is their responsibility to adopt a more cautious approach toward politically sensitive medicalization and to seek alternative solutions to the negative effects of rapid political change. As a result, several informants' initial attempts to be empathetic and understand the "context" in which perpetrators commit violence acts remained an unrealized and even superficial aim. This is aptly demonstrated in one such teacher's shift in focus, from the attempt to be empathetic of young people's lived experiences to a reductionistic definition of youth aggression based on a "lack of respect":

> You have to put yourself in their shoes. You should try to understand their behavior, the reasons behind it, what they are going through in society and even here at the school—but now, that does not mean you are going to allow a lack of respect...If you are not clear about what you expect from students, if the expectations change and you have not set clear limits, then this creates problems for them.

The shift toward a more disparaging view of youth violence, together with a concern to find solutions, enabled several of these informants to justify the endorsement of greater institutional intervention as a way of curbing youth violence. In developing these justifications, informants most frequently referred to the importance of "placing limits," or instated clear rules, on young people's behaviors and attitudes, as highlighted by the informant cited above. Therefore, the importance of raising political awareness, initially given so much attention, quickly paled in comparison with the need to create more absolutist and institutionalized mechanisms of controlling youth violence. Some school staff, for example, frequently identified specific schools that were particularly effective at controlling youth violence—not because they had effectively implemented politically sensitive and psi-informed approaches to youth problems, but because the "structure" of the school kept violence from becoming ubiquitous. As one school director argued,

> I always tell parents of these young people, and the young person as well, that changing schools sometimes helps, we've known it to help, they change environments, the structure of things, change teachers...It's a question of structure, but also, in a new school, they no longer represent a problem to the school staff, a threat or symbol of aggression, and this definitely helps them [to get out of the cycle].

A handful of psi and school professionals claimed that the lack of structure found in many schools can be attributed to professionals' erroneous understandings of how to implement democratic principles. One psi-pedagogic expert, for example, argued that the fear of reproducing repressive aspects of the military dictatorship has led those in positions of leadership in schools and the medical establishment to confuse "authoritarian" attitudes with the much-needed instating of institutional "authority." Teachers, pedagogic experts, and some psi professionals themselves have learned to turn a blind eye to the importance of actively socializing youth and of making them take responsibility for their actions:

> It's probably easiest to describe it by saying that authority and authoritarianism are two different things: authoritarianism is something more aggressive and destructive, but authority...is very important and that is what is needed. Someone to say, "ok, that's enough, cut it out." When the adolescent is like this, he needs someone to simply tell him what to do.

Attitudes in favor of regulating—rather than understanding and "giving voice" to—youth violence were also displayed by some psi professionals who, upon reflecting on specific cases of young patients they had seen in their clinical practice, ultimately endorsed a more "top-down" therapeutic approach to violence than their stated ideals would have originally supported. These informants insinuated that the enthusiasm with which more liberal segments of the psychiatric community took up the cause of political liberation, while inspiring, shows a lack of understanding of the ill effects of uncontrolled liberalization on the psychological health of young Brazilians. As one old-school psychoanalyst highlighted, in trying to explain the reasons for the decline in clinical interest in psychoanalysis,

> Certain elements of training and exigencies in training became lax, particularly in the bigger centers like in Rio, because [the professionals there] espoused, socially, a sort of liberalization above all, not a liberalization in terms of maturity of thinking, but a sort of irresponsible liberalization. And then what happened, well, they stopped being able to respond effectively and practically to the clinical demands that were coming...

As this and other informants claimed, such misunderstandings have led to significant clinical naiveté regarding the assumed benefits of allowing perpetrators of violence to engage in free-flowing and unguided psychotherapy. Rather than use these more classical psychotherapeutic principles with young patients who suffer from "aggressive tendencies," these informants argued that more directive therapeutic measures should be used.

Conclusion

The postdictatorship rise of the particular Brazilian policy approach to youth violence built on a politically sensitive medicalized platform seemed at first glance to be potentially extremely interesting and rewarding. It arguably constitutes a means of bridging the divide between standard policies that construct youth in inappropriate and vilifying ways, on the one hand, and clinical forms of medicalization that constitute the issue in terms of objective individualized pathology, on the other. In adopting this framework, professionals initially try to avoid straightforward medicalizing or vilifying understandings of youth violence and, instead, try to understand how youth violence is produced by the wider social and economic context.

To some extent, politically sensitive medicalization did provide a beneficial solution to professionals' concern with inappropriate vilification of youth, at least at the level of ideology. Informants demonstrated an elaborate and heightened concern with the social production of violence, one which allowed them to create a localized institutionalized response to youth violence based on attempts to modify social contexts rather than individual psyche. However, despite the best intentions of Brazilian psi professionals, a number of practical constraints emerged. Perhaps the most glaring constraint relates to the class-based nature of interactions between professional and young perpetrator, one where underling concerns regarding how to deal with Brazil's "underclass" keep professionals from being able to fully empathize and engage with the youth violence. As shown, in response to actual experiences, several professionals ultimately adopted a conservative and vilifying approach to young perpetrators of violence.

The vilifying tendencies that some professionals adopted can be interpreted in at least two main ways. On the one hand, professionals who came to conceptualize youth violence as a consequence of excessive liberalization are adopting quite conservative attitudes, which serve to blame and vilify poor "uneducated" youth. In part, these attitudes can be attributed to a traditional and elitist form of psychoanalysis that has been present in Pelotas for more than a century (Béhague 2004). At the same time, professionals also experienced a number of practical constraints, to the extent that their conservative tendencies partially reflect a cautious response to a new, challenging, and wide-ranging multidimensional set of practical goals that psi professionals have set for themselves. In other words, by assuming a more conservative stance, they are in fact reacting to their own powerlessness to act within a state that struggles to back the ideology of political representation and freedom with real opportunities and functioning institutions.

Indeed, the chapter has shown that the medicalized framework professionals developed has thus far failed to fully engage with the question of professionals' and young people's agency. To retain a socially sensitive outlook and understanding of the causes of violence, while at the same engaging directly with the individual's agency, requires professional and personal confidence, intricate sociological knowledge of institutional phenomenon, and the ability to galvanize change at the institutional—rather than simply individual—level. These are certainly challenging goals, for which most informants seemed ill prepared. What is more, the broad-based nature of the politically sensitive medicalization platform described in this chapter appears to have paralyzed professionals and inhibited the development of practical solutions, for it fails to encourage any real engagement with questions of how to promote social change. As a result, the psychologization of violence that some professionals eventually adopted as a result of this paralysis not only focused on individual character flaws and culpability, it also encouraged professionals to divert the locus of change from encouraging youth empowerment to increasing institutional control and regulation.

Note

Many thanks to Cesar Victora and Helen Gonçalves for their help and support in innumerable aspects of the research upon which this chapter is based. Funding for this research was provided by a National Science Foundation doctoral fellowhips and post-doctoral funding from The Wellcome Trust (Grant GR077175MA).

Bibliography

Alvarez, S. E. 1997. Reweaving the fabric of collective action: Social movements and challenges to "actually existing democracy" in Brazil, in R. G. Fox and O. Starn (eds.), *Between Resistance and Revolution: Cultural Politics and Social Protest*, New Brunswick: Rutgers University Press, pp. 83–117.

Alves, M. H. M. 1985. *State and Opposition in Military Brazil*, Austin: University of Texas Press.

Amann, E., and W. Baer. 2002. Neoliberalism and its consequences in Brazil, *Journal of Latin American Studies*, vol. 34, no. 4, pp. 945–959.

Ammann, S. B. 1991. *Movimento Popular de Bairro: De Frente para o Estado em Busca do Parlamento*, Sao Paulo: Cortez Editora.

Bacchus, W. A. 1990. *Mission in Mufti: Brazil's Military Regimes, 1964–1985*, New York, Greenwood Press.

Béhague, D. 2004. *The Shaping of Adolescent Pathology in the Wake of Brazil's New Democracy*, Doctoral Thesis: 451, Department of Anthropology, Montreal: McGill University.

Caldeira, T. P. 2000. *City of Walls: Crime, Segregation and Citizenship in São Paulo*, Berkeley: University of California Press.

Caldeira, T. P. R. 1996. Building up walls: The new pattern of spatial segregation in Sao Paulo, *International Social Science Journal*, vol. 48, no. 1, pp. 55–66.

Cardia, N., S. Adorno, and F. Poleto. 2003. Homicide rates and human rights violations in São Paulo, Brazil: 1990 to 2002, *Health and Human Rights*, vol. 6, no. 2, pp. 14–33.

Cardoso, R. 1983. Movimentos sociais urbanos: Balanco critico, in B. Sorj and M. H. Tavares de Almeida (eds.), *Sociedade e Politica no Brasil Pos-64*, Sao Paulo: Brasiliense, pp. 215–239.

Cardoso, R. C. L. 1989. *Popular Movements in the Context of the Consolidation of Democracy*, Notre Dame: The Helen Kellogg Institute for International Studies.

Cooper, B., and B. Singh. 2000. Population research and mental health policy: Bridging the gap, *British Journal of Psychiatry*, vol. 176, no. 5, pp. 407–411.

Costa, M. R. d. 1998. Juveniles and violence: The production of conservative subjectivities, *MARGEM*, vol. 7, pp. 159–173.

de Oliveira, W. F. 2007. Educacao social de rua: Bases historicas, politicas e pedagogicas, *Hist Cienc Saude Manguinhos*, vol. 14, no. 1, pp. 135–158.

Duarte, L. F. D. 1999–2000. Person and psychologization in Brazil: A study in moral regulation, *Journal of Latin American Anthropology*, vol. 4–5, no. 2–1, pp. 142–171.

Edwards, R., A. Ceilleachair, T. Bywater, D. A. Hughes, and J. Hutchings. 2007. Parenting programme for parents of children at risk of developing conduct disorder: Cost effectiveness analysis, *British Medical Journal*, vol. 334, no. 7595, pp. 682–685.

Fassin, D. 2002. The suffering of the world. Anthropological considerations on contemporary polities of compassion, *Evolution Psychiatrique*, vol. 67, no. 4, pp. 676–689.

Ferrándiz, F. 2004. The body as wound—Possession, malandros and everyday violence in Venezuela, *Critique of Anthropology*, vol. 24, no. 2, pp. 107–133.

Fryer, S., C. McGee, G. Matt, E. Riley, and S. Mattson. 2007. Evaluation of psychopathological conditions in children with heavy prenatal alcohol exposure, *Pediatrics*, vol. 119, no. 3, pp. 733–741.

Gilligan, J., and B. Lee. 2004. The psychopharmacologic treatment of violent youth: Youth violence: Scientific approaches to prevention, *Annals of the New York Academy of Sciences*, vol. 1036, pp. 356–381.

Goldstein, D. 2003. "In our own hands": Lynching, justice, and the law in Bolivia, *American Ethnologist*, vol. 30, no. 1, pp. 22–43.

Gomes, I. L. V., R. Caetano, and M. S. B. Jorge. 2008. A crianca e seus direitos na familia e na sociedade: Uma cartografia das leis e resolucoes, *Rev Bras Enferm*, vol. 61, no. 1, pp. 61–65.

Gregori, M., and C. Silva. 2000. *Meninos de Rua e Instituições: Tramas, Disputas e Desmanche*, São Paulo, Contexto.

Grunbaum, J., L. Kann, S. Kinchen, B. Williams, J. Ross, R. Lowry, and L. Kolbe. 2002. Youth risk behavior surveillance—United States, 2001, *Journal of School Health*, vol. 72, no. 8, pp. 313–28.

Jacobi, P. 1987. Movimentos sociais urbanos numa época de transição: Limites e potencialidades, in E. Sader (ed.), *Movimentos Sociais na Transição Democrática*, São Paulo: Cortez, pp. 11–22.

Jones, K. W. 1999. *Taming the Troublesome Child: American Families, Child Guidance and the Limits of Psychiatric Authority*, Cambridge: Harvard University Press.

Korbin, J. 2003. Children, childhoods, and violence, *Annual Review of Anthropology*, vol. 32, pp. 431–446.

Lessa, S. 1997. The situation of Marxism in Brazil, *Latin American Perspectives*, vol. 25, no.1, pp. 94–108.

Levisky, D. L. 2001. *Adolescência e Violência: Ações Comunitárias na Prevenção— Conhecendo, Articulando, Integrando e Multiplicando*, São Paulo: Casa do Psicólogo.

Morelli, A. J., E. Silvestre, and T. M. Gomes. 2000. Desenho da politica dos direitos da crianca e do adolescente, *Psicologia em Estudo*, vol. 1, no. 5, pp. 65–84.

Myers, D. J., and H. A. Dietz. 2002. *Capital City Politics in Latin America: Democratization and Empowerment*, Boulder: Lynne Rienner.

Nigg, J., and N. Breslau. 2007. Prenatal smoking exposure, low birth weight, and disruptive behavior disorders, *Journal of American Academy Child Adolescent Psychiatry*, vol. 46, no. 3, pp. 362–369.

O'Shaughnessy, R. 2004. Violent adolescents: Psychiatry, philosophy, and politics, *Journal of the American Academy of Psychiatry and the Law*, vol. 32, no. 1, pp. 12–20.

Passetti, E. 1999. Crianças carentes e políticas públicas, in M. D. Priore (ed.), *História das Crianças no Brasil*, São Paulo, Context, pp. 347–375.

Pinheiro, P. S. 1997. Popular responses to state-sponsored violence in Brazil, in D. A. Chalmers, C. M. Vilas, K. Hite, S. B. Martin, K. Piester, and M. Segarra. (eds.), *The New Politics of Inequality in Latin America—Rethinking Participation and Representation*, Oxford, Oxford University Press, pp. 261–280.

Riviere, C. 2004. Political violence in black Africa, *Anthropos*, vol. 99, no. 1, pp. 15–24.

Rohde, L., G. Barbosa, G. Polanczyk, M. Eizirik, E. Rasmussen, R. Neuman, and R. Todd. 2001. Factor and latent class analysis of DSM-IVADHD symptoms in a school sample of Brazilian adolescents, *Journal American Academy Child Adolescent Psychiatry*, vol. 40, no. 6, pp. 711–719.

Russo, J. A. 1993. Psiquiatria, manicômio e cidadania no Brasil, in J. da Silva Filho and J. Russo (eds.), *Duzentos Anos de Psiquiatria*, Rio de Janeiro: Relume-Dumará, UFRJ, pp. 7–10.

Sawyer, S. M., and G. Bowes. 1999. Adolescence on the health agenda, *The Lancet*, vol. 354, Supp. II, September 25, pp. 31–34.

Scheper-Hughes, N. 1992. *Death without Weeping: The Violence of Everyday Life in Brazil*, Berkeley: University of California Press.

Scheper-Hughes, N. 1996. Small wars and invisible genocides, *Social Science and Medicine*, vol. 43, no. 5, pp. 889–900.

Schraiber, L., A. D'Oliveira, and M. Couto. 2006. Violence and health: Recent scientific studies, *Revista de Saude Publica*, vol. 40, special issue, pp. 112–120.

Sheriff, R. E. 2001. *Dreaming Equality: Color, Race, and Racism in Urban Brazil*, New Brunswick: Rutgers University Press.

da Silva, L. A. V., R. F. Oliveira, and A. L. e. S. Franco. 1998. The role of the psychologist in programs of primary care with adolescents: An experience in Salvador, Brazil, *Psicologia: Reflexao e Critica*, vol. 11, no. 3, pp. 605–620.

de Souza, E. 2000. Reforma psiquiatrica: Um grande desafio, *Psicologia em Estudo*, vol. 1, no. 5, pp. 45–63.

Spencer, J. 2005. It's not as simple as it seems: Ambiguous culpability and ambivalent affect in news representations of violent youth, *Symbolic Interaction*, vol. 28, no. 1, pp. 47–65.

Tenorio, F. 2002. A reforma psiquiátrica brasileira, da década de 1980 aos dias atuais: História e conceito, *História, Ciências, Saúde—Manguinhos*, vol. 9, no. 1, pp. 25–59.

Thomas, C., and J. Penn. 2002. Juvenile justice mental health services, *Child and Adolescent Psychiatric Clinics of North America*, vol. 11, no. 4, pp. 731–748.

Victora, C. G., F. C. Barros, R. C. Lima, D. P. Behague, H. Gonçalves, B. L. Horta, D. P. Gigante, and J. P. Vaughan. 2003. The Pelotas (Brazil) Birth Cohort Study, 1982–2001, *Cadernos de Saúde Pública*, vol.18, no. 5, pp. 1241–1256.

Watts, I., and N. Erevelles. 2004. These deadly times: Reconceptualizing school violence by using critical race theory and disability studies, *American Educational Research Journal*, vol. 41, no. 2, pp. 271–299.

WHO (World Health Organization). 2000. *Health and Health Behaviour among Young People*, Denmark: World Health Organization Regional Office for Europe.

WHO. 2003. *Caring for Children and Adolescents with Mental Disorders*, Geneva: World Health Organization: 31.

Young, A. 2002. The self-traumatized perpetrator as a "transient mental illness," *Evolution Psychiatrique*, vol. 67, no. 4, pp. 630–650.

Zaluar, A. 1994. *Cidadões Não Vão ao Paraíso*, Campinas: Escuta, Editora da Unicamp.

Zaluar, A. 1995. The drug trade, crime and policies of repression in Brazil, *Dialectical Anthropology*, vol. 20, pp. 95–108.

Zaluar, A. 2000. Perverse integration: Drug trafficking and youth in the Favelas of Rio de Janeiro, *Journal of International Affairs*, vol. 53, no. 2, pp. 653–671.

Chapter 8

Understanding the Logic of Nicaraguan Juvenile Justice

José Luis Rocha Gómez

Introduction

As occurred in many other postconflict societies in Latin America, Nicaragua witnessed a massive rise in youth violence following the end of its almost decade-long revolutionary civil war in 1990. Gangs, in particular, emerged as a chronic source of citizen insecurity (Rocha 2000a, 2000b, 2005b, 2006b; Rodgers 1997, 2006a), and the Nicaraguan National Police—who, during the 1980s, had mainly preoccupied itself with the threat of U.S.-financed counterrevolutionaries—increasingly turned its attention to so-called common delinquency (Granera Sacasa and Cuarezma Terán 1997; Policía Nacional 1999). Similar to its counterparts in other Central American countries, the National Police did so by stepping up coercion, although in a much "softer" manner than most other states in the region (see Ungar this volume). At the same time, however, the contemporary Nicaraguan juvenile justice system is paradoxically also associated with regionally unique efforts to promote the protection of the rights of children and adolescents through the adoption in 1998 of an internationally lauded Code of Children and Adolescents (hereafter, the Code), whose application is supervised by a specially created state organ, the Office of the Special Ombudsman for Children and Adolescents (hereafter, the Ombudsman's Office).

This chapter seeks to understand the logic of this seemingly contradictory system, focusing on the underlying dynamics of the Police and the Ombudsman's Office. In theory these could be seen as having rather complementary roles. The former focuses on apprehending those who break the law, and managing their internment in carceral confinement centers, while the latter exists to make sure that this occurs in a manner that respects certain basic principles. In actual fact, however, relations between two organizations have been extremely conflictual, to the extent that they have constituted a significant source of internal tension within the postrevolutionary Nicaraguan state (see Rocha 2005c). The Ombudsman's Office has frequently condemned police action,[1] for example, while the Police has publicly expressed major doubts about the Code, for instance denouncing it as an obstruction to effective policing. Such incongruities are linked to the fact that the National Police and the Ombudsman's Office have different modes and sources of legitimization, which affect their organizations and forms of operation in specific ways, and ultimately reflect the particular nature of the broader political economy of postrevolutionary Nicaragua.

This chapter explores the divergent strategies that both organizations have deployed over the past decade, emphasizing the internal dynamics that have led to such behavior patterns. Part one focuses on the methodological means through which I obtained insight into the opposing dynamics and organizational heterogeneity of the National Police and Ombudsman's Office. I recount how I gained significant insight from my membership of the Advisory Council of the Nicaraguan Youth Secretariat, which I then combined with the theoretical application of ideas drawn from the work of Jürgen Habermas. Part two lays out the work of the Ombudsman's Office, through a detailed analysis of the origins of the Code that embodies the Office's work. Part three looks at the National Police, and explains the existence of incongruent internal networks that shape the institution's interaction with the Ombudsman's Office and the Code in particular ways. Finally, the last part of this chapter considers how the return to power of the *Frente Sandinista de Liberación Nacional* (Sandinista National Liberation Front, FSLN) in January 2007 has reconfigured the logic of juvenile justice in Nicaragua.

A Note on Methodology

This chapter draws on research conducted for a broader project on Nicaraguan youth violence that focused on the clash between informal and formal norms concerning gang violence in a poor neighborhood of South-Eastern Managua called Reparto Schick.[2] During the course of interviews with past and present gang members, neighborhood residents, and local police officers, there emerged a profound and what seemed to me paradoxical discontent with the newly adopted and internationally praised 1998 Code. This was widely perceived by both local residents and police officers as having led to a climate of impunity, insofar as it was causing gang members to systematically declare themselves within the age range protected by the Code whenever detained or arrested, and as a consequence, allowing them to avoid criminal charges (Rocha 2005a, 2005c, 2006c).[3] Not only did this mean that incidences of gang violence were only rarely denounced by exasperated local inhabitants, but moreover that the police had increasingly begun to resort to extrajudicial forms of punishments such as on-the-spot beatings of youth and adolescents whom they suspected were gang members, and detention without due process.

The divergence between police action and the juvenile justice system that I observed at the neighborhood level was also reported more generally in the Ombudsman's Office annual reports (e.g., PDDH 2002), as well as by third parties such as the Nicaraguan Centre for Human Rights (*Centro Nicaragüense de Derechos Humanos*, CENIDH 2004). These denounced the extensive abuses of youth rights by the police. It quickly became apparent, however, that in order to understand this dissonance better, I needed to pursue my investigations beyond the micro-level. I decided as a result to draw up the institutional profiles of the two key organizations involved in this divergence of the juvenile justice system in Nicaragua, namely the National Police and the Ombudsman's Office. I initially set about collecting and reading official reports and studies, and conducted a number of formal interviews with selected officials from both organizations. This provided me with two sets of sometimes complementary, sometimes contradictory discourses that gave me little sense of how and why these conflicting visions had come into being, and I began to feel increasingly frustrated. A few months before starting my neighborhood-level research, however, I had been invited to join the newly formed Youth Secretariat Advisory Council, a state entity created and directly overseen by the then President, Enrique Bolaños (2002–2007). My membership almost immediately began to provide me with a lens through which to survey the institutional and organizational labyrinths that were leading to ambiguous forms of interaction between the National Police and the Ombudsman's Office.

At this point it is important to note that I did not join the Council in order to study it. To a certain extent, the participant observation I ended up carrying out can be seen as a form of covert research because it was not officially condoned, although I freely shared my insights in informal conversations with other Council members and openly sought to interview Secretariat officials, many of whom acceded to my request, and indeed often provided me with essential information. The particular nature of this kind of research meant that I do not feel it appropriate to directly use specific information obtained from these sessions. Effectively, I treated my situation as analogous to the one faced by an anthropologist friend, who also happens to be a priest, and who found that confessions by members of his congregation provided him with key information for a study of indigenous youth he was carrying out. Whilst canonically prohibited from revealing this information, even under a pseudonym, it inevitably indirectly informed his analysis and his writings. This is what my membership of the Council gave me: critical clues about who might have answers, which officials were worth interviewing, what interests were at stake, and how informal processes intersected with more formal ones. To this extent, research can often be said to be shaped by indirectly related events.

During its brief existence of approximately a year and a half, the Council included current and former members of a diverse range of organizations: former members of the National Police, university researchers, consultants, nongovernmental organization (NGO) representatives, as well as members of other governmental bodies and multilateral institutions. The supposed objective of the Council was to generate an authoritative consensus regarding youth policy. It was, furthermore, assumed that its varied membership would provide the Secretariat with access to strategic resources: information about other key bodies, good relations with political parties, coordination with civil society, technical advice, and funding. At the same time, members had their own objectives for staying on the Council. The officials from the multilateral institutions saw their presence on the Council as a means to extend lobbying and advocacy work. Academics like myself had the—perhaps vain—hope that our research might influence policy, as well as—in some cases—a poorly hidden desire to be hired as consultants. In format, Council sessions consisted of little more than an extended working lunch, during which the director of the Secretariat invariably tried to present himself as someone who controlled more information than he was authorized to communicate, and generally tried to extract as much information as possible from us, rather than promote any form of substantive exchange. Some sessions were dedicated to studying reports and plans, while others involved outside guest speakers, including representatives from the Ombudsman's Office and the National Police, who rapidly emerged as the key players—and rivals—in juvenile justice policy determination.

Not surprisingly, perhaps, few of the policies adopted by the Secretariat were the fruit of the Council's deliberations. This was at least partly due to the fact that the full-time technical advisors of the Secretariat had a profile that was often very similar to that of the Council members, and jealously guarded what they saw as their policy-formulating prerogatives. They did not attend Council discussions and generally ignored us. At the same time, the Council can be said to have existed principally as a response to certain political imperatives. The presence of representatives of the United Nations (UN) and other agencies was perceived as legitimizing, and therefore highly prized by a government that could be described as something of a "low-intensity" administration, insofar as most important organs of state government, such as the National Assembly, the Judiciary, or the Supreme Electoral Council, were all in the hands of its political adversaries, the FSLN led by Daniel Ortega, and the Constitutionalist Liberal Party (PLC) controlled by former President Arnoldo Alemán (1996–2002). The fact that the Council was inefficient made it a useful multiparty body for the Bolaños government to brandish as an example of attempted multipartisanship. This particular political role was well highlighted when the Council was dissolved at a moment the Bolaños government came to feel increasingly cornered by its political adversaries, and therefore decided to eliminate any space through which information and funds might potentially be filtered to them.

Although my time on the Council confirmed that neither it nor the Secretariat ultimately decided the nature of the government's youth policy, my experiences nevertheless allowed me to observe processes of policy formulation close up, to learn who was participating in their negotiation, and the nature of the debates being played out. The Council sessions were principally a forum where different interest groups—the Secretariat, the Bolaños government, international donors, NGOs, academics, the FSLN, the PLC, the National Police, and the Ombudsman's Office—attempted to be seen as influencing the country's youth policy. Certain Council members pushed the agendas of the political parties they were associated with, while others promoted more particular institutional or corporate agendas. I was therefore able to witness in the Council not only the "finished texts" or "implemented actions" of the different discourses and interests around youth that I had obtained through my interviews, but their conflictual incubation, their interaction with each other and the numerous ways in which attempts are made to impose each of them over the others.

Going beyond a simple description of such processes, however, requires a conceptual framework that addresses the dysfunctions of the state in a more nuanced fashion than traditional Weberian explanations, which focus on underlying deficiencies in the state's bureaucratic apparatus such as fragile institutional memory, lack of financial resources, and deficient human capital endowments. This kind of analysis often fails to grasp the complexities of both state and political action, including in particular those deriving from the fact that both states and political processes are invariably embedded within wider socioeconomic contexts. This is perhaps clearest in relation to the processes and problems that Habermas (2000) has theorized as pertaining to the domain of "legitimization," something that he contends is the necessary basis for any sustainable political system. Habermas replaces the classic epistemological paradigm of politics being based on an unproblematic "subject-object relation" (Horkheimer and Adorno 2004: 59–64) with one that sees political action as deriving from "communicative reason." He argues that in order to be sustainable as an embodiment of political will, policies and laws have to be the result of intersubjective negotiations, in so far as deliberation and the achievement of a "communicative dynamic" between members of the "juridical community"—"the plurality of constellations of interests and value orientations" (Habermas 2000: 232)—are what imbue a political system or policy with legitimizing "consensus."

This approach offers a potentially extremely interesting perspective and conceptual apparatus for analyzing policies, relations among state institutions, and the production of policies in terms of "communicative procedures" (Habermas 2000: 169). While traditional approaches to policy determination do sometimes formulate dysfunctional outcomes in terms of a problem of lack of legitimacy, they generally do not analyze the more detailed components of this legitimacy that reveal the political dynamics of the state. In particular, they tend not to pay attention to the consequences of having different coexisting and competing sources of legitimacy and policy implementation mechanisms. Habermas, on the other hand, offers a variety of concepts that allow for an "unpacking" of this context, including the ideas of "juridical validity," "legal legitimacy," and "instrumentalization," all of which I will refer to in the following two chapter subsections as I explore the underlying logics of the Ombudsman's Office and the National Police, with a view to understanding the roots of their conflictual relationship.

Searching for External Legitimacy:
The Ombudsman's Office and the Code

Most of my information regarding the Ombudsman's Office was obtained through interviews with members of its directorate. My position as a writer for the Nicaraguan current affairs magazine *Envío* opened a number of doors for me, as officials were extremely willing to talk to the representative of a publication that was widely read within the international community in Nicaragua. The institution's dependence on international donor funds, as we shall see, made this a potentially interesting means of increasing its visibility among a key constituency. At the same time, however, the chief Ombudsman was a member of the PLC, and the deputy prosecutor and special ombudsman for children and adolescents were FSLN sympathizers, something that my experiences with the Council made me realize would significantly affect the information that they would provide. To use Goffman's (1959: 22–34) terms regarding distinction, there was a great space between the "front stage" and "back stage" of these officials as a result of their political allegiances. I thus sought to uncover the nature of the Ombudsman's Office by characterizing its institutional history and more specifically its relationship to Law No. 287, the Nicaraguan Code of Children and Adolescents, approved by the Nicaraguan National Assembly on May 12, 1998, (PDDH 2000). This law embodied the work of the Ombudsman's Office, which was established in 2000 as a dependency of the Ombudsman for the Defense of Human Rights, with the explicit brief to foster "a culture of promotion, defense and respect for the human rights of children and adolescents" (PDDH 2001: 9).

The Ombudsman's Office was in other words created to enforce the Code, which upholds the idea that children and adolescents are full members of a society who must be able to exercise constitutionally guaranteed rights. By opening a space for these new subjects of law, the membership of the juridical community was expanded and the new members were granted an autonomy that upset traditional values as enshrined in the 1973 law based on the concept of state guardianship over minors. The Code regulates all aspects of child and adolescent development, with a special emphasis on the juvenile justice system, which is the subject of 132 of the Code's 222 articles. The system exempts minors of 13 years and under from criminal responsibility, prohibits the deprivation of liberty for minors under 15 years of age and concedes protection to adolescents between 13 and 18 years old who commit crimes, in particular making the trial a formative process and establishing specialized penal centers for adolescents. As a result of the new system, the number of Nicaraguan youth deprived of their liberty dropped from 449 in 1998 to 36 in 2003 (CENIDH 2004: 31).

As Maclure and Sotelo (2003: 672–673) observe, the unanimity with which the Code was approved by the National Assembly was short-lived, as politicians from both the political Left and Right quickly began to challenge the Code, presenting it as a form of protection for juvenile delinquents. The most belligerent opposition came from the small populist Christian Way party that was, in fact, in danger of extinction. Christian Way went so far as to present a bill to reform the Code in April 2002, proposing that it more closely approximate adult criminal justice, including especially suggesting the implementation of a broader gamut of sanctions in responses to youth crimes, as well as classifying youth gangs as criminal associations (see Bancada Camino Cristiano 2002). To a large extent, this opposition stemmed from the fact that the Code was not promulgated as a result of a political consensus—in the Habermasian sense—but was rather instrumentally approved in a global context where such legal reforms were being strongly promoted as part of a general "good governance" agenda, with the ratification of international conventions and protocols recognizing human rights constituting a major concern of donors in post–Cold War Latin America. The Code effectively put the Convention on the Rights of the Child into full legal effect in Nicaragua, and as such can be seen as an expression of "legal globalization," implying the transnationalization of particular models of justice (Sieder 2009).

At the same time, however, this transnational process was dependent on a particular domestic political context. Both the Code (1998) and the Ombudsman's Office (2000), like the Law to Promote the Comprehensive Development of the Youth of Nicaragua (2001), and the Comprehensive National Development Plan for Youth (2001), were approved during the Alemán government (1997–2002), which was characterized by acrimonious relations with the governments of the European Union, the United States, and international development organizations in general. In promoting the passage of the Code, Alemán may have been calculating that he could minimize the corruption scandals in which his government was involved through a proliferation of legal initiatives linked to the internationally promoted "good governance" agenda. Indeed, the Code's supporters did not delude themselves about the circumstances that made its approval possible. They knew that the political conjuncture made legal reform a real possibility and pushed for the Code's passage accordingly in an explicitly instrumental manner. As the Special Ombudsman for Children and Adolescents, Carlos Emilio López, recognized frankly during an interview in March 2003, "the conventions have been ratified because the issues of children and human rights sell well nationally and internationally. In that context it was possible to produce and pass the Code."

The passage of the Code was, however, by no means sufficient to guarantee its legitimization. To comprehend the magnitude of the distance between the existence of the Code and its legitimization, it is illuminating to turn to Habermas' (2000) distinction between "juridical validity" and "legal legitimacy." Validity is produced when "the state authority declares that a norm put into effect has been sufficiently justified" (Habermas 2000: 223), which was what the Alemán government and National Assembly did in passing the Code in 1998, responding to the international context. In contrast, legal legitimacy relates to "an equitable consideration of all interests and values distributed" in a juridical community (Habermas 2000: 224). This had clearly not occurred at the national level within Nicaragua, as the local-level opposition to the Code that I encountered in the Reparto Schick, the opposition of politicians, as well as that of sections of the National Police, all illustrate well. In other words the Code achieved validity but not legitimacy because the moment of "rational acceptability" did not coincide with the moment of "social acceptance," to use another Habermasian distinction. Or put differently, there existed little social approval of the Code within Nicaragua, whatever the international consensus regarding such laws.

To Habermas (2002: 172), approval for policies is often purposefully created, but in this respect, the Ombudsman's Office earmarked few resources for shaping public opinion regarding the Code, despite the Special Ombudsman for Children, Carlos Emilio López, acknowledging during an interview that the Code's "great adversary" is "all of public opinion," "for ideological reasons" and "lack of information." The lack of knowledge, debate, and awareness-building about the Code has been amply documented, for example by the *Fundación de Protección de Niños, niñas y adolescentes infractores de la ley* (Foundation for the Protection of Delinquent Children and Adolescents; FUNPRODE, 2003: 80). Part of the problem was the fact that the Ombudsman's Office itself depends on external sources of legitimacy in its defense of the Code, and this meant that it tended to respond to the challenges to the Code by invoking its nature as an "ambassadorial" piece of legislation with regards to the international donor community, rather than alluding to any of the benefits putatively deriving from its application (Procuraduría Especial de la Niñez y la Adolescencia 2002). To a certain extent, this is a function of the precariousness of the Ombudsman's Office's budget and its reliance on international donor funds. Of the 15.5 million córdobas (U.S.$ 1,026,055) that the Ombudsman's Office for the Defense of Human Rights received from central state funds in 2003 (Ministerio de Hacienda y Crédito Público 2000–2005), only 930,000 *córdobas* (U.S.$ 61,563), or 6 percent, were for the Office of the Ombudsman for Children, according to the Special Ombudsman for Children and Adolescents, which in turn made up only 19 percent of its total income if we add the 4,877,857 *córdobas* (U.S.$ 322,900) it received from international donors (PDDH 2004: 49).[4]

In addition to the precarious budget, the weak attempts by the Ombudsman's Office to promote the Code also derived from the fact that the law was not the fruit of a broader consensus. The dialogue that led to its adoption was not an "equitable consideration of all interests and values distributed" in the Nicaraguan "juridical community" (Habermas 2000: 224), because it was not a piece of "self-legislation" whereby its beneficiaries were also its authors (Habermas 2000: 169). The Code represents a clear case of "instrumentalization," a process whereby "the logic of domination" determines the perversion of "Reason," thereby making "Reason" an instrument at the service of domination (see Horkheimer 2002: 65). Or in other words, dominant political interests seek to legitimize themselves through means of legally established law: "The reciprocal constitution of law and political power creates a connection between both moments that open and perpetuate the latent possibility of an instrumentalization of law at the service of a strategic use of power" (Habermas 2000: 237). The Alemán government, which clearly suffered a deficit with regard to internal legitimacy and was, at the same time, questioned by the international community, used a globally legitimated instrument to provide itself with some measure of legitimacy. It compensated for the deficits in its own legitimization through the deliberate manipulation of the existence of multiple sources of legitimization (see Habermas 1999: 126) that were, furthermore, operating in a context characterized by deficient "communicative reason" (Habermas 2000: 218).

Incongruent Networks within the National Police

This situation was dramatically highlighted in 1999 when the National Police implemented a new gang prevention policy (Policía Nacional 1999). The document outlining the policy displayed a contradictory mix of rehabilitative rhetoric with a program of repression. Youth gangs were presented as a critical threat that needed to be (literally) "beheaded," yet the Plan also made explicit reference to the Code and its rhetoric of rights. In practice, the Plan was unambiguously repressive, with over 400 adolescents, the majority of them less than 15, being arrested within the first few weeks, in open disregard of article 95 of the Code (Maclure and Sotelo 2003: 681). The Ombudsman's Office and some NGOs denounced these abuses (FUNPRODE 2003: 66), but the Ministry of the Interior responded by claiming that financial restrictions made it difficult for police officers to respect the Code (Ministerio de Gobernación 2002: 19; FUNPRODE 2003: 72). The National Police went even further, however, and argued that the Code "promote[d] impunity because it [took] longer to capture [juvenile delinquents] than it [took] the judicial authorities to release them," and certain senior officers even went on record saying that the Code made them feel "helpless," and that they saw it as a "legal obstruction" to the "re-establishment of public order" in Nicaragua (PDDH 2002: 71). Such declarations at the same time contradicted those made by other senior police officers, who claimed that Nicaragua was an unquestionably secure society, with less violent gangs than other Central American countries.

To understand these contradictions, it is necessary to realize that today's Nicaraguan National Police inherited its members, command structures, vision, and *modus operandi* from the Sandinista Police, founded in July 1979 as an entity designed to defend the revolution. The organization was thus characterized by a counterinsurgent military vision (Rocha 2001). Police officers, like soldiers of the Sandinista Popular Army, were trained to fend off attacks by counterrevolutionaries and their organizational legitimacy depended on the consensus generated by the revolutionary project. After the FSLN's electoral defeat in February 1990, however, the police apparatus became a focal point of the highly polarized postrevolutionary political settlement. Because the defeated FSLN continued to enjoy a significant support (Bautista Lara 1999: 31), the victorious opposition actively sought to dismantle any potential sources of institutionalization of this support by pushing for a reform of both the police and army apparatuses (Cajina 1997: 51–52). This move took the form of attempts to replace the police and army apparatuses with the counterrevolutionary *Contra* guerrilla apparatus, thereby signaling a rejection of the "inter-subjective understanding" indispensable to generating true social integration (Habermas 2000: 148). Ultimately, the 1992 Police Law was passed, defining the organization as an armed entity of a civic, apolitical, nonparty and nondeliberating nature (Bautista Lara 2004: 21).

The National Police therefore relies on dispersed and sometimes contradictory sources of legitimacy in contemporary Nicaragua, including its Sandinista origin, the rising crime rate, its protection of private enterprise, its rhetoric promoting preventative action against gangs, its violent operations, its unconditional backing of governmental decisions, and its projection of Nicaragua as a "safe" country. The key to understanding this seemingly nonsensical and contradictory combination was provided to me by my membership of the Council when it was recommended that I interview a former government minister.[5] I ended up having extended conversations with this person in August 2005, during which I presented some of my preliminary ideas about the underlying nature of the Nicaraguan juvenile justice system in terms of an institutional confrontation over legitimization between the National Police and the Ombudsman's Office. In particular I asked the ex-minister about the seemingly contradictory institutional nature of the former, to which he responded with a vast quantity of new information that obliged me to change my working hypotheses, in particular concerning the puzzle of the National Police's institutional dynamics.

Although the command structure of the National Police is widely known to be in the hands of 40 revolutionary combatants and 400 founding officers, with their crosscutting networks woven over the 25 years of the force's existence projecting a certain sense of organizational homogeneity, my ex-minister informant insisted that there were, in fact, two distinct groups, and that it was this that went to the heart of the National Police's contradictory response to the Code. On the one hand, some of its high-ranking officers were members of the traditional elite, who had joined the police after being combatants in the Sandinista guerrilla organization that took power in 1979 (see Wheelock Román 1985).[6] The strength of these (class) ties was visible in their numerous business associations, as many high-ranking officers from this group were welcomed on retirement as board members of certain companies.[7] These ties also explained the "special services" that the National Police notoriously provides to the elite in Nicaragua, such as differential treatment for white collar criminals (including perhaps most famously for the ex-president Arnoldo Alemán), the posting of riot police around buildings belonging to wealthy families during demonstrations, or the focused policing that occurs in elite areas of cities, to the detriment of poor areas.

The second group within the National Police was made up of ex-combatants of more diverse social origins, and whose economic and political fortunes depended principally on their links to the new Sandinista elite that emerged when the upper echelons of the FSLN pillaged the Nicaraguan state following their electoral defeat in 1990, a process known as the *piñata*,[8] and which set up FSLN cadres as a corporate economic interest group on a par with traditional elite conglomerates (see Rodgers 2008). This Sandinista Police group is highly loyal to the FSLN and its political directives, and has in particular sought to maintain channels open to youth gangs in order to be able to mobilize them to play disruptive roles during the student and public transport strikes that are routinely encouraged by the FSLN in order to demonstrate that it "controls the streets." The Sandinista network within the police has, as a result, successfully projected the Nicaraguan National Police as favoring a model for treating youth violence that stands in marked contrast with the policies applied by the other Central American police apparatuses. Instead of the various *Mano Dura*-style plans and antigang laws promulgated in Guatemala, Honduras, and El Salvador (see Carranza 2004: 75 & 154), the Nicaraguan Police claims to follow community involvement models (Bautista Lara 2003: 12–13), focused on arranging truces, amnesties, and job reinsertion for gang members, all of which implicitly support the aims and ideals of the Code (Rocha and Bellanger 2004: 359).

Most of these actions are clearly more symbolic than anything else, and such operations and the rhetoric underpinning them do not correspond to the reality of police operations on the ground. This contradiction clearly derives from the fact that both networks simultaneously want to project a sense of insecurity, yet, at the same time, also a sense that they have the security situation under control. As a result, the two networks often find their corporate strategies contingently synchronized. For example, the Sandinista network's rhetorical emphasis on preventative action vis-à-vis youth violence implicitly supports the ludicrous governmental claim that Nicaragua is "the safest country in Central America," a discourse that is designed to attract foreign investment, something in which the traditional elite network within the police has a direct interest (Bautista Lara 2004: 112). At the same time, certain sections of the traditional elite police network have an interest in the promotion of a sense of insecurity insofar as they control the majority of the private security companies that have proliferated in Nicaragua over the past decade,[9] with police officers often moonlighting as security guards, while sections of the Sandinista network control the country's flourishing small arms trade.

There are further points of coincidence, insofar as the existence of strong relations between the police and the traditional elite is a major factor explaining the confidence that the National Police inspires among the non-Sandinista postrevolutionary rulers of Nicaragua, the Sandinista associations of a large section of the institution notwithstanding, and despite this latter group colluding with gangs in order to provoke symbolically important instances of violent disorder so as to reinforce the FSLN's power. This has translated in both financial and institutional terms. In 2005, for example, the police received an 11 percent budget increase, while the entire public sector received an average of only 0.7 percent. Sustained increases have meant that the police budget went from 2.4 to 3.8 percent of the state budget in the past 5 years. Between 2000 and 2005, the number of police personnel increased by 2,091 or 33 percent, that is to say 18 percentage points more than general population growth (Ministerio de Hacienda y Crédito Público 2000–2005).[10] In terms of the National Police's relationship to the Code, however, the simultaneous coincidence and divergence of interests between the two networks leads to a certain ambiguity, which ultimately points to the fact that the "law, which in modern societies bears the primary burden for social integration, has no choice but to submit to the *profane* pressure of the systemic imperatives of society's reproduction, while simultaneously being subjected to coercion…which obliges it to legitimize those imperatives" (Habermas 2000: 58).

Conclusion

This chapter has explored the underlying contradictory logics of two key actors of the contemporary Nicaraguan juvenile justice system, namely the National Police and the Ombudsman's Office. Drawing on Jürgen Habermas' ideas concerning legitimacy and instrumentalization, as well as notions concerning legal globalization and more classic notions of political economy, I have described how the two organizations respond to divergent pressures and interests, attempt to justify their existence in relation to different constituencies, and are themselves heterogeneous and internally contradictory institutions. I have also shown how the interactions between the National Police and the Ombudsman's Office are to a large extent a reflection of Nicaragua's postrevolutionary political economy, and more specifically of a political settlement involving a range of interest groups that have both divergent and convergent interests, as well as contradictory modes of action. It is this last factor that is probably most critical to understanding the conflictual interaction between the two organizations, and their ambiguous relationship to the Code of Children and Adolescents, which can ultimately be said to have juridical validity but no legal legitimacy as a result. To this extent, following Habermas (2000: 103), we can say that ultimately it is the distance between the "idealism" of law and the "materialism" of the juridical order that drives Nicaragua's particular juvenile justice system.

In many ways this is not surprising, insofar as social policy is always the product of a particular context, whether exogenously imposed or endogenously generated, and once a particular law or policy is in place, it must necessarily interact with its environment. Moreover, laws and policies are inevitably applied and enacted by institutions and organizations that have a range of corporate and individual interpretations, pressures, and reference points that will also affect their actions, and therefore the outcomes of their actions. In the case outlined in this chapter, both the National Police and the Ombudsman's Office's actions were guided by their own corporate survival imperatives, the particular political networks traversing them, and their divergent sources of legitimization—legal globalization in the case of the latter, elite economic interests in the case of the former, whether in relation to the traditional or the new Sandinista oligarchy. The obvious question that this contextualized analysis raises is what happens when the political context changes significantly, as is arguably what happened in Nicaragua in January 2007, when the FSLN returned to power after Daniel Ortega's victory in the November 2006 elections.

The impact of the FSLN return to power on the Nicaraguan juvenile justice system has not been what might be expected in view of the analysis presented above. Two years after, the transformation wrought by this regime change can be summarized as the construction of a more homogenous, compact executive authority that has sought to dominate all other channels of state power. Since gaining the Presidency, the FSLN has also managed to leverage control over the Supreme Electoral Council, the Supreme Court of Justice, the Comptroller's Office, the Office of the Ombudsman for the Defense of Human Rights, the Presidency of the National Assembly, as well as most of the latter's major internal commissions. In addition, the FSLN has also consolidated its grip on the army, purging it of potentially disloyal officers. The only major state institution that it has not been able to control completely is the National Police, due to a rather idiosyncratic bureaucratic rule allowing an outgoing President to name the head of the Police shortly before transferring power to their successor-elect. President Bolaños named Aminta Granera, an ex-Catholic nun and ex-guerrilla who has long cultivated her relations with NGOs, the international community, the media, and religious groups, all of whom currently oppose the new FSLN regime (albeit not all for the same reasons), and who has also displayed no small measure of independence.

The response of President Ortega has been to make use of the legislative privileges that allow him to force the retirement of senior police officers, clearly in order to undermine Granera—or perhaps even to seek her resignation—as he has acted principally against officers known to be close to Granera, or else whose loyalty to the FSLN cause is suspect. Ultimately, the aim is clearly to engineer the National Police's fall into the hands of the FSLN, in order to ensure a certain political homogeneity to the Nicaraguan state apparatus. This homogeneity could well be achieved in July 2009, when all senior police officers who have fulfilled 30 years of service will be forced by law to retirement, a measure that will apply to almost all current senior Police officers. The homogenization of the Nicaraguan state arguably constitutes a new phase in postrevolutionary Nicaraguan oligarchic settlement (see Rodgers 2006b). The nature of this new phase is well illustrated by the increasing instrumentalization of gangs by the Police. Many gang members who had become inactive or "retired" were recruited by the FSLN in order to repress opposition protests against the FSLN's electoral fraud in the November 2008 municipal elections. It has widely been documented that FSLN militants went to poor neighborhoods and distributed pistols, machetes, and mortars to youth gang members, offering to hire their services to attack the proliferating opposition demonstrations. The resulting violence—as opposition protests were attacked, demonstrators beaten up and injured, and vehicles burned and destroyed—occurred in total impunity, with the Police frequently present but actively ignoring all brutality, and youth being actively egged on by Rosario Murillo, the first lady of Nicaragua, who described them as an exemplification of the "vigor" of Sandinismo's defense of the FSLN's electoral "victory." Not surprisingly, perhaps, once the demonstrations and the attacks ceased, the youth involved returned to their neighborhoods and turned their violence against local inhabitants and themselves, and levels of violence have increased, with homicide levels in particular rising dramatically (see Rocha 2008).

More generally, this instrumental legitimation of youth violence clearly undermines any coherent application of the Code. Instead of promoting a special juvenile justice system, the State is seen as encouraging specific forms of youth violence, and guaranteeing the impunity of perpetrators. To this extent, the instrumentalization of youth violence that is allowing the FSLN to consolidate its grip on power and homogenize the institutions of the State is arguably expanding the deficit of social approval that the Nicaraguan juvenile justice system in general, and the Code in particular, suffered from previously. Because the FSLN is emerging as an example of what Habermas (2000: 102) calls a "constellation of unfiltered normative interests," there is little chance of intersubjective negotiations occurring in the context of contemporary Nicaragua. At the same time, however, the FSLN's move away from negotiation and consensus toward the instrumental imposition of its own agenda is in many ways a double-edged sword, with the manipulation of youth violence in particular a mode of operation that is likely to have tragic consequences, not only in the political arena, but also beyond.

Notes

1. According to the Ombudsman's Office, 47 percent of all adolescents detained in 2001 were subject to mistreatment during their arrest. Specifically, 62.5 percent received blows and kicks, 12.5 percent suffered blows and verbal abuse, and 7.5 percent were subjected to blows and other types of abuse. A further 11 percent were interrogated without a lawyer being present (PDDH 2002: 87–121).
2. This investigation was based on field research conducted in 2003—which partly built on 6 months of research previously carried out on the neighborhood's local youth gang in 1999—as well as a range of interviews carried out in 2006, 2007, and 2008.
3. There are clear parallels here with Sieder's (2004) investigations in Guatemala, where she found that many citizens blame the new Penal Procedures Code for an increase in crime and impunity.
4. Calculated on the basis of an average 2003 exchange rate of 15.1064 *córdobas* to U.S.$ 1.
5. I am deliberately remaining very vague about this person's identity in order to protect their anonymity. I have had to be selective in my use of the information

they provided me, as revealing too much could endanger my source, although obviously the information that I am concealing nevertheless impinges on my analysis.

6. A significant section of the traditional Nicaraguan elite joined the FSLN in its fight against the Somoza dictatorship following the latter's increasingly venal governance of the country during the 1970s and his ordering the murder of a prominent member of the elite, Pedro Joaquin Chamorro, in 1978.

7. Accelerated retirement plans for the police force furthermore operated as a huge incentive for cultivating these links, thus maintaining networks of relations between economic and police elites in a manner similar to those described by Wright Mills (1960: 269–273).

8. A *piñata* is a papier-mâché figure that is filled with sweets and is an obligatory feature of Nicaraguan parties, where it is struck with a stick until its contents spill out, and a scramble ensues as everybody attempts to grab as many treats as possible.

9. There were 47 private security companies operating in Nicaragua in 2000, employing 6,536 guards (Godnick *at el.* 2002: 11), and by 2005 there were 67 companies and 9,329 guards (Policía Nacional 2005).

10. This coincidence of interests has not prevented infighting between the two networks, especially visible during the struggles between candidates for the post of first commissioner. The appointment depends directly on the president, and every time a new first commissioner is appointed, two or three other senior commissioners—those who would have also been eligible to direct the force—have to retire, which clearly stirs up significant internal rifts (see Romero 2006). Not belonging to either of the two networks within the National Police can actually smooth the path to becoming first commissioner, but at a price. In 2001, for example, President Alemán chose Edwin Cordero as first commissioner precisely because he had no links to either the traditional or the Sandinista elites. His independence, however, left him in a fragile position, and when he injudiciously disclosed that the police often paid its informants with confiscated cocaine, he was obliged to retract his remarks by an unprecedented alliance of high-ranking members of the two networks that, moreover, came together to refute his declarations at a collective press conference held, somewhat brazenly, in the National Police headquarters, where they also asked him to resign (see Romero 2003).

Bibliography

Bancada Camino Cristiano. 2002. *Iniciativa de Ley de Reforma a la Ley No. 287 Código de la Niñez y la Adolescencia*, Managua: Bancada Camino Cristiano.

Bautista Lara, F. 1999. La utopía posible de la nueva policía, *Visión Policial*, vol. 1, no. 6, pp. 31–32.

Bautista Lara, F. 2003. Causas de la violencia social y delictiva de niños, niñas y adolescentes, *Visión Policial*, vol. 4, no. 4, pp. 12–13.

Bautista Lara, F. 2004. *Policía, Seguridad Ciudadana y Violencia en Nicaragua*, Managua: PAVSA.

Rocha, J. L., and W. Bellanger. 2004. Políticas juveniles y rehabilitación de pandilleros en Nicaragua, in ERIC, IDIES, IUDOP, NITLAPAN, and DIRINPRO (eds.), *Maras y Pandillas en Centroamérica: Políticas Juveniles y Rehabilitación*, vol. 3, Managua: UCA Publicaciones, pp. 293–399.

Cajina, R. 1997. *Transición Política y Reconversión Militar en Nicaragua, 1990–1995,* Managua: Coordinadora Regional de Investigaciones Económicas y Sociales (CRIES).

Carranza, M. 2004. Políticas juveniles y rehabilitación de mareros en El Salvador, in ERIC, IDIES, IUDOP, NITLAPAN, and DIRINPRO (eds.), *Maras y Pandillas en Centroamérica: Políticas Juveniles y Rehabilitación,* vol. 3, Managua: UCA Publicaciones, pp. 15–88.

CENIDH. 2004. *¿Dónde Están los Derechos? Aplicación e Impacto de las Medidas de la Justicia Penal Especializada del Adolescente,* Managua: CENIDH.

FUNPRODE. 2003. *Informe Final del Proyecto Justicia Penal Especializada,* Managua: FUNPRODE.

Godnick, W., R. Muggah, and C. Waszink. 2002. *Balas Perdidas: El Impacto del Mal Uso de Armas Pequeñas en Centroamérica,* Geneva and Oslo: Small Arms Survey and Norwegian Initiative on Small Arms Transfers.

Goffman, E. 1959. *The Presentation of Self in Everyday Life,* New York: Anchor Books.

Granera Sacasa, A., and S. Cuarezma Terán. 1997. *Evolución del Delito en Nicaragua (1980–1995),* Managua: Editorial UCA.

Habermas, J. 1999. *Problemas de Legitimación en el Capitalismo Tardío,* Madrid: Ediciones Cátedra.

Habermas, J. 2000. *Facticidad y Validez,* Madrid: Editorial Trotta.

Horkheimer, M. 2002. *Crítica de la Razón Instrumental,* Madrid: Editorial Trotta.

Horkheimer, M., and T. W. Adorno. 2004. *Dialéctica de la Ilustración,* Madrid: Editorial Trotta.

Maclure, R., and M. Sotelo. 2003. Children's rights as residual social policy in Nicaragua: State priorities and the code of childhood and adolescence, *Third World Quarterly,* vol. 24, no. 4, pp. 671–689.

Ministerio de Gobernación. 2002. *Resumen Ejecutivo—Diagnóstico de Seguridad Ciudadana en Nicaragua,* Managua: Ministerio de Gobernación.

Ministerio de Hacienda y Crédito Público. 2000–2005. *Presupuesto General de la República,* Managua: Ministerio de Hacienda y Crédito Público.

Policía Nacional. 1999. *Plan de Prevención de las Pandillas 1999,* Managua: Policía Nacional.

Policía Nacional. 2005. *Registro Nacional de Empresas de Vigilancia,* Managua: Policía Nacional.

Procuraduría Especial de la Niñez y la Adolescencia. 2002. *Contra-Argumentos a Iniciativas de Reforma al Código de la Niñez y la Adolescencia,* Managua: PDDH and Red de Alcaldes Amigos de las Niñas y los Niños.

PDDH (Procuraduría para la Defensa de los Derechos Humanos). 2000. *Código de la Niñez y la Adolescencia Comentado por 27 Personalidades Nicaragüenses,* Managua: PDDH.

PDDH. 2001. *Informe Anual de Gestión 2001,* Managua: PDDH.

PDDH. 2002. *¿Cara o Sol? Investigación Socio-jurídica de Adolescentes que se Encuentran en Privación de Libertad en los Departamentos de la Policía a Nivel Nacional,* Managua: PDDH.

PDDH. 2004. *Informe Quinquenal del Procurador Especial de la Niñez y la Adolescencia: Noviembre 1999–Junio 2004,* Managua: PDDH.

Rocha, J. L. 2000a. Pandilleros: La mano que empuña el mortero, *Envío,* vol. 216, pp. 17–25.

Rocha, J. L. 2000b. Pandillas: Una cárcel cultural, *Envío*, vol. 219, pp. 13–22.

Rocha, J. L. 2001. Breve, necesaria y tormentosa historia del FUAC, *Envío*, vol. 232, pp. 10–22.

Rocha, J. L. 2005a. Código de la niñez y la adolescencia: Una ley incomprendida, *Envío*, vol. 278, pp. 19–25.

Rocha, J. L. 2005b. El traido: Clave de la continuidad de las pandillas, *Envío*, vol. 280, pp. 35–41.

Rocha, J. L. 2005c. *The Political Economy of Nicaragua's Institutional and Organisational Framework for Dealing with Youth Violence*, Crisis States Programme Working Paper No. 65, London: Crisis Status Research Centre.

Rocha, J. L. 2006b. Mareros y pandilleros: ¿Nuevos insurgentes, criminales?, *Pueblos, Revista de Información y Debate*, http://www.revistapueblos.org/article.php3?id_article=450 [accessed August 8, 2006].

Rocha, J. L. 2006c. Pandilleros del siglo XXI: Con hambre de alucinaciones y de transnacionalismo, *Envío*, vol. 294, pp. 25–34.

Rocha, J. L. 2008. On the track of political gangs: Has Mara 19 been born in Nicaragua?, *Envío*, vol. 329, http://www.envio.org.ni/articulo/3921 [accessed February 4, 2008].

Rodgers, D. 1997. Un antropólogo-pandillero en un barrio de Managua, *Envío*, vol. 184, pp. 10–16.

Rodgers, D. 2006a. Living in the shadow of death: Gangs, violence and social order in urban Nicaragua, 1996–2002, *Journal of Latin American Studies*, vol. 38, no. 2, pp. 267–292.

Rodgers, D. 2006b. The state as a gang: Conceptualizing the governmentality of violence in contemporary Nicaragua, *Critique of Anthropology*, vol. 26, no. 3, pp. 315–330.

Rodgers, D. 2008. A symptom called Managua, *New Left Review*, vol. 49 (January–February), pp. 103–120.

Romero, E. 2003. Desautorizan a Cordero, *La Prensa*, July 10, http://www-ni.laprensa.com.ni/archivo/2003/julio/10/nacionales/nacionales-20030710-11.html [accessed November 10, 2006].

Romero, E. 2006. Granera será la nueva directora de la policía, *La Prensa*, July 18, http://www.laprensa.com.ni/archivo/2006/julio/18/noticias/ultimahora/ [accessed November 22, 2006].

Sieder, R. 2004. Renegotiating "law and order": Judicial reform and citizen responses in post-war Guatemala, in S. Gloppen, R. Gargarella, and E. Sklaar (eds.), *Democratization and the Judiciary: The Accountability Function of Courts in New Democracies*, London: Frank Cass, pp. 137–160.

Sieder, R. 2009. Legal globalization and human rights: Constructing the "rule of law" in post-conflict Guatemala, in P. Pitarch, S. Speed, and X. Leyva (eds.), *Human Rights in the Maya Region: Global Politics, Cultural Contentions and Moral Engagements*, Durham: Duke University Press, pp. 67–88.

Wheelock Román, J. 1985. *Imperialismo y Dictadura*, Managua: Editorial Nueva Nicaragua.

Wright Mills, C. 1960. *La Élite del Poder*, Ciudad de México: Fondo de Cultura Económica.

Chapter 9

Deadly Symbiosis? The PCC, the State, and the Institutionalization of Violence in São Paulo, Brazil

Graham Denyer Willis

Introduction

Soon after the democratic opening of the Brazilian political system in 1985, the city of São Paulo began to experience rapidly escalating violence. Homicide rates rose to levels expected under conditions of open warfare, with some 10,845 people killed in 1999 (SSP 2007). This violence was particularly acute in the periphery of the city, where many neighborhoods suffered upwards of 100 murders per 100,000 people per year (SEADE 2007), over five times the Latin American average. The prognosis for public security at the turn of the millennium was thus highly negative. To almost universal surprise, however, violence in São Paulo experienced a remarkable decline from 2000 onwards. By 2005, the overall number of homicides had dropped by 48 percent compared to the 1999 peak (SSP 2007). One of the most significant factors underlying this decline was a dramatic reduction in homicide rates in some of the city's most violent peripheral neighborhoods. The homicide rate in the District of *Cidade Tiradentes*, for example, which had been 107 per 100,000 in 2000, had declined to 13 per 100,000 by 2006 (SEADE 2007).

This decline has been widely attributed to the introduction of "zero tolerance" policies by the state of São Paulo during the past decade and a half (Goertzel and Khan 2007). This approach, pioneered in New York during Rudy Giuliani's municipal administration, places great emphasis on strict law enforcement and the repressive control of "visible" social disorder (Greene 1999). Police means are increased, and law enforcement officers are provided with greater latitude in their deployment of violence, especially when targeting so-called problem areas and problem demographics. The approach has become very popular throughout Latin America (see Davis 2007), and proved particularly attractive to policy makers in São Paulo within the context of geographically concentrated violence in the cities' poor peripheral communities.[1] The result was that zero tolerance style policies were vigorously put into application from the late 1990s onwards (Wendel and Curtis 2002). Nevertheless, in May 2006 São Paulo was brought to a standstill by an unprecedented series of attacks on police stations, banks, and other public buildings throughout the city that lasted 10 days, killed 493 people, and caused a wholesale paralysis of business, transportation, education, and urban public life. These attacks were carried out by the *Primeiro Comando da Capital* (PCC), an organization that James Holston (2007: 273) has pithily labeled a "gang cartel," but is in many ways much more complex, insofar as it originated as a small-scale prison gang which has now evolved into a highly organized, centralized, and hierarchical syndicate structure of thousands of members that is a ubiquitous fixture of São Paulo's peripheral communities.

The PCC attacks, which were spurred by the abrupt transfer of imprisoned PCC leaders to an isolated maximum security detention regime, marked the first time in São Paulo's recent history that violence had reached out from the periphery into the heart of the city. As such, they clearly seemed to indicate the failure of zero tolerance measures. The reality is arguably much more complex, however, with the dynamics of violence regulation in São Paulo very different to the portrait conventionally presented. The argument that is made in this chapter is that the attacks were a reflection of the inherent fragility of the perverse symbiotic institutionalization of state and nonstate violence in São Paulo. Zero tolerance policies effectively fostered the emergence of the PCC, which paradoxically had a positive effect on levels of violence in the urban periphery by imposing monopolistic forms of order in areas where the state was unable or unwilling to do so. The PCC does not represent a "parallel power" (Leeds 1996), however, but is symbiotically linked to the state in a way that is leading to particular societal perceptions of violence that are ominous for the future. The first part of the chapter explores the origins of the PCC, highlighting its connections to the introduction of zero tolerance policies, and its initial logic as a prison self-protection group. Drawing on the example of the neighborhood of São Gotardo,[2] the second section then describes how the PCC has spread into poor peripheral communities in São Paulo where the state is either absent or only partially present, and how this movement led to declining levels of violence in these areas of the city. Finally, a last section looks at the fragile symbiosis that exists between the PCC and state authorities, focusing specifically on the corrosive consequences of this particular institutionalization of violence, including especially vis-à-vis the emergence of a discourse calling for the revocation of human rights.

Zero Tolerance: Planting the Seeds of the PCC

Although the declining number of homicides in São Paulo is widely claimed to reflect the success of zero tolerance policies, the evidence on the ground supporting this assertion is not obvious (World Bank 2006). A multitude of other efforts have also been invoked to explain the radical decline, including, for example, the recent implementation of a diffuse collection of public security programs (Goertzel and Khan 2007). These include the regulation of "dry communities," the creation of community policing pilot projects, and the use of Geographical Information Systems (GIS) mapping to identify and prioritize crime hotspots, even if these have been implemented in a rather desultory manner, scattered throughout the metropolitan area of São Paulo.[3] One often overlooked phenomenon that can be unambiguously linked to the introduction of zero tolerance is the massive increase in the São Paulo prison population, however. Between 1994 and 2006, this population grew from 55,021 to 144,430, an increase of greater than 160 percent (SAP 2007).

The rapidly expanding inmate population became more densely concentrated in inadequate penitentiary complexes, leading to overcrowding and a seemingly perpetual wave of violence and rioting over prison conditions (Salla 2006). These were, more often than not, violently put down by the state. One such incident, the 1991 massacre of 111 inmates in the Carandiru Detention Centre, sparked the genesis of the PCC, which was founded 2 years later in the nearby Taubaté prison complex, following the transfer of Warden José Ismael Pedrosa from Carandiru. Pedrosa—who was assassinated in 2005 by suspected PCC members—rapidly began implementing a repressive management structure in Taubaté similar to the one that motivated the riots in Carandiru, and this legitimated the formation of an inmate self-protection group calling itself the *Primeiro Comando da Capital*. The group drew up a statute (PCC 1993, my translation), which outlined key rules relating to its *raison d'être*, articulated as follows:

> The *Primeiro Comando da Capital* (PCC), founded in 1993 during a tireless and formidable fight against oppression and injustice in the concentration camps that are Carandiru and Taubaté, has as absolute focus liberty, justice and peace. We will stay organized and united to avoid a massacre such as, or worse than, that which happened in Carandiru, on October 2nd 1992 where 111 inmates were cowardly murdered in a massacre that will never be forgotten by the Brazilian conscience.

The founding of the PCC can therefore be seen as a reaction to the inhumane and repressive conditions rife within the São Paulo prison system (Adorno and Salla 2007). The organization very rapidly imposed a strict internal order inside Taubaté, and drastically improved conditions by imposing strict rules concerning inmate behavior, despite opposition by the official authorities. In the face of the organization's growing influence, the state decided in the mid 1990s to disperse the PCC leadership throughout different prisons in São Paulo. This strategy only served to spread the gang throughout the entire prison system, however, fostering the development of a large-scale network that either co-opted or eliminated any rival groups—generally parochial and poorly coordinated—and rapidly established itself as a dominant authority within prisons (Mingardi 2007). Once an initial presence was established, the PCC used violence to enforce order and reform prisoner conditions—often taking guards hostage in negotiations, for example—and also developed an extensive smuggling network to ensure both the basic and luxury needs of inmates. Supplies such as toiletries, adequate clothing, and sufficient food are sourced by PCC members, lawyers, or family outside the prison and transferred through this illicit network (Câmara dos Deputados 2006a; Salla 2007; Silveira 2007).

The PCC has had a remarkable impact on violence within the prison system. In the mid 1990s, lawyers, prison clergy, and even prison guards noted that the rise of the PCC in Taubaté had brought undeniable benefits to detainees. A PCC monopoly brought a decline in prison deaths and a decrease in the number of victims of all types of prison violence, including incidents of interpersonal violence and violent sexual assaults, such as rape (Mingardi 2007). As of 2006, the organization had such a degree of control over its members that it succeeded in enforcing a unilateral and outright ban on the use of crack cocaine within the prison system of the State (Câmara dos Deputados 2006a). In many ways, therefore, the PCC can be said to have usurped many of the responsibilities and prerogatives of the state in São Paulo's prisons. Largely impotent to inject meaningful reform without the cooperation of the group—and perhaps relieved to have such a responsibility "outsourced"—the state administration of the prison system has adapted to coexistence and, in some cases, actively cooperates with the group. In a formal deposition given behind closed doors in 2006, the putative leader of the PCC, Marcos Willians Herbas Camacho—known as "Marcola"[4]—for example, remarked that prisoners who enter the São Paulo penitentiary system are sorted out according to gang affiliation, in order to be sent to prisons that are controlled by their gang rather than fueling violence by sending them to prisons where rival gangs were fighting over control.[5] Similarly, during a rash of prison murders in 2003, the Secretary of Public Security of São Paulo State, Nagashi Furukawa, approached the PCC, as the dominant prison gang, to talk about reining in prison violence. Promising a "humanization" of the prison system if there were no murders for 1 year, the Secretary requested that the PCC use its network to improve the situation. For the next 2 years, there was a significant drop in prison killings, which was reflected in the official statistics of the Secretary for Penitentiary Administration (Câmara dos Deputados 2006a; SAP 2007).[6]

From a small band of prisoners in the Taubaté prison complex in the early 1990s the PCC rapidly expanded to a network of hundreds of thousands of affiliates within the São Paulo penitentiary system, making a transition to nonprison contexts from the mid 1990s onwards as it gained a presence in the city's peripheral communities. Part of the reason for this transition is that most inmates in São Paulo's prisons originate from the metropolis' socioeconomically marginalized periphery, and when released, return there. They clearly retain their links to the PCC after doing so, partly through obligation, but also because the organization needs members outside prisons in order to be able to source goods to be transferred to those still inside. Indeed, the PCC has a differentiated membership structure. Incarcerated members, while benefiting from protection, food, and basic goods provided by the group, are not required to remit membership payments. Outside the prison, members considered to be "in good standing" must pay monthly membership dues. These funds provide goods for incarcerated members, finance the costs of lawyers, and may also contribute to community based donations or cover funeral costs. Members in good standing must remit payment of their monthly fees without fail; as per the statute and PCC practice, nonpayment or delayed payment of dues is punished severely, often culminating in summary execution (Holston 2007; PCC 1993). Although some money is received from local businesses in the neighborhoods that the PCC controls, most of these revenues are generated through drug trafficking that occurs in the peripheral neighborhoods of São Paulo, beyond the reach of the state authorities, and facilitated by the existence of the PCC network, which is one further reason why PCC members remain members after leaving prison.

São Gotardo: The View from the Periphery

The vast periphery of São Paulo is home to a marginalized population that has been subjected to large scale processes of exclusion and discrimination. While the periphery is not economically homogenous, it is, on average, a more socioeconomically vulnerable area. Residents are predominantly working class, often employed in nominal-paying service-oriented employment as maids, nannies, groundskeepers, or security guards in wealthier areas of the city. The periphery has been shunned by large businesses and substantive economic infrastructure such as financial institutions and shopping malls. Locally owned small businesses, such as bakeries, hair salons, and bars predominate. There is comparatively little state investment and most public resources are allocated to the wealthier central areas of the city, which are substantially better serviced and policed (Hughes 2004). Residents of the periphery are, in large part, regional migrants to the city of São Paulo. Processes of urbanization through the second half of the twenty-first century saw the arrival of thousands of migrants from all areas of the country (Caldeira 2000). Migrant inflows to the city were dominated by large numbers from the Northeastern region, an economically depressed area with strongly racialized characteristics. The influx of poor and darker skinned migrants that settled in underserved and informal periurban areas has contributed to the creation of a stereotypical image of the periphery as being black, poor, and uneducated.

This notion that the periphery is populated by "the other" has been reinforced during the past three decades by the fact that São Paulo's peripheral neighborhoods often serve as nuclei of the drug economy. As with the dynamics of *favelas* (informal settlements) in Rio de Janeiro—see Enrique Desmond Arias (2006), Luke Dowdney (2005), and Ben Penglase (2007), for example—peripheral neighborhoods in São Paulo constitute a convenient, poorly accessible space, where the drug economy can be sheltered among local residents and a complex built environment. Most importantly of all, as has been pointed out by Raquel Rolnik (1999) and Teresa Caldeira (2002), the state is notable for its absence, which creates a space for so-called violence entrepreneurs to emerge unchallenged (Collier et al. 2003; Hazlehurst and Hazlehurst, 1998: 12). These features have become central to the problematic of violence in the periphery, as they promote high levels of volatility and insecurity.

The community of São Gotardo, in the Eastern zone of São Paulo, is a case in point. At the end of the twentieth century, São Gotardo was among the most insecure communities in the city, labeled one of the five greatest "factories" of underage offenders by the youth corrections system (FEBEM 2000). Plagued by youth gangs engaged in small-scale violent drug-market-based rivalries and anarchic economic criminals, homicide rates in São Gotardo among males aged 15–19 stood at 326 per 100,000 in 2000 (SEADE 2002), and the general homicide rate was between 40 and 80 times higher than that of the central districts of São Paulo (SEADE 2007). The security environment was, in other words, exceptionally poor, with armed robberies occurring frequently on the community's main streets, to the extent that they had become socially conceptualized as routine (Willis 2007). In 1998, for example, nearly 800 metropolitan buses—more than two per day on average—were robbed at gun or knifepoint in the borough (Netto and Silva 2002). In other words, at the turn of the millennia, São Gotardo can be said to have succumbed to a high degree of loss of social control.

Such circumstances might logically be thought to have made São Gotardo ripe for zero tolerance measures, and at first glance it would seem that such policies were indeed applied, quite successfully albeit rather heavy-handedly judging from the numerous reports of extrajudicial killings that affected the community (see OVP-SP 2007). Certainly, by 2004, 4 years after the introduction of zero tolerance policies in São Paulo, the homicide rate in São Gotardo had dropped by some 45 percent (SEADE 2007). From persistently being the leading cause of mortality in the community, homicides fell to being the third in 2005, behind more conventional ones such as heart disease and stroke. Overall, since 2000, the local homicide rate plummeted from some 85 per 100,000 to less than 20 per 100,000 (SEADE 2007). During the course of interviews carried out with São Gotardo inhabitants in December 2006, however, state authorities emerged as being highly mistrusted and were not perceived as responsible for the reduction in violence. Instead, residents pointed to the PCC's arrival during the latter half of 2003 as having fostered an unprecedented regime of order in the community. Following years of living in a state of fear and heightened unpredictability, residents now claimed to be living with levels of security never before seen or experienced. The nature of this order was clearly spelt out in the formal statutes of the PCC, which stipulated general rules of conduct not only for its members but also the inhabitants of the local communities it occupied. Under this "regulation" criminal activity, engagement with state authorities, and even economic activity was not to occur without the consent of the group.

This meant that very little common delinquency now occurred in São Gotardo, for example. At the same time, the PCC's monopoly over power in São Gotardo left little space for these rules to be questioned by local residents, who were well aware of the penalties for noncompliance. Transgressions were punished by summary execution, and in some cases, beheading. But despite this brutality, residents of São Gotardo did not reject the violence of the PCC, but rather accommodated themselves to its presence, even extolling its virtues. This attitude was highlighted during a conversation I had with a local woman named Aguenilda,[7] who had settled in the community as a teenager nearly two decades previously from the impoverished northeastern state of Bahia:

> This place has never been safer in the 18 years that I have lived here. Before, we used to have to hide and not go out at night because of the violence and gun fights. Now, with [the PCC] here…things are better than they have ever been. You have to be careful though, always blind, deaf and dumb…

This sense of security—having to be "blind, deaf, and dumb" notwithstanding—went beyond mere individuals. According to another São Gotardo resident called Adriane, local health clinics benefited from the protection of the PCC and were no longer threatened by theft and robberies of supplies and medication. As a result, access to healthcare in the neighborhood had improved, as clinic staff members were less fearful, and residents could travel freely to the clinic without risk of being assaulted. Such protection generally did not come without cost, however. As Vanessa, another neighborhood inhabitant described, local businesses such as bakeries were guaranteed physical protection from theft and violence, but had to provide members of the PCC with free food and drinks. Compared to life in the past, characterized by high and unpredictable violence, this was deemed by many to be a small price to pay, especially as PCC members often actively helped local inhabitants in both financial and nonfinancial ways. As a result, according to police official Da Rosa, whom I interviewed in December 2006,

> The outlook for the PCC is growth, and it will only grow…Why are these drug traffickers liked in the favelas? Because they take the role of the state. People here like traffickers because they don't let any thieves steal. [They tell them:] "If you steal here, I'll kill you." No one messes around with anyone, [and] no one denounces anything that they do. People from the favela love [the trafficker] because he takes care of the community. He helps out. He buys food. He gives work. He provides credit. He's hiding here, and the police are there. No one will say anything. Often times the traffickers are seen as heroes.

State-PCC Relations

Although there is no doubt that the state is less present in urban peripheries, and that this is an important element to understanding the rise of the PCC in such communities, as Enrique Desmond Arias (2006a: 39) has pointed out, "essential to understanding the persistence of violence in Brazil is an examination of the necessary links that criminals sustain with actors in state and society—actors who have reciprocal interests in maintaining connections to criminals in order to accomplish personal and political goals" (see also Arias 2006b; Caldeira 2002; Leeds 1996). Arias's observations concern the networks that exist between drug organizations and state actors in Rio de Janeiro, but they have equal pertinence and currency in São Paulo. It has been suggested that the PCC and state authorities in São Paulo constitute "parallel powers" (Macaulay 2007), along the lines that Elizabeth Leeds (1996) has discussed in relation to drug gangs in the *favelas* of Rio de Janeiro. Two issues caution against such an interpretation. Firstly, as described above, the state's actions have been directly causal of the PCC's emergence. Zero tolerance, violence within the prison system, and a withdrawn state have all created conditions amenable to the birth and expansion of the PCC. Secondly, the PCC and the state do not operate in isolation of each other; there exist strong informal networks between them that allow for unhindered drug running, arms trafficking, and the transmission of contraband into the prison system.

The complicity of state actors in promoting the interests of the PCC has strengthened the capacity of the armed group politically, economically, and socially, to the extent that it is perhaps more accurate to talk of there being a "symbiosis" between the PCC and the São Paulo state (Mingardi 2007). Not only does the PCC clearly benefit from its association with the state, but the state also benefits from the PCC. The solid control that the PCC has over both the prison system and peripheral communities allows the state to distance itself from politically unpopular and problematic demographics— the poor—and problematic areas—the periphery. Numerous individuals within the state apparatus also clearly benefit from their association with the PCC. Within the prison system, prison guards who make just U.S.$ 340 a month often complement their salaries with bribes, something that is inextricably tied to the fact that they "come from the same *favela*" (Câmara dos Deputados 2006a: 130), a factor that further threatens the integrity of the state. Such tight linkages and influence allow for illicit articles to be transferred into prisons unhindered. In one recent case, a heavy machine gun broke through the bottom of an otherwise unsearched mail package being carried through to prisoners at a major prison facility (Câmara dos Deputados 2006b). More generally, a significant portion of the firearms in the possession of groups like the PCC have been shown to originate from within the public security system and/or the army (Câmara dos Deputados 2006c).

Connections between the state and the PCC also exist within the judicial system. The judiciary of São Paulo is notoriously hierarchical, with more wealthy individuals regularly escaping formal accountability. In general, the way the legal system works is a function of the uneven and discriminatory processes at work in society; the wealthy avoid incarceration as a result of their ability to respond to the financial propositions of their investigators (Pinheiro et al. 2000). For organized armed groups such as the PCC, unless the case has received significant media attention, individuals may benefit from influential treatment (Câmara dos Deputados 2006a). The third level of PCC involvement with the state is in the political arena (Câmara dos Deputados 2006b). Contrary to sensational reports that characterize the PCC as Marxist-Leninist, the PCC does not have overt political aspirations (Câmara dos Deputados 2006a; PCC 1993), even if the PCC network—which numbers in the hundreds of thousands even without counting prisoners who are not allowed to vote—could be sufficient to elect multiple federal congressmen. When questioned about the intentions of the PCC and its potential to translate its size into electoral influence, the PCC leader Marcola expressed apathy, referring to the inefficacy of the Brazilian political system and stating that putting a representative in Congress through voting is much more difficult than simply "buying" a congressman who has already been elected (Câmara dos Deputados 2006a).

The permeability of the state is an important facet of the expansion of the PCC beyond the walls of the penitentiary system. As the PCC began to establish itself in the marginalized periphery, it benefited from the paucity of state institutions of control, a factor that allowed it to violently consolidate the drug economy and wipe clean the landscape of individualistic crime and gang violence. The state, which is by and large a bystander to nonstate violent activity in marginalized communities, had little deterrent effect on the arrival of the armed group. In fact, evidence suggests that certain actions of the state facilitated the growth of the PCC in the periphery (Mingardi 2007). Experiences of arbitrary and extrajudicial police violence in these communities have conditioned the population to be fearful and suspicious of state agents of control, even as residents demand greater security and safety. For these communities the PCC offers unmistakable order and control, which are two things that have made it particularly attractive to populations accustomed to exclusion, active state repression, and histories of sporadic, warlike violence.

Rights, the PCC, and the Institutionalization of State Violence

The arrival of the order-oriented PCC has been seen as positive by local communities, since the permanence of the organization and its instrumental use of violence has resulted in fewer killings. But the idea of the PCC intrinsically acting to defend the interests of the marginalized has been challenged by James Holston (2007), who suggests that the PCC is nothing more than a "prison-based gang" that advantageously co-opts the language of resistance to state repression as a way of obscuring the organization's criminal nature. Holston proposes that the PCC spuriously utilizes such language to portray "...themselves as the victims of entrenched social inequalities, abuses, and violence..." (Holston 2007: 307). This interpretation is echoed by Fiona

Macaulay (2007: 638), who has suggested that the PCC's use of poor prison conditions as a justification for violence against the state is "nothing but a smokescreen." While the organization is quite definitely steeped in violence, contending that it is nothing but a criminal organization overlooks the empirical evidence of life in poor peripheral neighborhoods such as São Gotardo, where the PCC clearly provides a sense of order that was previously lacking. Furthermore, there is no doubt that the conditions of incarceration of prison inmates has improved markedly as a result of the PCC's organization.

The PCC controversially makes explicit use of human rights language in laying its claims to better living conditions in prisons. This is not fortuitous. During the past decade, zero tolerance policies have underpinned a discourse of rights revocation calling for the use of greater violence against suspected and "confirmed" criminals. An article written by the lawyer Leo Alves (2003, my translation), for example, portrays crime in Brazil as "terrorism against the honest," and contends that,

> Criminals, for their part, do not honor their obligations. They abuse their own freedoms to run over the rights of others, even the fundamental kind—like the right to life—of their fellow citizens. With this in mind, it is time to review the role of the State. The State should either protect everyone indiscriminately, and, in this case, run the risk of offending the honest; or, it should limit the rights of *marginais* [marginals] in the name of security for the majority of the rest.[8]

By employing the term *marginais* Alves is effectively criminalizing a particular demographic, namely the poor inhabitants of the periphery of São Paulo, something that can obviously have dramatic consequences. At the same time, however, and rather ominously, such a perspective has also been interpreted very differently. During an interview conducted in December 2006, police deputy Soares of the Civil Police compared the PCC with the Colombian rebel group FARC (*Fuerzas Armadas Revolucionarias de Colombia*), and suggested semiadmiringly that the order that both groups imposed was highly adapted to their respective contexts:

> It's clear how it works. What happens, you see…its like when Roberto Cabrini went to see the FARC in Colombia. He asked the FARC commander, "So, I'm here in this small town in Colombia…are there no thieves? No one steals?" And the commander says to him, "Listen, there is nothing like that here. Feel free to sleep with the door open. No one will steal anything." You see, they know that they will be stood up against a wall and filled with lead by a machine gun. It should be that way, because most people don't get it, they need strictness. Most people don't understand any other language. It's different if you're speaking with an educated person, who is doing a doctorate or something, than if you're speaking with an ignorant person. The ignorant guy only understands one

language: beatings. If you hit him he'll be quiet. But if you say "be quiet," he won't be. Unfortunately, how do we do it? By respect, or through fear? Here it has to be through fear, by terrorizing them. They'll do it because they fear you, because they know that they will get it otherwise.

Deputy Soares's discourse highlights two key issues that are acquiring increasing importance within debates concerning state policy toward urban violence in São Paulo. Firstly, the growing support for the notion that repressive violence is a necessary component of enforcing order and control over "uneducated" or "ignorant" people. Secondly, the fact that nonstate armed groups such as the FARC or the PCC are not formally bound by the rules in the way state authorities are is what allows them to effectively maintain order. Implicitly, it is a small step to arguing that public security forces ought to be allowed to utilize similar levels and styles of violence, and certainly the São Paulo public security forces seem to be increasingly stepping beyond the bound of human rights (see Cardia 2000; Cavallaro 1997; Pinheiro and Mesquita Neto 1999). Statistics show that police routinely kill civilians with impunity in the city. In the year between March 2007 and April 2008, for example, police killed 315 individuals (SSP 2007). Police have also been involved in the unregulated deployment of violence more informally. Martha Huggins (1997) suggests that rights obligations for on-duty police has lead to the creation of death squads of off-duty police that carry out operations that would not be possible through formal policing methods. Incidents involving men using state vehicles, weapons and, on occasion, uniforms, suggest that there is a connection between some extrajudicial groups and public security forces (OVP-SP 2007).[9]

Conclusion

This chapter has argued that the major drop in homicides witnessed in São Paulo during the past decade has been less a function of the application of zero tolerance measures, and more the result of the rise of the PCC, a gang-like syndicate that dominates prisons and numerous peripheral communities of the city. The strength and control of the PCC in the peripheral communities of the city has been overlooked by those responsible for public security management and policy, but has clearly transformed the environment of violence in the periphery. The PCC imposes a brutal order that is nevertheless predictable in an otherwise anarchic context in which the state is either absent or incompletely present. This has led some to describe the PCC as a form of "parallel power" in São Paulo (Macaulay 2007). At the same time, however, groups like the PCC cannot exist without significant connection to state authorities, and the group's illicit activities both inside and outside the prisons that gave birth to the organization are based on a network of linkages with prison guards, the police, politicians, and the legal system. Corrupt activities on the part of specific state agents have allowed the PCC to maintain a drug economy, acquire guns, and smuggle contraband into the prison system.

Seen in this light, the PCC does not so much emerge as a form of "parallel power," but is rather symbiotically linked to the state. This symbiosis represents a particular systemic institutionalization of state and nonstate violence that is clearly leading to the emergence of particular societal perceptions of violence, namely in the form of a discourse calling for the revocation of human rights. This presents a number of very significant challenges for the future of security (public and otherwise) in São Paulo. Although homicides are decreasing, security is clearly not improving, and this is a situation that the new rights revocation regime is unlikely to enhance. As the May 2006 PCC attacks starkly demonstrated, violence has begun to affect society well beyond the boundaries of the periphery, and this is at least partly fed by the growing rights revocation discourse. The existence of two distinct, but interlinked security regimes in São Paulo obviously makes it difficult to make any prediction as to the future course of violence in the city, but one thing that is clear is that the systemic institutionalization of state and nonstate violence in São Paulo is not an answer.

Notes

1. As Loïc Wacquant (2003) has remarked, another reason why such policies become popular is that they transpose crime and violence onto negative stereotypical categories such as "the poor," "the darker skinned," "the uneducated," thereby comforting the elites and the middle class in their perception that crime has to do with "the other."
2. A pseudonym.
3. The much-touted recent reform of firearms legislation, thought undoubtedly invaluable, has had a minimal impact (World Bank 2007).
4. The nickname Marcola is a product of Camacho's youth, insofar as it is a combination of Marcos and the Portuguese word for glue, "cola," which Marcola was addicted to as a street child in 1980s' São Paulo (Câmara dos Deputados 2006a).
5. At the same time, however, Marcola also suggests that when state authorities wish to "eliminate" a particular gang member, "...they throw him [into a prison that is controlled by an opposing gang] and he will die, the outcome is already known..." (Câmara dos Deputados 2006a: 196, my translation).
6. Despite the apparently successful fulfillment of Furukawa's request, little humanization was forthcoming.
7. A pseudonym.
8. The call to restrict the rights of criminals for the purpose of ensuring security has also been raised in some unusual quarters. Following the PCC's May 2006 attacks, for example, Congressman Fernando Gabeira, a dictatorship-era political prisoner, a former revolutionary, and the founder of the Brazilian Green Party, argued that "the human rights movement in Brazil needs to mature. It has been structured in the defence of the individual against state abuses; prisons, police, asylums and other institutions. This model is valid when the state holds a monopoly on violence. Organized crime is a new thing which threatens less scrupulously than the state does. It needs a creative revision" (quoted in Barros 2006).

9. Vestiges of the military dictatorship of the 1960s and 1970s, such as the continued presence of death squads, also play an important role in explaining this extrajudicial violence (Macaulay 2007). Furthermore, unlike most other Latin American countries that experienced dictatorship, Brazil still maintains a national security law—the *Lei de Segurança Nacional*—for activities considered to put national integrity, security, the democratic process, and public power at risk. Crimes can be prosecuted under this law for political nonconformism, political and social subversion, and class conflict. Proceedings investigated under the national security law are closed and do not require evidence to be released. Recent events suggest that this law may be experiencing a revival in the context of socioeconomic insurgence. In April of 2008, following the occupation of a farm in Rio Grande do Sul by the *Movimento dos Trabalhadores Rurais Sem Terra* (Movement of Landless Rural Workers, MST), a federal judge invoked the *Lei de Segurança Nacional* against the leaders of the group for "political non-conformism" (Valle 2008). If successful, such an application of the law would potentially represent a new phase in the criminalization of the poor in Brazil.

Bibliography

Adorno, S., and F. Salla. 2007. Criminalidade organizada nas prisões e os ataques do PCC, *Estudos Avançados*, vol. 21, no. 61, pp. 7–29.

Alves, L. d. S. 2003. Restrição dos direitos no enfrentamento ao terror, *Jus Navigandi*, vol. 8, no. 227, http://jus2.uol.com.br/doutrina/texto.asp?id=4854 [accessed February 19, 2008].

Arias, D. E. 2006a. *Drugs and Democracy in Rio de Janeiro: Trafficking, Social Networks and Public Security*, Chapel Hill: University of North Carolina.

Arias, D. E. 2006b. The dynamics of criminal governance: Networks and social order in Rio de Janeiro, *Journal of Latin American Studies*, vol. 38, no. 2, pp. 293–325.

Barros, A. 2006. Não existem direitos humanos á brasileira, *O Estado de São Paulo*, June 4.

Caldeira, T. P. R. 2000. *City of Walls: Crime Segregation and Citizenship in São Paulo*, Berkeley: University of California Press.

Caldeira, T. P. R. 2002. The paradox of police violence in democratic Brazil, *Ethnography*, vol. 3, no. 3, pp. 235–63.

Câmara dos Deputados. 2006a. *Transcrição Ipsis Verbis: Depoente Marcos Willians Herbas Camacho, CPI-Tráfico de Armas*, Brasília, http://www1.folha.uol.com.br/folha/cotidiano/20060708-marcos_camacho.pdf [accessed March 23, 2008].

Câmara dos Deputados. 2006b. *Transcrição Ipsis Verbis: Depoentes Ruy Ferraz e Godofredo Bittencourt, CPI-Tráfico de Armas*, Brasília, http://congressoemfoco.ig.com.br/Noticia.aspx?id=6367 [accessed March 23, 2008]. Câmara dos Deputados. 2006c. *Transcrição Ipsis Verbis: Depoente Pablo Dreyfus, CPI-Tráfico de armas*, http://www2.camara.gov.br/comissoes/temporarias/cpi/cpiarmas/notas/nt120405.pdf [accessed April 3, 2007].

Cardia, N. 2000. *Urban Violence in São Paulo*, Comparative Urban Studies Papers Series, No. 33. Washington DC: Woodrow Wilson Center for International Scholars.

Cavallaro, J. 1997. *Police Brutality in Urban Brazil*, New York: Human Rights Watch.

Collier, P., V. L. Elliott, H. Hegre, A. Hoeffler, M. Reynal-Querol, and N. Sambanis. 2003. *Breaking the Conflict Trap: Civil War and Development Policy*, Washington: World Bank and Oxford University Press.

Davis, D. 2007. El factor Giuliani: Delincuencia, la "cero tolerancia" en el trabajo policiaco y la transformación de la esfera pública en el centro de la ciudad de México, *Estudios Sociológicos*, vol. 25, no. 75, pp. 639–683.

Dowdney, L. 2005. *Neither War nor Peace: International Comparisons of Children and Youth in Organized Armed Violence*, Rio de Janeiro: COAV.

Federal Bureau of Investigation. 2006. *Expanded Offence Data*, http://www.fbi.gov/ucr/cius2006/offenses/expanded_information/index.html [accessed April 12, 2008].

FEBEM (Fundação para o Bem-Estar do Menor). 2000. *Levantamento de Dados de Jovens Internados*, São Paulo: FEBEM.

Greene, J. A. 1999. Zero tolerance: A case study of police policies and practices in New York City, *Crime and Delinquency*, vol. 45, no. 2, pp. 171–187.

Goetzel, T., and T. Khan. 2007. The unsung story of São Paulo's murder rate drop, *New American Media*, June 10, http://news.newamericamedia.org/news/view_article.html?article_id=0a7ee25d39a7d2b0737cef8c76bc84b5 [accessed February 28, 2008].

Hazlehurst, C., and K. M. Hazlehurst. 1998. Gangs in cross-cultural perspective, in K. M. Hazlehurst and C. Hazlehurst (eds.), *Gangs and Youth Subcultures: International Explorations*, New Brunswick: Transaction Publishers, pp. 1–34.

Holston, J. 2007. *Insurgent Citizenship: Disjunctions of Democracy and Modernity in Brazil*, Princeton: Princeton University Press.

Huggins, M. 1997. From bureaucratic consolidation to structural devolution, *Policing and Society*, vol. 7, no. 4, pp. 221–224.

Hughes, J. P. A. 2004. Segregação socioespacial e violência na cidade de São Paulo: Referências para a formulação de políticas públicas, *São Paulo em Perspectiva*, vol. 18, no. 4, pp. 93–102.

Leeds, E. 1996. Cocaine and parallel polities on the Brazilian urban periphery: Constraints on local level democratization, *Latin American Research Review*, vol. 31, no. 3, pp. 47–84.

Macaulay, F. 2007. Knowledge production, framing and criminal justice reform in Latin America, *Journal of Latin American Studies*, vol. 39, no. 4, pp. 627–651.

Mingardi, G. 2007. O trabalho da inteligência no controle do crime organizado, *Estudos Avançados*, vol. 21, no. 61, pp. 51–69.

Netto, J. P., and J. V. Silva. 2002. *Roubo a Ónibus Na Cidade de São Paulo: Epidemologia Do Crime e Análise Do Problema Policial*, São Paulo: Instituto Fernand Braudel de Economia Mundial.

OVP-SP (*Observatório Das Violências Policiaca—São Paulo*) 2007. *São Paulo*. Centro de Estudos de História da América Latina, Pontifícia Universidade Católica de São Paulo, www.ovp-sp.org [accessed March 17, 2008].

Penglase, B. 2007. Barbarians on the beach: Media narratives of violence in Rio de Janeiro, Brazil, *Crime, Media and Culture*, vol. 3, no. 3, pp. 305–325.

Pinheiro, P. S., and P. Mesquita Neto, 1999. *Primeiro Relatório Nacional sobre Direitos Humanos no Brasil*, São Paulo: Núcleo de Estudos da Violência.

Pinheiro, P. S., J. E. Mendez, and G. O'Donnell (eds.). 2000. *The (Un)Rule of Law and the Underprivileged in Latin America*, Notre Dame: University of Notre Dame Press.

Primeiro Comando da Capital (PCC). 1993. *O Estatuto*, http://pt.wikisource.org/wiki/Estatuto_do_PCC [accessed January 18, 2007].

Rolnik, R. 1999. *Territorial Exclusion and Violence: The Case of São Paulo, Brazil*, Comparative Urban Studies Project Occasional Papers Series No. 26, Washington: Woodrow Wilson Centre for Scholars.

Salla, F. 2006. As rebeliões nas prisões: Novos significados a partir da experiência brasileira, *Sociologias*, vol. 16, no. 8, pp. 274–307.

Salla, F. 2007. De Montoro a Lembo: As políticas peneténciarias de São Paulo, *Revista Brasileira de Segurança Pública*, vol.1, no. 1, pp. 72–90.

SAP (Secretaria da Administração Penetenciária). 2007. *População Carcerária No Estado de São Paulo de 1994 a 2006*, http://www.sap.sp.gov.br/common/dti/estatisticas.html [accessed April 14, 2008].

SEADE (Fundação Sistema Estadual de Análise de Dados). 2002. *Índice de Vulnerabilidade Júvenil*, http://www.seade.gov.br/produtos/ivj/index.php [accessed February 22, 2008].

SEADE (Fundação Sistema Estadual de Análise de Dados). 2007. *Informações Dos Distritos Da Capital*, http://www.seade.gov.br/produtos/imp/distritos/ [accessed between January 3, 2008 and April 26, 2008].

Silveira, V. J. 2007. A realidade dos presídios na visão da Pastoral Carcerária: Entrevista com o Padre Valdir João Silveira, *Estudos Avançados*, vol. 21, no. 61, pp. 209–220.

SSP (Secretaria de Estado da Segurança Pública). 2007. *Estatística Trimestriais*, http://www.ssp.sp.gov.br/estatisticas/portrimestre.aspx [accessed April 16, 2008].

Valle, D. do. 2008. Sem-terra são denunciados no RS por crime contra segurança nacional, *A Folha Online*, April 19, http://www1.folha.uol.com.br/folha/brasil/ult96u393708.shtml [accessed April 30, 2008].

Wacquant, L. 2003. Toward a dictatorship over the poor? Notes on the penalization of poverty in Brazil, *Punishment and Society*, vol. 5, no. 2, pp. 197–205.

Wendel, T., and R. Curtis. 2002. Tolerância zero: A má interpretação dos resultados, *Horizontes Antropológicos*, vol. 8, no.18, pp. 267–278.

Willis, G. 2007. *The Pedagogy of Violence and Fear in São Paulo*, completed in partial fulfillment of MA degree, Victoria: Royal Roads University.

World Bank. 2006. *Crime, Violence and Economic Development in Brazil: Elements for Effective Public Policy*, Report No. 36525, http://www.unodc.org/pdf/brazil/Crime_and_Violence_jan_2007.pdf [accessed April 3, 2008].

Chapter 10

Mean Streets: Youth, Violence, and Daily Life in Mexico City

Héctor Castillo Berthier and Gareth A. Jones

Introduction

In a country that contented itself with being "exceptional" among Latin American nations, avoiding civil wars, major guerrilla movements, or a significant presence of gangs in the latter part of the twentieth century, contemporary Mexico has been exposed to levels and an intensity of violence unheard of in its recent history and even in contrast to the rest of the region. Dramatic events such as the 1997 massacre at Acteal, lynchings, and the "femicides" in Ciudad Juárez (Staudt 2008; Vilas 2001) appear small scale against the *narcoviolencia*. The "war" between drug cartels and security forces has claimed over 8,000 lives in 2007 and 2008, and introduced new actors such as Los Zetas and Los Negros, mostly former military personnel now working for the Gulf and Sinaloa cartels, capable of deploying enormous firepower against competitors or the state. It is claimed that transnational gangs, especially the Mara Salvatrucha MS-13 and Calle 18, have a growing presence in Mexico, while "Mexican" gangs are said to be using more violent methods to secure the market for drugs and contraband. Robberies, mugging and kidnapping seem both more prevalent and violent. Almost inconceivable 20 years ago, today everyone in Mexico has an anecdote that relates to violence as an experienced or potentially personal event. The pervasive sense of vulnerability to violence dominates casual conversation and social actions. Going to restaurants, concerts, or simply strolling are activities now conducted with the possibility that the evening may witness a holdup, the sound of gunfire, or the arrival of police. Newspapers and billboards carry advertisements for self-defense classes, kidnap insurance, and psychological counseling.[1] Private security now watches over everywhere from high-end boutiques to the corner pharmacy.[2]

As noted in a recent newspaper article by former cabinet minister and ambassador to the United States, Federico Reyes Heroles, the Mexican public has become "intoxicated" with violence and the sense of helplessness that is presumed to be a consequence (Reforma December 2, 2008: 16). Violence has infused itself into daily life, serving as a "shared idiom" through which a host of social and political conditions can be discussed and tackled (Arteaga 2004). In launching the *Plan Mexico Seguro* at the start of his presidential term, Vicente Fox (2000–2006) stated he would win the battle with "delinquency," which he was keen to stress involved gangs, street children, and petty criminals. The shared idiom, however, increasingly allies "delinquents" with "enemies" and "terrorists," providing legitimacy to both discourse and actions that increasingly invoke public security as coterminus with and possibly superseded by national security, and thus supporting a militarization of policing. The argument, extended during the administration of President Calderón (2006–2012), is that cartels, gangs, and crime syndicates pose greater threats to the state than the guerrilla organizations of the past, and should be considered a new form of political violence. An article in the influential Reforma newspaper considered, rhetorically, whether the present violence now merited consideration of Mexico as a "failed state" (December 13, 2008).[3]

In this chapter we do not want to argue *against* violence in Mexico as anything other than serious, vicious, and anxiety inducing for many. The chapter seeks to argue for the need to retain and understand violence as social, constitutive of what Whitehead (2004) terms a "poetics" or a discursive amplification that is assimilated into daily practices. More particularly, we want to problematize a prominent "figure" in contemporary images and discourses of violence, namely the (male) "youth" who is characterized as the main perpetrator, increasingly identified with being a "gang member." Based on ethnographic work with young people we want to capture the texture of lives framed by violence on a daily basis. Rather than rely on the ever-increasing accumulation of news stories and data on violence we are interested in how young people exercise what Charles Wright Mills termed their "sociological imagination," or as he put it,

> Today men often feel that their private lives are a series of traps. They sense that within their everyday worlds, they cannot overcome their troubles, and in this feeling, they are quite often correct...What they (citizens) need, and what they feel they need, is a quality of mind that will help them to use information and to develop reason in order to achieve lucid summations of what is going on in the world and of what may be happening in themselves (Mills 1970: 3–5).[4]

The chapter considers the "lucid summations" of violence that are expected and tolerated in daily life. In seeking to understand what might be termed the "social" dimensions of violence, we are interested in how young people talk of violence and in so doing make dramatic, frightening events ordinary.

To put these accounts in context, the chapter first discusses the upsurge of violence in contemporary Mexico and predominant representations as "political." Using the example of a gang member in Mexico City we note that within these conditions many gangs are operating "business as usual," combining the economic imperative of their actions with the social status that wealth and a potential recourse to violence conveys. We then outline how public policy has elevated the threat of gangs, and especially of the maras, legitimating tougher securitized policing measures. To counter this perspective, we present an extended narrative replete with violence and organized criminal behavior but which, we argue, also demonstrates its generally circumscribed nature, in stark contrast to the more widespread sensationalist discourses. In the final section we raise concerns for the consequences that representing "youth violence" as a security threat may be having for young people who are not involved in gangs, showing through two specific examples how the violence that affects them is most often the outcome of relations with the state or security personnel, conditioned in particular ways by the dominant discourse about youth violence in Mexico.

Security and "Political" Violence: Initial Implications for Youth

Violence is infused into Mexican daily life through the media and political action. Displays of violence have long been prominent in the public sphere. Images of victims' bloody bodies are the stock in trade of the *Nota Roja* newspapers devoted to killings, robbery, and traffic accidents (Monsivais 1997), and form a central theme of cinema and literature (Jones and Moreno-Carranco forthcoming; Polit-Dueñas 2008).[5] With official statistics of criminality and violence widely considered to be untrustworthy (see Arango 2003; Jiménez 2003), both citizens and the state rely on representations of violence and the subjectivity of encounters to confirm impressions that trends are upward, that crime, delinquency, and violence are more prevalent, less predictable, and more vicious. Personal anecdote and rumor, therefore, are supported by a performative expression of violence. Drug cartels have been quick to appreciate representations of violence as a means to spread fear. Senior police officers, judges, and journalists have been assassinated, often in crowded public spaces.[6] The Zetas especially use Internet and media exposure to publicize their actions, with their "signature" being—in a mimicry of Al-Qaeda and the Mahdi Army in Iraq—the dumping of decapitated bodies and severed heads as warnings to the government to "show respect." The victims' prior torture and execution has sometimes been uploaded onto YouTube.

Concern at the levels and type of violence, and the incompetence of the state's response, has motivated the formation of a number of civil society organizations.[7] The *Ya Basta* campaign organized by *México Unido contra la Delincuencia* is perhaps the most widely known and national. Demonstrations against killings, kidnaps, and assaults have been prominent in most major cities.[8] On June 27, 2004, upwards of 1.5 million people marched through Mexico City demanding that the then mayor, Manuel López Obrador, take firmer action against kidnappers and gangs, and pursue reform of the police, an event repeated in August 2008 with perhaps 100,000 participants.[9] Business groups have sought to gain control over police deployment, a move formally recognized with the creation of the *Policía Bancaria e Industrial*, a specialized unit dedicated to the protection of banks, malls, and offices, and which is partly privately funded.[10] More individualistic responses have been the appearance of the *narco-manta* on bridges and flyovers identifying drug dealers, corrupt police officers, and state officials.[11]

The inescapable representation is that violence in Mexico is pervasive and a potential threat to the internal security and the legitimacy of the state. With 400,000 serving officers and a 40-fold increase in the budget for security and justice between 1996 and 2000, and a total budget of U.S.$ 11.7 billion by 2008, Mexico does not suffer from a lack of manpower or resources (Lopez Portillo 2004; Suárez de Garay 2006). By common consent, however, policing is inefficient and often corrupt, and attempts to raise professional standards have in fact motivated use of excessive force in order to "get results," or else deepened links with criminal networks to make up for low pay and limited promotion prospects (Pansters and Castillo 2007; Davis 2006). The opposition to reform and/or the apparent ineffectiveness of the outcome has motivated a shift from "policing" to "security." Under President Fox internal security was passed to the newly created *Agencia Federal de Investigación* (AFI, akin to the FBI) and President Felipe Calderón formed a federal antikidnapping unit in 2008 under the National Security Council. With Calderón especially, frustration at the police locally and federally has prompted the extensive deployment of military forces and the secondment or recruitment of military personnel to police agencies, notably the *Policía Federal Preventativa* (PFP) and the AFI.[12] By October 2008, 40,000 troops were involved in domestic security.

The shared idiom of violence has underpinned an attitude to tougher policing and support for zero tolerance measures. A quantifiable effect of greater and tougher policing has been a growing prison population, rising by about 50 percent during the Zedillo administration (1996–2000), and doubling under President Fox (2000–2006).[13] According to government data, 43 percent of those sentenced for federal crimes during 2003 were aged 16 to 29, and the majority of Mexico's prison population is less than 30 years old and almost one-half aged between 18 and 23.[14] Some of these inmates will be detained as a result of police harassment or as zero tolerance laws have made activities such as graffiti a criminal offence or prohibited the meeting of young men in small groups (Cruz Salazar 2004; Debroise 2005). According to Emilio Álvarez Icaza, president of the Federal District Human Rights Commission, "In a period of 12 months, 10% of young people in the Federal District were detained for [allegedly] committing a crime" (Reforma November 29, 2006). Many will have been picked up in sweeps of markets, highway intersections or nightclubs in operations known as *redadas, razzias,* or more popularly *apañones* (literally, pick ups).[15]

These are long standing tactics that demonstrate the state's capacity for operative coordination—combining municipal, riot, cavalry, and airborne units—against youth and especially "*los chavos banda.*" Blamed for violence and social breakdown—"*matan, roban, violan y dan miedo*" according to successive Mexico City governments—the state aims to break up or deter *banda* formation through operations known as "Dispan" (*dispersión de pandillas*) (Castillo Berthier 2000). While there is no evidence that these operations reduce violence, they are becoming common across Mexico. According to official reports for the city of Monterrey, each weekend upwards of 2,000 young people from poor areas of the city are identified as *pandilleros* and detained.[16] But even if gangs are caught in the sweeps, their formation and activities are unlikely to be disrupted for long, especially for gangs with the right contacts.

In 2005, Héctor met with "El Cholo," a gang member who manages a wide network of contacts across low income neighborhoods of Mexico City. At the meeting, El Cholo was dressed in smart jeans, a tight shirt, and a colorful leather jacket, gold watch, and chains down his chest, and a gun tucked into the belt behind his back. His car was a new silver VW Passat with sport rims, and a mega stereo and speaker system that almost filled the trunk. After checking if Hector was a policeman or a journalist, and assured that he was a university researcher, Cholo instructed "Get in, let's get out of here. The area is really jacked up [dangerous]." There followed a tour through different barrios, bars, pool halls, parking lots, and street corners, collecting the week's income and giving instructions for the next week to the young people—mostly teenagers—working for him, that lasted until 4:00 a.m. the next morning.

> Cholo: Don't freak out. The car's legal, it's not "hot" and plus, all the fuzz [police] from here know me and we work without any problems...
>
> We advanced through the streets.
>
> Héctor: What does the word "safety" mean to you?
>
> Cholo: [laughing]...Look, real easy: That they don't mess with me, that they don't go around harassing me, that the kids [who work for him] apply themselves, that they don't get me into any shit, and that the fuzz get that they aren't going to have any shit with me, and that their payoff is a cinch [certain] with me.
>
> Héctor: Do you have many connections in the police?
>
> Cholo: Well not a lot, but yeah, the most effective ones. They tell you when the raids are going to come, where, at what time, when the bosses are going to pass by, when they have to nail [detain] someone. I mean, they know the world, the environment, they know who we are and they don't want any shit either. Plus it doesn't come on the cheap, they charge and their dough has to be paid before anything else.

For Cholo dealing with the police is an unavoidable but manageable hazard of his gang's business. He complains that he has to pay the police more and more ("They can never get their fill"), although he is careful not to indicate how much. He is admired by the young people of the neighborhoods who come up to touch his car—a graffiti in the area reads

"Better to die young and rich, than old and poor." El Cholo is beyond the archetype *pandillero* typified by the hanging out, alcohol and drug use, and has moved into organized criminal activity on a regular basis. Cholo's attitude to violence is conveyed as an extension to the business rationale, and includes a challenge to the prevailing representations of violence and gangs.

> Héctor: And the violence? How do you interpret violence?
> Cholo: I don't like it, for real [honestly], but you've got to be firm. They can't see you with fear in your eyes, nor with your hand shaking... In fact, the more of a bully you are, and the more you act like a shit, the more they respect you. Those assholes are children of the bad life and they like to be knocked around...
> Héctor: But, are there deaths? Are there a lot of murders?... The news...
> Cholo: Look [he interrupts]. What they say on the tube [television] is nothing more than pure lies. Yes, there are a few little deaths, but they're asking for it, they want to overstep the mark or look after number one, or they even go so far as telling on you, those mother fuckers!... The snitches have no place here. They'd better go there across the way [pointing to the cemetery].
> Héctor: Have you ever killed someone?...
> Cholo: That's none of your damn business... [the implication is clear]

In some respects Cholo's insiders' self-analysis contains few surprises. He presents the robberies, car thefts, the sale of drugs, and even the homicides as part of a daily routine. He sees the accounts of these activities given by others, especially the media, as exaggerations and outside of his world. He objects to the stigma projected onto him, and young people from poorer neighborhoods, and identifies his criminal and gang activities as linked to a system of policing and kickbacks, and highlights how actions are governed by rules (no snitching, work hard, don't attract attention, etc.), and is not threatening to the state and only occasionally to others. Yet Cholo knows he must be careful. Actions against gangs that used to be relatively unsystematic "police" operations have become matters of "security" in response to *narcoviolencia* and perceived increase in gang activity, murder, and violent crime.

From Pandillero to Mara Jomboi

The unsystematic nature of past police operations against gangs—in contrast to the antigang laws and actions becoming common across Central America—fitted nicely with the comforting image of Mexican exceptionalism. But measures such as the setting up by the *Secretaría de Seguridad Pública* of an antigang operation called *Operación* ACERO in 2003, an anti-Mara unit in the Federal District, and the use of the military, especially in Chiapas and border cities, speak to a more coordinated and "security" oriented approach.[17] Driving the shift are reports of infiltration into Mexico of maras from Central America. It has long been known that cities such as Ciudad Hidalgo and Tapachula in Chiapas have had a maras presence, and concentrations have been identified in Oaxaca, Veracruz, and the border (Lara Klahr 2006; Valenzuela Arce 2007). But recent Mexican and U.S. government reports suggest the maras to be a growing presence, linked to drug and gun smuggling, and a national as well as localized public security threat (Lara Klahr 2006). The Mexican intelligence agency, the *Centro de Investigación y Seguridad Nacional* (CISEN), for example, has asserted that there may be at least 5,000 mareros in Mexico (cited in Fernández Menéndez and Ronquillo 2006) while USAID (United States Agency for International Development) claims as many as 200 gangs and 3,000 mareros in the southern border states and 17,000 along the northern border (USAID 2006). An unsubstantiated claim made by a representative of the Federal District *Asamblea Legislativa* put the number of *Mara Salvatrucha* members in Mexico City at over 1,000 (El Universal February 25, 2004).

The empirical validity of these numbers is not the point. While we are both familiar with the figures, and the presence of maras to the South, our personal experiences have not entailed run-ins with maras in Mexico City. Indeed, it is possibly telling that newspaper articles attempting to provide a shock exposé of maras mention only small groups and individuals (La Crónica December 9, 2005). Moreover, according to the Mexican government's own data on apprehensions, the majority of mareros detained in Mexico are Mexican, not Central American (Crónica April 3, 2008; also Nateras Domínguez 2007). This is not to say that these young men are not gang members, possibly associated with well-established networks such as the Vatos Locos, Vagos, or Hecho en Mexico. The appropriation of a "maras-look" or identification as maras however is deceptive. Gangs are, after all, about identity and image, and great care is taken in the selection of clothing, tattoos, uses of slang, and names, that allude to broader counterculture youth identities (Castillo Berthier 2002; Hernández León 1999; Marcial 1997; Nateras Domínguez 2007). With the widespread availability of DVDs and video arcade games, and possibly personal experiences of time in the United States, most young people, gang members or not, are aware of the maras dress codes, slang phrases, and hand signs, most of which are indeterminate from or fusions of *cholo* styles, themselves appropriated by the maras from the United States. Thus, while public policy and media representations may have converted *banda* to *pandilla*, and subsequently in a context of national and regional antigang initiatives, to maras, for most young men "gang" identities remain fluid, reliant on (potential) sociability and deriving meaning from the intersections of everyday youth culture and criminal activity.

This was well illustrated by one of our contacts, Jovany Avilés, known as *el Jovax*, who lives in the *Unidad Habitacional* Vicente Guerrero in Iztapalapa, an area marked by poverty and overcrowding. He provided us with the following narrative about an individual called *el Yanko*, which highlights the multifaceted nature of youth violence. Defining himself as "...almost a

sociologist, a community interventionist, and a result of popular subculture," Jovax traces how what he terms the *banda* centered around culture,
family, and crime, and involved competition, drugs, and violence:

I met *el Yanko* when his brother *el Picos* took some props (propaganda)
from me about a ska gig that we were organizing in the barrio. *El Picos*
was wearing a mesh net over his head, low-rider pants, and he was one
of the barrio's crackerjacks who stole cars; his brother, of course, was the
leader of the *banda*. One year later, *el Picos* had left the gangbangers in
order to become one of the most promising musicians from his street;
he had formed a ska band and played at all the parties in the hood, the
CONALEP [National College for Technical and Professional Education],
and the Vocational school. He traded his AK-47 for a low brand Yamaha,
which they had tricked him into for two lines of coke and two tabs of
ecstasy.

One day, *el Picos* dropped by to invite me to organize a gig on the
apartment complex's soccer field: we got three ska groups, one hip-hop
group, and as support a friend from the block had his band come, which
one weekend before had won the Hard Rock Café Battle of the Bands. We
took out copies of the props and passed them out around the schools in
the barrio... Even the stuck-up princesses from the "Chunditec" [pejora-
tive name for the UNITEC technological college] ended up at the feast.
The whole *banda* was in on the organization, some selling beers and others kicking out the assholes that wanted to sneak in; some paid the full
amount and others pooled their money to get in.

At night, as was usual in that barrio, the concert ended in fights. No
one knows who started the squabble. Some say that the guys from the La
Bola 8 barrio had ordered *el Yanko* to be killed because he hadn't included
them in a rumored plan for "the robbery of the century." What the guys
from La Bola 8 didn't know... is that when the gig was about half-way
through, in Pachuca, Hidalgo, *el Yanko* was pulling out his sawn-off shot-
gun to rob the downtown branch of Banamex. In less than three minutes,
el Yanko entered the branch, let out a shot killing a man who was filling
out the deposit slip for his first self-financing car payment for a Tsuru
car... and threatened the tellers, while *el Dani* and *el Vale* grabbed the
money and took the manager hostage in order to leave the bank. Upon
approaching the door they realized that *el Morro*, who was the driver, was
having an epileptic attack that had left him stuck between the steering
wheel and the truck's gearshift, a Ram Charger that had often served as
our transportation to go to the El Callejón [bar]. El *Yanko*, upon seeing
the situation, stopped the first car on the road and killed the driver, who
was a woman on her way to her first romantic date,... 4 years after the
signing of her divorce.

By the time that *el Nene* [from La Bola 8] started the fight, el *Yanko* was
in room 18 of the Miraflor hotel, counting the stolen money and snort-
ing more than ten lines of coke to celebrate. They say that nothing would

have happened if they had come back that night like the plan had called
for...[but] *el Morro* suggested they go buy fireworks in a nearby town that
he knew on the way to the D.F. and *el Yanko*, having done more than 3
tabs of ecstasy and 8 or 10 lines of coke, accepted the idea of returning
to our barrio triumphant with fireworks. While making the detour they
found themselves at a strip club, [where] they made the owner kick out
all the people and close the establishment so that they could be the only
clients. *El Yanko*, as the leader, was the first to choose his "kaylie," then *el
Vale* and *el Dani*, and finally, and because he was the youngest, *el Morro*.

They left the place like at 8:00 in the morning and before going directly
to the highway they ran into a couple of patrol cops that signaled to pull
over for a routine check. *El Yanko* accelerated with euphoria crashing into
a minibus; the passengers got out with the intention of lynching them.
Three of the *banda* members ran from the truck, but not *el Yanko as* he
had poliomyelitis from the age of 5. *El Dani* was the only one that went
back for him, took him by the belt and threw him over his shoulder. They
say that *el Dani* ran while *el Yanko* was shooting. He killed three or four
civilians and one of the police officers before they stopped him. They
killed *el Morro* and *el Vale* in the chase and they held *el Yanko* and *el Dani*
for 10 years in jail, solely on charges of possessing military weapons.

During the 8 years of *el Yanko's* lock-up the barrio changed. The rest of
the *banda* migrated to the United States with the excuse that "this barrio
is too hot." With the passing of the years the styles changed and the gangbangers slowly disappeared—just like the [Volkswagen] "Beetles"—and
were replaced by armed kids ready for holdups. *El Picos* and his family
reformed. His dad had bought a minibus, his sisters had gone back to
school, and *el Picos* had become a popular African genre musician...Little
by little the barrio was taken over with new car theft and synthetic drug
sales (*bandas*), though now there was more organization. There was peace
between the bandas that worked together: One would take care of stealing,
others of transforming cars or hiding them,...but unlike 8 years before,
the car thieves weren't violent with the people from the barrio. They went
to electro parties and fashionable nightclubs...they wore brand-name
clothes, and most knew Cancún, Zipolite, or Playa del Carmen.

It was at a party at my house when I heard that they were saying to *el
Picos*, who was making out with a Canadian [name deleted], "*Picos*, your
hommie *el Yanko* just arrived at your house." The rumor spread through
the party and the uncertainty was felt in the whole barrio, because three
years earlier when *el Chikín* had gone to visit *el Yanko* in jail he returned
with the message: "*Tell them all that when I get out of here, Troy is going
to burn in the barrio, since no one is going to be left alive. The barrio sewer
is going to be filled with the blood of every asshole and bitch that enjoyed
my dead presidents when I was away.*" This included all of us that were
at the party that night. Fortunately, the new leader...is the diplomatic
type...[and] he took care of *el Yanko*. A year passed [with el Yanko] stealing for the new leader. He bought himself a new truck, one of those

that they call "chocolate" (illegal) and had three kids with three different women.

Three months after *el Yanko* got out of jail, *el Cachas*, leader of *Los Bola 8*, got out too. They say that one night at the celebration of Saint Judas Thaddeus, *el Yanko* and *el Cachas* met up, drank a bottle of Torres Diez and recognized each other as the most "A1 fucking leaders" to have ever existed. That's how they started robbing trailers at the exit to the highway to Puebla and doing express kidnaps. One day, *el Yanko* told us that for three nights he dreamt of *el Cachas* on the top of a very big wall and that behind the wall his three kids were crying without their mothers. *El Yanko* interpreted the dream as having a problem with *el Cachas* in which his kids were in danger, so the next day he dissolved the partnership, sold his truck, and swore before the Virgin of Guadalupe that he would no longer steal or get high. He bought himself a taxi and started to roll around the streets closest to the barrio. *El Cachas* carried on [as before], creating a reputation for *el Yanko* as a "fag" among the other gangs in our barrio, Ciudad Azteca, Tepito, San Fernando, and many more.

One day, *el Yanko* picked up one of *el Cachas's* ex-girlfriends as a passenger. He asked her out and they went to drink some beers at the *Bodegón*. After two weeks of wooing her, *el Yanko* decided to end the relationship using his kids as an excuse. To get back at him, the girl, I don't remember her name, told *el Cachas* that *el Yanko* had hit her and jerked her around in front of a lot of people, so *el Cachas* went to the taxi base where *el Yanko* worked and gave him a ferocious fucked-up beating from behind. A few hours later *el Yanko* woke up, he went to his house, took a 45 caliber pistol and without asking for back-up from anyone, headed to *el Cachas's* house where he was with his kids, brothers, and his mother, having *pambazos* and quesadillas for dinner. *El Yanko* entered the house and took *el Cachas* by the hair, and said, "Let me get it out of me, asshole; you caught me from behind." *El Cachas* didn't want to fight but just as one of his brothers pulled out a gun, *el Yanko* put a bullet between his nose and upper lip, turned the weapon and shot eight bullets into *el Cachas's* abdomen, [before] he shot 4 year-old Dylan and 6 year-old Fernandita in the head.

Today, no one knows where *el Yanko* is. The barrio is "hot." *El Picos* and his family also left and they say that if *el Yanko* ever returns, it will only be to fulfill the threat of killing everyone that enjoyed his money while he was the *banda* leader.

How far the events in *el Jovax's* somewhat melodramatic tale are exaggerated is difficult to discern. Even allowing for such a possibility—which would suggest an interpretation of violence as performative—the violence of the account is evident. Yet, the narrative also demonstrates the wide range of domains of everyday life and contradictory impulses that goes beyond the stereotypical notions of gangs presented in policy pronouncements. Young people that might be identified as *bandas* or *pandillas* can morph into family members, employers, sports associations and relate to youth identities such as hip-hop (crew), punks or *skatos*. Narrating the actions of El Yanko, violence makes sense to Jovax within a set of daily practices, with each giving the other meaning, whereas for the state violence is perceived as outside "normal" daily practice, it is aberrant to the function of society.

The Lucid Summations of Youth

The antidelinquency discourse, toughened further through eliding youth involved with violence with gangs, and increasingly a concern for the maras, and in the context of an escalating *narcoviolencia*, is less discriminating with regard to youth involved in various counterculture activities. "Security" policing is less discerning of youth involved in street crime, vandalism and graffiti, drinking, use of drugs, or congregating in groups of "darks" or "Emos."[18] Young peoples' actions are part of a problem for a state that has failed to integrate youth into social, political, and cultural life, where the education system ill prepares young people for an economy that has undergone massive restructuring in the last two decades, and in which many institutions, notably the church and political parties, are keen to promote a restricted "moral agenda."[19] Youth not involved in gangs are not immune from either the "zero tolerance" measures or the stigmas attributed to them. The following narratives of two young people seek to explore how each presents an explanation, a "lucid summation," of their life in relation to the world around them that is rational, iterative, and mediated by violence.

The first narrative was provided to us by Víctor Mendoza, *el Ponkas*, from the Unidad Habitacional El Rosario located in the north of Mexico City. A graffiti artist from the age of 12, *El Ponkas* works with different groups of *graffiteros* to support the professionalization of their work and to defend them against the city's police department's "anti-graffiti" program.[20] His narrative recalls an exchange he had with a young artist called *el Jáver*, 12, about the time he and his friend *el Waco*, 13, were caught as they painted subway cars "just for the fun of it":

> The police jacked us good, asshole! . . . *El Waco* and I always go to Garibaldi [station] to paint. When the subway goes to change lines we stay hidden under the seats and we wait for the "dead weight" to get off and then, when everyone gets off, we pull out the tools (permanent markers) pretty damn quick and we start to throw out some tags. That time, it was off the hinges how we fucked up the subway car. It was . . . chock-full of signatures! Then when the line changed, we were still assed-up seeing the whole thing and taking some pictures, when suddenly all the people started to board again. And pow! The subway guys (security) were on. The shit is we only painted tags and we took a video of the whole process . . . Our styles were really decadent! The shit of it is that the subway car stank of the marker paint, even though it was "dry line," those ones that you throw square and really rough lines.

The first shit was that we were on at the line change, and after the terrible smell, within a minute the security guys come up to us and then we felt like everything was falling down on us. They said to us, "Let's see, let's see, fucking kids get out." Then, they took us through the hallway in the middle of Garibaldi Subway station,...taken by the arm with our heads bent down, until they put us in an office. They cornered us there and they made us wait a good while. Yeah, we were really fucked. *El Waco* thought that he had managed to throw away the marker that we had painted with. But no way, man, the jackass didn't throw it. And then he passed it to me and I pushed it up, you know where. I went overboard, really "raunchy," and then you know...total shit! Ha ha ha. From the [office] they moved us to another room and once inside the security guys told us that we had to sign a letter. They wanted to steamroll us into signing it and that they would fuck us. But it was bull. The letter was like a kind of Subway Regulation, saying a shitload of sanctions and things like that. But no way, we didn't sign it; they wanted to stick us with "the dumbass's rule." But, well we already know all about it, and so we had to endure the headbanging.

At that point the pigs arrived, real dicks, with those thingies that are metal detectors, and that's when I began to sweat. Because I was carrying the load, but the shit is that I got a dipshit of a cop, because he didn't pass the stick really cool. Plus, he didn't look at my family jewels and so he didn't realize that I was carrying the marker in my butthole. So we got off since they didn't find any evidence on us that we painted the subway car and then they didn't have a witness...When they caught us, they started saying, "What? You don't know that painting the subway is a crime?" And with that we could go without stopping and directly to the "*Juve*" [court]. But, holy shit! If they had found the marker on me we wouldn't have gotten off, not even with a beating. When we were in the office, after they "passed the thingie," they searched my backpack and my notebooks, checking that I didn't have paints or any tags to be able to pin it on me. But the cool thing was that I was carrying an almost new notebook, if I had brought the Black Book [with tagging designs] it would have been lockdown.

Not finding any proof on us they couldn't present us to the authorities, but they were still set up to fuck us. Before getting off the "TroMe" [Metro backward], the dudes in suits took out their cameras and took some "clicks" of the tags. In the second office that they put us in...there were some computers and while some of them were talking I managed to see the screen when the suits started to download the pictures of our tags. They were saying amongst themselves: "Check the picture file from the last 3 months to see if these graffiti are there, since something tells me that they're from these brats." They opened a file with a shitload of pictures that they had registered and they started to compare them. It was a data base, where they reviewed and compared the tags, looking for some that were similar to the ones we had done. The good thing was that *el Waco* did his tag different. Why, fuck off! They had loads of pictures. From me they only had like three or four pictures, but from *el Waco* they had a shitload. Imagine that on the computer they opened the files and blew up the pictures to screen size and then they start to pass one by one...Shit, a really loaded file, really super-sized. Plus, they even have pictures of *Chuchito 100% ley*. Pure crap, huh? But they only have tags registered, no bombers, nor stickers, and, yeah, there's the rest of the *banda* that has gone in to paint subway cars and tunnels. The material they had was only from Line 8.

One of the things that was really whack was that when they started to pass us the pictures, they asked us about the tag in a picture—"Do you know this dude?" And well, yeah, we knew two or three *bandas* that they had had registered. But we said, "No way! We didn't run into any one. We didn't even do that." And they said to us: "Like hell, fucking brats, they're from your group, you should know them! Name them and you're off, you can go; cough up this group and just tell us you are from their crew."...Yeah, we fucked them over, but it was done...Finally the well-dressed dudes tell us: "This time you got off, brats, but we already have a picture of you. So, if you ever fuck-up, we already have you identified, so you're warned." They took us out of the office and gave us a kick in the butt and told us: "Watch out, fags." When we left, we moved pretty damn quick. We raced to take the train for the "Consti" (station Constitución de 1917), [but] we still managed to see the look on the face of one of them and we raised a finger. Then, we were like ha, ha, ha, and laughing it up.

The second narrative concerns Claudia Espinosa, *la Yaya*, who participates in the *barra* (hooligan) and *porra* (organized fan) groups that support the National University's football team, "Los Pumas." In recent years the more violent *barras* have gained a greater presence in the stadiums previously controlled by the *porra*, and the possibility of infiltration by gangs has attracted the attention of the state and the Football Federation (Lara Klahr 2006). The *barras* have formed identity pathways, sources of work, friendships, and even political organizations, and hold rivalries with other teams' groups. Her narrative suggests a strongly gendered world, in which women potentially suffer from being part of groups that build solidarity through masculinized rituals, codes and languages, and from the violence that occasionally results from participation. Yet it also suggests that security officials, managing team executives, and even the *barra* leaders themselves often see these groups as a "mass" of marginalized youth who are "delinquents, addicts, violent, empty," effectively treating them as they would gang members. The following excerpt from an interview with *la Yaya* narrates events after a soccer game attended by about 30,000 or more people.

The game? Well, way cool, the fans sang and sang, there were a shitload of us and since we were visitors, we all stayed together: The *barra*, the *porra*, and the normal fans, a ton of kiddies that were with their old man and old lady. Everyone really happy, impressed with how our songs sounded. At that time, the legislation that said *barras* leave after a 20 or 30 minute gap still wasn't being applied. They took us out all together and along the same routes, which gave the chance for really hardcore clashes outside the stadium. That day was no exception...At the exit, some were throwing the beer coolers along the ramps, others were taking out the toilets from the bathrooms, and some were breaking wires, tubes, and whatever could be untied. The intention wasn't to kick anyone's ass, but to fuck-up the stadium...the majority of the *banda* was just walking, and celebrating the burning of the other team's flags or t-shirts.

The security measures outlined the exit route for the *barras* from both teams: The same street! We could not even try to move toward another...the mounted police officers stopped it and forced us to walk toward where we all knew the opposite side's *barra* were. To the satis-faction of some and the concern of many, the clash occurred just a few meters from a famous street in the city...Nothing new: A few whacks, the "thirst for rags" [theft of flags], fallen pride, and presumptuous mascu-linities on the floor. After all, within the *barra* one way of gaining respect was an ability to use your fists...Many kids and families ran toward the back with the intention of getting away. [But the *banda* at the back was unable to join the fighting and the mounted police] instead of moving to let them pass, continued forward. Without listening to what several old ladies with their kids were telling them: "Move along now: Why are you throwing us back where the fights are, there in front they're doing some hardcore ass-kicking?" Those cops didn't budge an inch. Upon feeling the pressure, they started to charge with their horses...then began the onslaught of runners toward the front...In sum, all fucking hell broke loose between those that were running toward the back, those that were running toward the front, those that were kicking the banda's asses from the other side, and those that were receiving thumps from the mounted police, because fighting back with [those guys] means messing with the horse and with the riding whip...

Some [people] took advantage of the moment to do business. They gave you the chance to enter their house in exchange for a dead president [money] and once inside they would sell you a t-shirt or sweatshirt, so that you could take off your team's or *barra* top so that you could leave later, I mean, to keep you from more problems with the police or with the other *barra* or your own, because...being cowardly, well, it just doesn't fly. Some older ladies and gentlemen opened their doors just to see what was happening outside, and suddenly they had 20 or 30 kids in their houses...Being cool, some of them didn't throw them out; they gave them t-shirts, shirts, sweatshirts...They took out water and alcohol to clean the wounds of two or three guys that were walking around really fucked up, they let them use their phones, they lent them dead presi-dents...In one of those houses there were some 16 year-old kids. They were boyfriend and girlfriend and they were both badly fucked up...They had ripped off the girl's t-shirt and they broke one of the straps from her bra, they got a few good punches in on her face. The boy had his head bust open...Walking around grunge style, wearing long hair and a t-shirt from the *barra* was extremely provocative to the mounted police officer that had hit him on the back with a whip. His girlfriend jumped for him, "earning herself" an ass-kicking, taking with her the humiliation of her exposed body and the cop's mockery...

The two narratives present different relations to violence: Jáver and El Waco do not seek confrontation while La Yaya offers a more celebratory account; Jáver and El Waco are also acting alone, while La Yaya is part of an organized "mass." But both Jáver and El Waco, and La Yaya, have to face state power on a regular basis in which "combating" violence and delinquency affords legitimation to police and security personnel methods. For *grafiteros*, their moves are closely watched, their actions logged on computers and their bodies are searched, while the *barra* and the *banda* face cavalry units, dogs, and riot police. Jáver and El Waco rationalize this interaction as an extension of their "art"; dodging the Metro guards and police on the trains confirms their skills and youthfulness, and furthers their social solidarity. For La Yaya, too, violence highlights the strength of social bonds among the *barra* and with society (the "ladies and gentlemen" who opened their doors to help them escape the violence). This is who they are and what they do, although this is something that frequently comes at a price, as, for example, in the case of the girlfriend taking the blows for her boyfriend. Moreover, La Yaya is very much aware of how the political context shapes these encounters: the "Mexico City Government spends a wad on security [for] officers, helicopters, dogs, horses, that stuff that they claim makes games more 'comfortable' and recreates a familial environment...[as if there is] a more legitimate relationship with stadiums than the barras." Her experiences of violence have also provided insight, however: "fortunately for the administrative statistics everything is 'under control,'" while on the streets the "emergency measures end in basic algorithms: more officers plus more restrictions equals more security...A logic that legitimizes the treatment of the *hincha* (fan) as delinquents and security checks that make the girls put up with their breasts being touched and their bras lifted above their clothes..." In other words, in both the case of La Yaya, and Jáver and El Waco, these young people are aware of "what is going on in the world" and are able to invoke a "sociological imagination" to give sense to it.

Conclusion

Open a newspaper, listen to the radio or watch television in Mexico, and it is difficult to ignore the claim that the country is experiencing increasing, more violent, and more organized crime. The policy response has been to adopt tough military(-type) policing and more recently the use of the military in daily "security" operations. Most Mexicans are skeptical, and rightly so, that these measures are effective at dealing with criminal activity, as the case of el Cholo indicates at even a relatively low level. Nevertheless, perhaps distracted by discourses of "war," of nationalist sentiments against Central American gangs, and of fear that the car thefts, muggings, and kidnappings are indeed linked to wider networks, concerns at the presence of military and other security agencies on the streets are aired but tend to be put to one side. The "shared idiom" trumps a careful analysis of the best available statistics showing that the national murder rate at 10 to 14 per 100,000 inhabitants is lower than in 1994 when it reached 19 (Reforma December 2, 2008).[21]

Young people in Mexico are caught in the crossfire, literally and metaphorically, of violence, its representations and the states responses. Data show that murder, for example, disproportionately affects young people[22] and young peoples' daily lives have to negotiate violence as potential victims of robberies, muggings, and as bystanders to operations by security forces, cartels, or gangs. But many young peoples' social worlds are obliged to relate to a poetics of violence in particular ways. "Counterculture" (the term is itself revealing of a normative expectation of moral order) collective identities of crews, skatos, punks, or as *banda* and even in *pandillas*, with their expressions of music, clothing, sexual and drug use, attending clubs or just hanging out, bring young people into relationships with authority and especially the police. To a certain extent, this has always been the case. But now, when a young person is stopped with paints in a rucksack it will be by a municipal officer keen to demonstrate his grasp of "zero tolerance"; possession of fireworks will bring the attention of the AFI; and antidrug raids at clubs are more likely to involve actual or former military personnel. In his biographical account of growing up on the *"Mean Streets"* of New York during the 1940s and 50s, Piri Thomas reveals how he made sense of the discrimination, poverty, and violence of everyday life, combining the excitement of friendships, drugs, sexual relations with the limits of expectations and the criminal justice system. Thomas's personal "social imagination" brought an awareness of how his youth was framed by racial identity and economic inequalities. In contemporary Mexico, the state, media, and civil society groups may present violence as political, but to most young people most of the time violence needs to be understood as social.

Notes

1. A *New York Times* article described the success of a store in Polanco selling body armor designer wear (October 12, 2008).
2. There are presently around 75,000 private security guards in Mexico, with 21,000 employed by over 600 companies in the Federal District alone.
3. In Ciudad Juarez alone there were 911 deaths in the first 9 months of 2008, raising the murder rate for the city to 65 per 100,000 against an official national statistic of about ten (Padilla 2008).
4. Mills is prompted by the individual's difficulty of understanding his or her position in history and "society," given the large-scale structural changes

around them, but his project is to trace the contribution of the social sciences to unearthing meaning amidst uncertainty.

5. Films such as *Amores Perros, de la Calle, Batalla en el Cielo,* and *La Zona* include central references to violence as murders, assassinations, child kidnap, and vigilantism.

6. Nuevo Laredo is the stand-out example with five police chiefs between 2002 and 2004, and three in just 1 year, with one appointee (Alejandro Dominguez) killed in a hail of gunfire during his first day of office.

7. Victimization surveys regularly show mistrust of the police and the attorney general's office, higher levels of real crime than reported in official data, and growing fear (see Pansters and Castillo Berthier 2007). Fewer than one in five crimes are reported, only about one-half of which are investigated and less than five per 100 result in identification of a perpetrator.

8. Official data put the number of kidnaps at thousands, aided by logging "express kidnaps" as robbery. A survey of 66,000 people, however, estimates 43,561 kidnaps in 2004 and 77,833 in 2006 (IKV PAX Christi 2008).

9. In 2001 the mayor generated ridicule following the lynching of two "suspected" police officers in Tláhuac when he explained the slow response of police units to the scene—they arrived some hours after television crews—by arguing that community action had to be understood as part of the social organization of indigenous communities and was beyond state purview.

10. In 2003 the *Secretaría de Seguridad Pública del Distrito Federal* and the *Procuraduría General de Justicia del Distrito Federal*, with funds from businessmen such as Carlos Slim, paid U.S.$ 4.3 million to bring Rudolph Giuliani and former police chief William Bratton to analyze the policing of Mexico City.

11. Narco-mantas are announcements painted onto large sheets, informing on the identity of narco associates in government and exhorting the authorities to take direct action against cartels and gangs, or conversely they are warnings issued by cartels against investigators and prosecutors.

12. A few days into office, in December 2006, President Calderon deployed 7,000 troops to Michoacán, and on June 14, 2007, he approved the national deployment of 25,000 troops and federal police.

13. A range of reforms to the penal code upgraded previously minor offences to merit a custodial sentence, despite prisons being 300 percent over capacity (Zepeda Lecuona 2004).

14. 70 percent of young detainees are "newbies" and around 70 percent are serving sentences for theft, one-quarter for goods worth less than U.S.$ 80.

15. In June 2008, a raid by Mexico City police on the News Divine disco in the barrio of Nueva Atzacoalco, apparently to stop drinking and drug consumption, killed eight in the stampede that followed in which the exits were blocked by police (three of whom also died) (Castillo Berthier 2009).

16. Release requires payment of a 300-peso "fine" for those under 18 years and a 500-peso fine for those over 18 years.

17. For Ciudad Juárez, Padilla (2008) claims that some "gangs" are army personnel acting as vigilante, taking out easy targets such as small-scale drug dealers, who are also killed by the cartels keen to "clear house" at a time of pressure.

18. "Emo" combines sexual ambivalence and feelings of victimhood that manifest as self-harm and suicide. A series of apparently orchestrated attacks on groups of Emo took place in early 2008 in Mexico City, Querétaro, and Tijuana.

19. Contrast the policing and security budget with the absence of public funds for youth in poorer areas of Mexico City such as Ixtapalapa, Ixtapaluca, and Chimalhuacan or with the reliance on partial and insecure funding such as for the intensely used FARO network of cultural centers (see http://www.cultura.df.gob.mx/culturama/secretaria/Recintos/FARO/indexN.html). [accessed December 18, 2008].

20. See www.grafittiarte.org. [accessed December 18, 2008].

21. According to the most recent data from the *Sistema Nacional de Seguridad Pública*, homicide numbers are similar in 2003 as in 1982: in the Federal District, there were 947 murders in 1982 and 975 in 2003; in the State of Mexico, there were 1,521 murders in 1982 and 1,912 in 2003; and for Sinaloa and Tamaulipas, two states associated with drug deaths, 489 and 325 murders, respectively, in 1982 and 419 and 227 murders in 2003.

22. *Sistema Nacional de Seguridad Pública* data indicate that of just over 10,000 murders in 2003, 3,765 victims were aged 10–29 years and about half that number aged 24–29 years.

Bibliography

Arango, A. 2003. *Indicadores de Seguridad Pública en México: La Construcción de un Sistema de Estadísticas Delictivas*, USMEX 2003–2004 Working Paper Series, http://repositories.cdlib.org/usmex/prajm/arango [accessed February 2, 2009].

Arteaga Botello, N. 2004. *En Busca de la Legitimidad: Violencia y Populismo Punitivo en México 1990–2000*, Mexico City: UACM.

Blancas Madrigal, D. 2008. Operan células de maras en el DF y en 22 estados; el 60% es de origen mexicano; en el sureste aparecen chiapatruchas,: CNDH, *La Crónica*, April 3.

Castillo Berthier, H. 2000. *Juventud Cultura y Política Social*, Mexico City: Instituto Mexicano de Juventud.

Castillo Berthier, H. 2002. De las bandas a las tribus urbanas, *Desacatos*, vol. 9, pp. 57–71.

Castillo Berthier, H. 2009. De los emos al new's divine: Rupturas, intolerancia e incomprensión, sin agenda pública, *Revista de Antropología de la INAH* (in press).

Cruz Salazar, T. 2004. Yo me aventé como tres anos haciendo tags, sí, la verdad, si fui ilegal! Grafiteros: arte callejero en la ciudad de México, *Desacatos*, vol. 14, pp. 197–226.

Davis, D. E. 2006. Undermining the rule of law: Democratization and the dark side of police reform in México, *Latin American Politics and Society*, vol. 48, no. 1, pp. 55–86.

Debroise, O. 2005. Back, in R. Olivares (ed.), *Exit México*, Mexico City: Universidad Nacional Autónoma de Mexico, pp. 118–125.

El Universal, 2004. Existen mil maras en el DF, afirma diputado, *El Universal*, February 25.

Fernández Menéndez, J., and V. Ronquillo. 2006. *De los Maras a los Zetas: Los secretos del narcotráfico, de Colombia a Chicago*, Mexico City: Grijalbo.

Hernández León, R. 1999. A la aventura!: Jovenes, pandillas y migración en la conexión Monterrey-Houston, in G. Mummert (ed.), *Fronteras Fragmentadas*, Zamora: El Colegio de Michoacán. pp. 115–143.

IKV PAX Christi. 2008. *Kidnapping is Booming Business: A Lucrative Political Instrument for Armed Groups Operating in Conflict Zones*, Utrecht: IKV Pax Christi.

Jiménez, C. 2005. Los Maras Cruzan centroamérica para buscar refugio en México y EU, *La Crónica*, December 9.

Jones, G. A., and M. Moreno-Carranco. The multiplex city: Uncovering Mexico City in contemporary film, *Space and Culture* (forthcoming).

Jiménez Ornelas, R. 2003. La cifra negra de la delincuencia en México: Sistema de encuestas sobre victimización, in S. García Ramírez and L. A. Vargas Casillas (eds.), *Proyectos Legislativas y Otros Temas Penales. Segundas Jornadas Sobre Justicia Penal*, Mexico City: Instituto de Investigaciones Jurídicas. pp. 167–190.

La Reforma, 2006. Violan Derechos de Jovenes, *La Reforma*, November 29.

Lara Klahr, M. 2006. *Hoy Te Toca la Muerte: El Imperio de las Maras Visto Desde Adentro*, Mexico City: Planeta.

López Portillo, E. 2004. La reforma a la seguridad pública, *Nexos*, vol. 323, pp. 17–24.

Marcial, R. 1997. *La Banda Rifa: Vida Cotidiana de Grupos Juveniles de Esquina en Zamora, Michoacán*, Zamora: El Colegio de Michoacán.

Mills, C. W. 1970. *The Sociological Imagination*, New York: Oxford University Press [orig. 1959].

Monsivais, C. 1997. *Mexican Postcards: Critical Studies in Latin America*, London: Verso.

Nateras Domínguez, A. 2007. Adscripciones juveniles y violencias transnacionales: Cholos y maras, in J. M. Valenzuela Arce, A. Nateras Domínguez, and R. Reguillo Cruz (eds.), *Las Maras: Identidades Juveniles al Limite*, Mexico City: Universidad Autónoma Metropolitana Iztapalapa. pp. 127–155.

Padilla, H. 2008. *Las Fronteras de la Gobernabilidad: El Caso de la Ciudad Juárez*, paper presented at the Coloquio Internacional Gobernabilidad, Gobernanza y Buen Gobierno, UAM-Iztapalapa, September 17–19.

Pansters, W., and H. Castillo Berthier. 2007. *Mexico City*, in K. Koonings and D. Kruijt (eds.), Fractured Cities: Social Exclusion, Urban Violence and Contested Spaces in Latin America, London: Zed Books. pp. 36–56.

Polit-Dueñas, G. 2008. On reading about violence, drug dealers and interpreting a field of literary production amidst the din of gunfire: Culiacán–Sinaloa, 2007, *Revista de Estudios Hispánicos*, vol. 42, no. 3, pp. 559–582.

Reyes Heroles, F. 2008. Diagnostico, *La Reforma*, December 2.

Staudt, K. 2008. *Violence and Activism at the Border: Gender, Fear, and Everyday Life in Ciudad Juárez*, Austin: University of Texas Press.

Suárez de Garay, M. E. 2006. *Los Policías: Una Averiguación Antropológica*, Guadalajara: ITESO.

Thomas, P. 1997. *Down These Mean Streets*, New York: Vintage [orig. 1967].

USAID. 2006. *Central America and México Gang Assessment*, Washington: USAID Bureau for Latin America and the Caribbean Office of Regional Sustainable Development.

Valenzuela Arce, J. M. 2007. La mara es mi familia, in J. M. Valenzuela Arce, A. Nateras Domínguez, and R. Reguillo Cruz (eds.), *Las Maras: Identidades Juveniles al Limite*, Mexico City: Universidad Autónoma Metropolitana Iztapalapa. pp. 33–61.

Vilas, C. M. 2001. Tristezas de Zapotitlán: Violencia e inseguridad en el mundo de la subalternidad, *Bajo el Volcán: Revista del Posgrado de Sociología*, vol. 3, pp. 123–142.

Whitehead, N. L. 2004. On the poetics of violence, in N. L. Whitehead (ed.), *Violence*, Santa Fe: School of American Research Press, pp. 55–77.

Zepeda Lecuona, G. 2004. *Crimen sin Castigo: Procuración de Justicia Penal y Ministerio Público en México*, Mexico City: Centro de Investigación para el Desarrollo A.C.

Chapter 11

Policing Youth in Latin America

Mark Ungar

Introduction

Among the host of ills afflicting Latin America today—from poverty to political instability—youth has become the primary focus of both blame and concern. One of the most serious of the many problems that disproportionately affect young people is violent crime—marked by a 41 percent rise in homicides that has made Latin America the world's deadliest region (PAHO 2002). Scholars and policymakers have brought out the causes of the rising crime rates, from poverty to authoritarian legacies. But they have neglected the centrality of youth—as both a group and as a concept—in understanding why crime has turned into a citizen security crisis in Latin America. The policing of youth, this chapter asserts, shows that the region's response to crime is stuck between its long-standing, centralized, repressive, and often iron fist (*mano dura*) response on the one hand and, on the other, preventative policing based on addressing crime's causes through citizen participation and institutional accountability. This impasse leads to contradictory and overly ambitious policies that allow police structures and practices to continue to be based on identifying, separating out, and cracking down on social sectors and areas regarded as inherently criminal—above all, on youth and in the spaces they congregate.

After a brief description of the causes of youth violence, the first section of this chapter will describe how the policing of youth exemplifies this larger tension between repressive and preventive approaches through three issues that highlight the causes, conflicts, and problems of youth policing: legal responsibility, public space, and gangs. To show the prevalence of these issues under the region's varying political and socioeconomic conditions, this analysis will draw on examples from industrialized Southern Cone countries such as Argentina to poor Andean countries like Bolivia. But the main case study will be Honduras, a country where youth gangs have proliferated and become policing's primary focus. The Honduran example is explored later in the chapter and dramatically highlights the difficulties inherent to moving beyond the opposing paradigms of repression and prevention in addressing

youth violence in Latin America. A final section discusses the growing movement toward community-oriented policing of youth, describing a range of
promising programs being enacted throughout the Latin American region.

The Context

Each year, nearly 200,000 people between the ages of 10 and 29 are mur-
dered, with a rate that ranges from 0.9 per 100,000 in high-income countries to 17.6 per 100,000 in Africa and 36.4 per 100,000 in Latin America
(WHO 2007). Violence—homicide, suicide, accidents—killed 80,000 Latin
America youth in 2006, more than any other group and at a rate higher than
in any other world region. Homicide among people between the ages of 15
and 25 increased 44 percent between 1984 and 1994, and is now the second
cause of death for this age cohort (UNICJRI 1995).[1] Also, 29 percent of
the region's murders occur among people 10–19 years of age, making youth
homicide up to three times higher than national homicide rates. And for
every killing, the WHO (World Health Organization) estimates that there
are between 20 and 40 victims of youth violence requiring hospital treatment. The three countries with the world's highest youth homicide rates are
Latin American: Colombia, Venezuela, and Brazil. In Venezuela, 54 percent
of all murder victims are younger than 25 and homicide is the primary cause
of death among young poor people (Sanjuan 2003: 122). In Brazil, youth
homicides have increased 77 percent since the late 1990s, compared to
48.4 percent for the population in general, to 51.7 homicides per 100,000
youth, a rate that is 100 times greater than that of the great majority of
countries around the world (UN-Habitat 2004). Trends in other countries
are not much better. In the Dominican Republic, for example, 45.7 percent
of all killings in 2001 involved individuals between 20 and 29 years of age.
In El Salvador, 15–17 year olds make up 93 percent of the homicide victims,[2]
and in Guatemala, the nongovernmental organization (NGO) Casa Alianza
documented 334 killings of minors in 2005, a 14 percent increase from
2004 (Casa Alianza 2006).

Such high rates of youth violence, of course, stem from the social, cultural,
and economic conditions in which most of the region's 140 million youth
live.[3] While education has gradually expanded, an estimated 37 percent of
young people still drop out before getting a high school certificate, half of
them prior to finishing their primary education. Over half of the children
who do not complete primary school, moreover, are from low-income homes
(CEPAL 2003). About 90 of the top income decile in Mexico completes primary education, but only 63 percent of the lower four deciles does, for example, while about 14 percent of Brazilian youth in the lowest 10 percent income
group are illiterate and just 4 percent are employed in the formal economy
(Grindle 2004; World Bank 2007). The rate of unemployment among youth
in the region is between 16 and 20 percent,[4] which is three times the adult
rate. Of those who do work, about 30 million do so under poor and unstable
conditions in the informal economy, while about 22 million others neither

work nor study. Argentina, one of Latin America's wealthiest countries, reveals how such conditions increase youth run-ins with the law. Of the 10 million Argentines between 14 and 24 years of age, between 47 and 67 percent are considered low-income[5]—nearly double the overall rate of 25 percent. Well over a million people under 24 do not study or work, and nearly 77 percent do not finish high school.[6] In the 1990s, the unemployment rate among people ages 15 to 19 was 35.9 percent which was among the highest recorded by the International Labor Organization (Hopenhayn 2004). In Buenos Aires province, the country's most populous and most developed, unemployment for that age range rose from 19.7 percent in 1990 to 34 percent in 2000 (Government of Argentina 2001). In the same period, cases in the province's Minor Courts rose 92 percent, and the government estimates that 80 percent of that increase stems from concurrent increases in poverty and inequality.

In addition to the direct impact of these conditions are the less direct impacts of cultural conditions. Many of those who assert that children exposed to violence are more likely to engage in it as youth point to the high rate of such exposure in Latin America through first hand experiences, media images, the availability of drugs and arms, and a growing emphasis on consumption among a sector without the resources to consume. By age 16, the average Colombian has seen 150,508 acts of violence and 17,520 murders on television, film, and other outlets (Boletín de la Asociación de Televisión por Cable 1993 cited in De Roux 1993: 10). In El Salvador, 48.3 percent of youth blame political parties and the media for making violence so prominent in their lives (Solís Robles 2004: 2). In cities throughout the region, large portions of young people expect to die, emigrate, or be incarcerated in the near future—creating an alienation in a region where social, economic, and political instability already warp the normal processes of youth development and socialization.

Traditional Policing, the Mano Dura, and Youth in Latin America

Even though there is little disagreement that such conditions cause crime, law enforcement around Latin America continues to be "iron fisted." The currently predominant basis for policing is zero tolerance, which stems from Kelling's (in)famous "broken windows" argument that antisocial behavior such as intimidation and harassment, along with deterioration of the built environment, scare off law-abiding citizens and allow crime to take root on a corner, street, or neighborhood. As law-abiding residents start avoiding the area and delinquents are drawn to it, a sense of public order slips out of the neighborhood's control even without actual criminal activity. Detentions for misdemeanors and antisocial behavior, this approach argues, thus prevent potential criminals from being emboldened into more serious crime. Combined with crime mapping and strong prosecution, such an approach also provides the police with information about general crime patterns as well as drugs, illegal arms, and other illicit possessions from detainees (Kelling and Coles 1996).

To be both effective and remain within the bounds of civil rights, though, zero tolerance policing requires solid legal training for all officers, coordination with social services, functioning courts, and oversight by accountability agencies, the judiciary, NGOs, and the media. Detentions for truancy, for example, only work if the courts are able to follow up on them and provide social services to prevent recurrence. Nowhere, of course, do such controls prevent abuses that come with greater police power. But in Latin America, "zero tolerance" is often applied without such supports or outside controls, turning it into a *mano dura* that is little more than a continuation of predemocratic policing. Comprising the bulk of those practices are edicts and other internal regulations that most Latin American police have been acquiring since the colonial era, empowering them to carry out detentions for a wide range of subjectively defined activities and behaviors, from "vagrancy" to "suspicion of criminal intent" (see Gentili 1995). Such edicts are supplemented by special operations that subsequently become institutionalized into law, as well as by routine practices such as checking for police record and verifying identification. In nearly every Latin American city, these edicts, special operations, and routine checks comprise the basis of the majority of police detentions. And as the most visible and least powerful target of such policing, youth are disproportionately affected. A growing percentage of special military-police operations, for instance, are against youth gangs. In Venezuela, for example, 90 percent of the victims of police abuse were men between the ages of 15 and 24, almost all of whom had darker skin and lived in poor neighborhoods (El Achkar 2007). In Guatemala, 80 percent of all detentions and arrests are for alleged misdemeanors (USAID 2005: 2). As the number of such detentions becomes the self-referential measure of success, policing only becomes more dependent on them.

Not only does this form of zero tolerance neglect the causes of crime, but it reflects a wider institutional and legal failure in Latin America. Neoliberal spending reductions, along with a decentralization that has broken up centralized agencies, have together reduced the capacity of Latin American governments to address crime with coherent, consistent, and adequately financed policies. Such failure is most apparent in the promising but ultimately inapplicable new penal process codes that 14 countries in Latin America adopted since the mid-1990s to strengthen criminal justice and due process by empowering prosecutors, restricting the police's role, introducing oral trials, and creating courts at the investigative and sentencing stages. A lack of training, funds, oversight, and agency cooperation has clearly curtailed these codes' benefits. An inability to meet the new codes' higher standards, amid continuing political pressure to crack down on crime, then allows the continuation of old practices, such as extended detention, which the new codes were supposed to end. In Peru, for example, 68 percent of teens who commit petty crimes are sentenced for up to 3 years of reclusion despite new due process guarantees and the country's progressive Child and Adolescent Code that provides an array of alternatives to prison.

Legal Responsibility

The focus of policing on criminal sectors rather than the criminal justice system itself is perhaps most vividly seen in a clamor around the region to reduce the age at which people can be tried in criminal court. The Minimum Rules of the United Nations (UN) for the Administration of Justice for Minors, commonly known as the Beijing Rules, state that legal responsibility "should not be fixed at an age that is too early, taking into consideration the circumstances that accompany emotional and intellectual maturity." The consensus of experts is that the earliest such age should be 15, which most countries' laws reflect. In most of Latin America, only adults over age 18 are considered fully responsible for laws that they break. Those between 16 and 18 are held responsible for their acts, but tried within a separate legal system as "minor offenders," while anyone under 16 is not considered legally responsible for their acts. But there is mounting pressure to reduce the age of legal responsibility down to 16 and for minor offenders down to 14 or even lower. In polls, 70 percent of Argentines favor reducing the age of culpability to 14 years, for example, and proposals to do so have been debated by the Senate's Penal Affairs Commission for the past several years (Kunz 2005). In Colombia, the media continually reports on young people as young as 14 being used by narco-traffickers to kill judges, officials, and journalists. Such concerns prompted President Álvaro Uribe, in his first electoral campaign, to promise "greater severity for the dangerous juvenile delinquent" and to "evaluate if 18 years should continue being the minimum age of legal responsibility" (Vieira 2005). In 2006, the Colombian Parliament—with support from a range of parties—enacted a Law of Infancy and Adolescence that sets several forms of criminal legal responsibility at age 14.

As with the application of zero tolerance in Latin America, such moves neglect the poor functioning of laws and institutions that treat youth offenders. In other words, the clamor for repressive laws grows not because preventive approaches have failed, but because they have not been fully tried. Both social programs for youth (such as educational and family projects for at-risk youth) as well as enforcement of prohibitions that heavily affect youth (such as alcohol, narcotics, and firearms) tend to lack necessary financial and administrative support. A Juvenile Penal Law that created alternative sentencing for youth has helped give Costa Rica one of the world's lowest youth imprisonment rates, for example, but many of its earmarked programs such as a drug treatment center for youth are, as an unattributed article in one newspaper put it, a "utopia".[7] Panama has high youth imprisonment rates because of a dearth of alternative sentencing options, while new training programs to reduce violence by guards in youth detention facilities lack the financial and political support for implementation.

Public Space

The law's dual repression of youth—harsher crackdowns amid weak institutions—plays out most visibly in Latin America's public spaces. As in many regions, the public's fear of crime is most clearly seen, expressed, and generated over the use of public space. The identity, self-esteem, and status of young people everywhere, of course, depends on how they act and react in public space. But the exposure of teen relationships, expression, and problems is amplified in Latin America, where there are few public spaces dedicated to youth. In the Dominican Republic, for example, 47 percent of young people interviewed about their use of public space said they hung out on the street (Bobea 2003). Since modern societies regard public street space for consumption and organized events, its use by youth is often seen as illegitimate. In neighborhood polls around the region, in fact, residents typically identify kids gathering in the street as the biggest "problem" affecting their daily lives, whether their activities are legal or not. Youth thus become objects of collective fear, seen not as individuals but for the anxieties they cause and the jarring cultural changes they are seen to embrace. The particular impulsiveness of youth, wrapped up in their hostility to tradition and authority, only serves to aggravate these tensions.

For the police, as a result, control of youth is almost always the priority to establish what the community regards as the proper public order—which is why edicts are such useful law enforcement instruments against youth. Nearly all serious confrontations in Argentina since the 1983 democratization, for example, have been between police and youth between 15 and 18 years of age after large events like concerts. In Mendoza province, where police complicity in a series of youth killings during the 1990s prompted a 1999 security overhaul, the use of checking for records to arbitrarily detain young people continues to be the norm. Along with such approaches, also undermining policing of youth is the fact that young people are more often victims—of abuse, violence, neglect, sexual exploitation—than victimizers. But as victims or witnesses, most of them do not go to the police—depriving them of adequate protection or attention. Youth are objects of rather than contributors to criminal policy as a result, and police action toward them is far more selective and discretionary than for other social sectors. Throughout Latin America, for example, youth are disproportionately stopped for police identity checks. In Argentina, as in other countries, the police are given far more political and legal leeway to break up groups of youth in public. In provinces such as Mendoza and La Rioja, nearly every unresolved case of police killings involved a youth victim. Such attitudes are pronounced in Latin America, where many officials say that legal and administrative controls have far less influence than their own view about different groups in how they face the range of issues, situations, and circumstances involved in daily policing.

Youth Gangs

The most threatening gathering of youth in public space, of course, are youth gangs. The number, size, and violence of youth gangs (usually called *pandillas* or *maras*) is increasing in virtually every Latin American country, with nearly every police agency citing gangs as their primary concern. Mexico City has about 1,500 gangs, for example, while Lima has about 500 *pandillas* with about 10,000 members of ages 11 to 23.[8] The Nicaraguan capital of Managua has more than 110 *pandillas* with approximately 8,000 members, who commit 50 percent of all crimes in Nicaragua and 60 percent of all crimes in Managua (Royal Canadian Mounted Police 2006). Medellín, Colombia, has an estimated 400 armed groups with 10,000 members—the majority of whom are under 18 years old.

But just as zero tolerance masks weak institutions, the reporting of such alarming numbers stems in part from a lack of common criteria or state policy in documenting, defining, and addressing gangs. Along with wide discrepancies in the actual number of gangs—Ecuador's estimates of how many gangs it has, for example, range from 480 to 1,050[9]—is a discord between analysis, policy, and politics. As with other social problems, many policies expediently reflect community demands and political needs: a pro-tourism campaign, for example, can turn a group of loitering youth into a gang in order to change policing practices. Much exaggeration and many misdirected programs also come from studies that use oversimplified categories, such as "violent" and "nonviolent," or fail to use time and geography, for example, to show precisely how and when neighborhood gangs get drawn into international crime. This lack of clear definition and approaches leaves police on their own in dealing with youth gangs, with greater leeway but not with more effective strategies. Most frustrating for police officers, the critical knowledge they have gained about gangs and potential gangs in their areas—such as on gangs' goals (like territory, competition, and economic gain), their actions (such as assaults and extortion); and philosophies (from music to fascism)—is not integrated into policy.

Nowhere are the results of such policy failure as spectacular as in Central America, which has seemingly been overrun by youth gangs over the past 10 years. The two largest and most dominant gangs in Central America are the super-*clikas Mara Salvatrucha* (known as MS-13) and *Mara Barrio 18*, with about 100,000 well-organized members together spread through El Salvador, Honduras, Guatemala, México, and 33 states in the United States. They have their own culture, language, and symbols that are appealing to children. More important and a continual source of recruitment, though, are the solidarity, belonging, and other needs that they provide that society does not. Once they take root, the *maras'* activities expand rapidly, typically starting with neighborhood "taxes" and supposedly extending to international drug trafficking. Such expansion is facilitated by highly developed communications networks that were created by *mara* leaders in Central America who are deportees from the United States, whose policy of deporting noncitizen residents with even minor criminal offenses swelled the region with jobless but often educated young men.

But since policy responses to the *maras* were developed well after the gangs themselves, their impact has been limited. Central America's fragile criminal justice systems lack follow-up with individuals or alternatives like mediation and conflict resolution, leaving many at-risk youth without support or attention. Such limits, combined with citizen panic over record crime rates and the very visible presence of tattooed *mareros*, have made zero tolerance the region's default form of policing. In El Salvador, for example, the national youth program, *Mano Amiga* (Friendly Hand) was overcome by the *Super Mano Dura* (Super Iron Fist) policy of harsh crackdowns. Even though a strongly pro-*Mano Dura* former army general lost the 2007 Presidential election in Guatemala, crackdowns remain popular. The government argues, despite objections from human rights organizations, that only its military— along with the 11,000-men brigades and civilian security groups it plans to assemble—is able to stop gang violence that killed over 5,500 people in 2005.

Youth Gangs in Honduras

The *maras* are particularly entrenched in Honduras, which ranks lower than nearly every country in Latin America on social indicators for youth. Over 15 percent of the country's urban youth neither work nor study, for example, and over 20 percent of 14–15 year olds have not completed the mandatory 6 years of schooling (Arriagada 2001). Although the country was largely spared from the prolonged civil wars that afflicted its neighbors in the last half of the twentieth Century, like them Honduras overhauled its security structure with the regional peace accords of the late 1990s. Constitutional reform in 1996 ended the armed forces' internal security authority, and the 1998 Police Law (*Ley Orgánica de la Policía Nacional,* LOPN) formed a new civilian police force under the Security Ministry. Introduced into the new security structure was the *Consejo Nacional de Seguridad Interior* (CONASIN, National Council for Internal Security), a body of NGOs and state agencies authorized to formulate security policy, advise the President, receive complaints about officials, and supervise police activities. Also established was the *Unidad de Asuntos Internos* (UAI, Internal Affairs Unit), empowered to investigate wrongdoings by police officers and detain them if necessary. A penal process code that was revised in 2002 introduced oral trials, alternative resolution mechanisms like mediation, and investigative and sentencing courts. Also created in 2002 was a national community policing program, Safer Community (*Comunidad Más Segura*), to address the causes of crime in the high crime areas through neighborhood-based officers, education programs for citizens and youth-centered prevention.

But public panic over growing crime put these reforms under strain after Ricardo Maduro was elected President in 2001 on a "zero tolerance" anti-crime platform. The new government's initial criminal policy included preventative, rehabilitative, and educational initiatives like the "Despertar" (Awake) workshop series for low-income parents (Castillo 2004). But such programs were quickly drowned out by *Mano Dura*. Upon taking office, Maduro expanded the police force, increased the budget of both the police and the military, and flooded the streets with 6,000 soldiers. He enacted

Presidential Decree 123–2002 to allow searches without a warrant, and established joint police-military patrols in the *Honduras Segura* program. Expanded police power was institutionalized by the 2002 *Ley de Policía y Convivencia Social* (LPCS, Law of Police and Social Coexistence), which authorizes the police to "control" the people in a certain area in order to fight crime and to arbitrarily detain "vagabonds"—people who lack an "honest" means of living or suspected of not having "licit" purposes in the neighborhood in which they are found. Much of the law's language—such as Article 100's focus on "suspicious form" and "societal danger"—gives the police wide discretion in the use of force. The LPCS was quickly taken up to drive home the argument, reiterated in daily reporting, that the root cause of crime is unredeemable criminals. The new law, one newspaper editorialized, makes "a clear differentiation between those who live within the law and those who break it" (Espinal Díaz 2004).

For Hondurans, the vast majority of such law breakers are *mareros*.[10] Although the percentage of deaths linked to the *maras* ranges from 13 to 25 percent—with police saying off the record that about 12 percent of *mareros* are criminally violent and that they commit about a third of violent crimes—they get blamed for nearly all crime and their activities saturate political rhetoric and media coverage.[11] With strong backing from the public, Congress, and the judiciary, policing has focused nearly exclusively on the hundreds of neighborhood gangs around the country, almost all of which have become integrated into Barrio 18 and MS-13.[12] The centerpiece of this focus is the August 2003 amendment of Penal Code Article 332—known as the *Ley Anti-Maras*—that punishes gang members with 6–12 years' imprisonment. A potent example of the criminalization of youth and the expansion of police power, 332 erodes basic civil rights—in particular, by allowing detention without a judicial order, by criminalizing association rather than specific acts, and by not specifying crimes but the possibility of committing them.

For example, Article 332 "punishes with nine to twelve years imprisonment and a fine of 10,000 to 200,000 *lempiras* the heads of *pandillas* and other groups whose purpose is to . . . commit any act that constitutes a crime. The same punishment of imprisonment . . . reduced by a third, will apply to the rest of the group members. Chiefs or ringleaders are those who stand out or identify as such and whose decisions influence the spirit and actions of the group." Of the 1,600 alleged *mareros* arrested under 332, usually after special operation roundups, many of those charged with being leaders described themselves as couriers, recruiters, drug runners, or as having other roles whereby they took orders rather than give them.[13] While such protestations support claims of innocence and so are not necessarily truthful, these diverse and detailed descriptions indicate a very elastic interpretation by officials, without much judicial control, of deciding "whose decisions influence" the group and can thus be charged as a "leader."

The law, ironically, also demonstrates policy and police weakness. On one level, no one knows how many *mareros* there are: The police estimate that there are between 50,000 and 70,000 *mareros*; executive officials

say there are between 60,000 and 100,000 *mara* members, collabora-
tors, and sympathizers;[14] and the press has suggested up to 140,000. All
these numbers are unsubstantiated by any independent methodology, are
far above estimates of no more than 12,000 *mareros* offered by some religious organizations,[15] and have since been discredited by the government of
Manuel Zelaya.[16] But even going by the government's own lowest calcula-
tions, the fact that police have detained less than one in 50 *mareros* demonstrates its ineffectiveness.

Instead of leading to new approaches based on criminological analysis,
though, this failure only seems to have pushed the police to step up the use
of its long-standing repression through an increasingly harsh *Mano Dura*.
Many activists and state officials even imply that, as part of this crackdown,
the government allows police to kill youths.[17] Most officials agree off the
record with the estimate of 2,300 extrajudicial killings of youth and children
from 1998 to 2005. Of the 1,600 such deaths of young people under the
age of 23 reported between 1998 and 2003, 61 percent were not adequately
investigated, and 39 percent had evidence of police responsibility.[18] In 2002,
no perpetrator was identified in 60 to 70 percent of the killings, and gangs
were suspected in 15 to 20 percent of them. Residents of poor neighborhoods
report unmarked vans roaming areas like basketball courts where youths
congregate, and the cities' estimated 7,500 street children and youth—who
are not in gangs but associated with them because of their tendency to be
addicted to sniffing glue and to commit petty crimes—complain of continual harassment.[19]

But the inability of even such punitive action to rein in the *maras* is
instead blamed on the standards that try to contain them within a rule of law.
Rooted in the view that there is a fundamental divide between a *Mano Dura*
repressive policing on the one hand and rights guarantees and preventative
policing on the other, the government has systematically undermined criminal justice laws and institutions. Maduro's Security Minister, for example,
asserted that the new penal code symbolizes the *garantista* approach—their
dismissive term for criminal justice rules and actions that privilege the rights
of the accused at the expense of victims and society—and that it should be
scrapped for being ineffective against crime.[20] Many gang members now
shun tattoos and other overt marks of gang membership, in particular, which
often leads prosecutors and judges to declare that there is insufficient proof
to convict under the 2002 penal process code (distinct from the penal code,
of which 332 is a provision). Of the 1,109 *mareros* netted at the height of
anti-*mara* operations between August and December 2003, for example,
561 were released.[21] This reluctance to prosecute has angered state officials,
aggravating the split between the *garantista* and *Mano Dura* approaches,
increasing the use of forced confessions, beatings, mass raids, extended
preventative detention—and probably encouraging police to kill suspected
mareros on the street.[22]

Also being undermined is the *Dirección General de Investigación Criminal*
(DGIC, the investigative police), which is critical to solving and thus

preventing patterns of crime. Instead, the *Policía Preventitativa* (PP, the preventative police), which gets about 90 percent of the police's budget, dominates law enforcement in Honduras. Although PP officers receive practically no investigative training, they pass themselves off as investigative police, intimidate witnesses, inadequately protect crime scenes, and conduct their own parallel investigations. Such action is implicitly supported by the government. Since it was created, in fact, the Security Secretariat has conducted a "process of counter-reform...characterized by halting the process of depuration of corrupt officers and those involved in right violations and in death squads" as well as a deliberate weakening of the DGIC (Castellanos 2002). Agencies trying to reverse these trends, meanwhile, also have been weakened. Prosecutors can investigate police wrongdoing, for example, but lack the institutional, political, and legal power to instigate change. The country's Human Rights Prosecutor complains that any of its investigations of police conduct is constantly delayed and obstructed, and that there is a lack of will and personnel to follow up on cases.[23] The accountability agencies that were a keystone of the 1990s reform, CONASIN and the UAI, have also been gutted. While CONASIN on paper has many powers, it cannot carry out any of them effectively if it is not convened—and the Security Minister, the head of CONASIN, is the only official empowered to convene it. In doing so only at times of institutional crisis when needing some political cover, the Secretariat has effectively excluded CONASIN from policy, planning, and internal controls. So although it does publish reports on criminal policy critical of the government, CONASIN has not been able to carry out its primary functions of being a check on criminal policy and helping to hold the police accountable.[24] The UAI, meanwhile, has been crippled because of its investigation of youth killings. In September 2002, UAI chief María Luisa Borjas implicated Security Ministry and police officials in 20 extrajudicial executions of children and youth. She immediately began to receive death threats, her staff was reduced, and two months later, was suspended for allegedly failing to present proof of her claims.[25] The new UAI, with a more reliable head and reduced staff, is more compliant. While its chief claims that they are never subject to political meddling, she also admits that they do not receive much financial support or opportunity to investigate serious cases.[26]

The logical but tragic impacts of such policing of youth reaches extreme forms in the country's prisons—the *Mano Dura*'s final step. In April 2002, for example, 69 inmates—61 of them *mareros*—were killed at El Porvenir, a 300-capacity penal center holding 500 prisoners.[27] According to the official report, the cause was an uprising triggered by a botched effort to disarm detainees only days after their transfer, without the staff at the center being notified that *mareros* from a rival gang were already being held at the prison. During the uprising, a large group of *mareros* took refuge in a cell, in which they were locked and then burned in a fire—with officials shooting at those who managed to flee the flames. But the many questions left unanswered in the official report—such as why the vast majority of victims were from *Mara 18*, why prisoners were given control of discipline, and where all the firearms came from, and why a cleanup was ordered right after the fire—demonstrated not only a lack of policy and control, but state complicity in the gang-linked activities such as arms and drugs trafficking. Despite the preventable conditions, 107 inmates died just 2 years later in a fire at San Pedro Sula central penal facility, a 400-person complex that crams in 1,200. "We only have a small space, and very few programs. Public defenders do not come regularly," said Oscar Jehovani Sevan, a prison inmate. "We don't get to leave this area, and they feed us through these gates—it's never enough, and there's a lot of competition to get what they have," said Melvin López, who died in the fire.[28] In a windowless area of about 650 square feet (200 square meters), where 180 MS-13 *mareros* were held, a fire broke out on the night of May 17. When prisoners tried to take equipment from firemen, the firemen left and prison officials did not help those trapped inside the burning cell.

Despite the focus on gangs, the few state institutions for rehabilitation serve only about 100 gang members. Nearly all other agencies helping *mareros* are Church groups and NGOs. There are rising demands to lower the age of criminal culpability below the current age of 18, even though youth between 12 and 18 years of age can already be tried in youth courts and just 5 percent of all crime is committed by those under 18 (and just 0.2% of those crimes were homicides). Teens in this age range in conflict with the law can be put for 1–8 years into the four centers (three for boys and one for girls, with a total of about 300 youth) run by *Instituto Hondureño de la Niñez y la Familia* (IHNFA, the Honduran Institute of Childhood and the Family). There are educational, vocational, therapeutic, community service, and labor programs there. But they lack sufficient personnel, and, with the IHNFA office outside of the youth center, personnel in charge of specific cases often do not have direct contact with the actual youth. Inside the centers, there are arms, drugs, physical mistreatment, and sexual abuse. While IHNFA guards are unarmed, the PP police at the facilities are, although many IHNFA officials want to get rid of them. IHNFA officials also complain that coordination with other youth agencies consists of little more than shifting around papers without real follow-up, and that there is no analysis of the causes of the country's high dropout rates because school officials seem to lack the interest or means to act when students are absent.[29] To shift policy toward prevention, they add, the agency needs triple the current budget of 100 million *lempiras* (about U.S.$ 5.5 million).

Community-Oriented Policing

Because minors will be a part of society for a long time, the best policing of youth must be preventative, as even *Mano Dura* proponents acknowledge. The spike in youth violence, in fact, has been a chief catalyst for community-oriented policing, one of the biggest and most promising waves of security reform in Latin America and other regions. As the broad alternative to increasingly ineffective *Mano Dura* policing, the preventive strategies that define community-oriented policing focus on addressing and resolving the conditions that cause crime by empowering citizens, building police-community partnerships, improving social services, and better using crime statistics. Street patrols, policy councils, social programs, infrastructural improvement (such as improved street lighting), and localized police structures (such as more foot patrols and independent precinct commissioners) are some of the many community policing programs being adopted around the world.

Because this strategy can be tailored to local conditions—one of its strongest appeals—it varies greatly among countries. But in Latin America, nearly all community policing programs have been centered directly or indirectly on youth, with policies that can be placed into three main categories. The first is better coordination among agencies that deal with youth, since a lack of communication has been the norm—particularly among education and social services on the one hand and criminal justice agencies on the other. The success of such approaches can be seen by improvements in a collective ability to bring together the many characteristics of at-risk individuals long treated separately—such as socioeconomic pressures, family stability, and the community attitudes. The second approach is to provide opportunities for youth in the basic needs of education, recreation, and employment—such as through supervised alternative spaces, improving public transport, and after-school jobs. Many countries have also established forms of community justice, ranging from locally elected judges in Venezuela and Peru to neighborhood councils in Bolivia and local justice centers in Argentina. Set up in community centers and run by locally elected officers, these forms of community justice are designed and empowered to hear and resolve minor conflicts that the police or courts are unable to resolve, from tenant complaints to public sanitation. With their better knowledge of local conditions and their use of mediation, community justice has also helped by allowing citizens to bring to the surface underlying problems like domestic violence and youth unemployment.

The third and most difficult category is changing police structure so that officers have the time, training, and incentives to learn about communities, their conditions, and their youth. Since about 80 percent of policing deals with noncriminal issues, there is usually ample room and information to help police address crime's causes without being paralyzed by them. Only by patrolling an area and knowing its residents, for example, can police determine the balance between benefits for gang members (such as recognition, socialization, protection, belonging, and excitement) and costs (such as physical danger and community discrimination) necessary for effective antigang policy. As the examples below highlight, the most successful and sustainable changes in the policing of youth in Latin America combine all three approaches. Better agency coordination to assess the level of risk for youth while also toughening up criminal prosecution—a strategy commonly known as "pulling levers"—has shown some positive results.

Some strategies target specific causes of crime, such as rampant use of firearms. Although it has only 14 percent of the world's population, Latin

America has nearly half of its firearm homicides (Bandeira and Bourgois 2006). Over 70 percent of homicides in Central America are carried out with the area's 1.6 million guns, of which only 500,000 are legally registered; indeed, in El Salvador alone, 78.5 percent of homicides in 2005 involved firearms (Pleitez Chávez 2006: 30). Brazil, where the firearm homicide rate grew from 7 to 21 deaths per 100,000 from 1982 to 2002, arms killed over 10,000 minors in 2000 and is the top cause of youth murders (Small Arms Survey 2007). Despite these alarming statistics, gun control is very weak and disarmament laws have been enacted in only a few countries and cities. But some areas are taking action to reverse this trend. In El Salvador, the town of San Martín enacted a Gun Free campaign in June 2005 centered on youth with dozens of cultural events in public spaces, including courses to encourage young people to learn about the issue, training courses in communications, and a weekly radio show produced by local teens. Between November 2005 and June 2006, homicides fell by 40.7 percent and crimes committed with guns fell by 29 percent.[30]

But the most significant community-oriented policing programs have been national in scope. While they all involve structural changes and criminal policies beyond a strictly community-oriented program, these reforms are all based on the type of preventative and citizen-based approaches associated with community policing. Honduras's Safer Communities policing program, *Comunidad Más Segura*, brought preventative strategies, such as regular community meetings and streetlight repairs, that have led to a marked decline in homicides, robberies, and domestic violence in the 30 neighborhoods in which it operates.[31] Uruguay's National Citizen Security Program gives more responsibility to local police commissioners, for example over criminal investigation. Other initiatives include regular community-police and national meetings of Neighborhood Security Commissions, more courses in the Police Academy and more educational opportunities for active officers. Most of all, Uruguay has set up a Center for National Rehabilitation that houses youth in a facility with work programs and a staff of psychologists, social workers, and others trained in rehabilitation.[32]

The long-term potential of such national programs can be seen in Costa Rica, which began one of Latin America's first community policing programs in 1994 by forming a community extension unit in the Police Academy to focus on citizen security research,[33] which was then applied with positive results in the high-crime area of El Hatillo. This was followed up by the Community Security Unit in 1998 which now has 92 permanent police and 200 civilian personnel. Based on more coordination among social service ministries and with more outreach to business, the program's prevention-centered approach focuses on greater police presence, groups at risk, and social reinsertion. To carry out this work, community police officers have more flexible schedules and different promotion criteria, and are supported by police lawyers called *alpha limas* and the National Learning Institute, which conducts trainings on crime and other areas of the law. Most of all, the program trains and empowers residents to develop security plans to address neighborhood crime problems, based on 11 two-month courses on issues ranging from criminology to child abuse. According to surveys, 62 percent feel more secure and 35 percent feel only as secure as before, while 46 percent feel close to the police and 44 percent feel that the situation is the same as before the program.[34]

Such results are even more impressive amid high levels of violence or poverty, such as in the large cities of Colombia. Starting in 1995, the capital of Bogotá cut down urban violence through citizen security schools, neighborhood "fronts" to discuss crime prevention, and community policing units. These programs reduced violence significantly and led to strong public support for such strategies. Medellín launched education and community mobilization against violence with programs such as counseling, sport, and work programs for 1,500 youth. Cali's Development, Security, and Peace program—run by representatives of unions, the Church, and private companies—included more education and services for police, community councils, public polls, and youth programs. After it helped significantly reduce the annual total of 600 homicides between 1994 and 1998, it became a national model.

In Brazil, Rio de Janeiro's Grupamento de Policiamento em Áreas Especiais (GPAE, Special Area Police Unit), was created in 2000 to bring community policing to violent *favelas* by proactive policing that uses mediation, constant contact with the community, and focuses on reducing risk factors for youth. The high-crime city of Diadema in Brazil's São Paulo state adopted a program in 2000 to address the crime through a combination of prevention and repression, starting out with a series of programs such as the "Teen Apprentice Project" to support teen education and employment, followed up by increasing citizen participation in the plan's expansion and evaluation. In the 6 years after the plan began, the number of homicides dropped from 31 to 6 per month. This attention to preventing crime includes focus on "situational prevention," such as street lighting, school safety, and bus stops, as well as community violence prevention, through attention to problems such as poverty, marginality, and families.

The Andean region has shown contrasting emphases in youth-oriented community policing. In Bolivia, this approach has drawn on a highly multicultural and mobilized citizenry. The first programs came with the 1994 Popular Participation Law, which led to formation of Vigilance Committees, community security forums, and the Support and Citizen Cooperation Patrol to handle youth delinquency, homelessness, and drug addiction. It then spurred formation of other citizen-based units around the country. One of the most popular are the school brigades, comprised mainly of student volunteers who cooperate with the police during cultural and sports events. "The school brigades allow us to get close to the parents of the students involved. Through the youth, we can get to know the parents, the big brothers, the neighbors," says the La Paz Department police chief, adding "This is the best way of being close to the community."[35]

In neighboring Peru, reform has instead stressed criminal justice. After the National Citizen Security Council promoted local initiatives to improve participatory cooperation with the police through citizen security councils, a consortium of public and private agencies began an innovative program of restorative justice that addresses youth in the criminal justice through a two stage response. The first is an "immediate defense" system upon the youth's initial contact with law enforcement, to develop noncustodial sentencing that promotes reparations for victims and the community, trying to make the youth's responsibility to the community the center of their treatment. The second stage is run by an Education Follow-Up Team, comprised of an education professional, a social worker, and a network coordinator to, establish educational goals for the youth.

Argentina has also seen an upsurge in community policing as the *Mano Dura's* limits become increasingly evident and as decentralization allows for more policy innovation. La Rioja province began one of the first comprehensive efforts in 2003 to improve police-community relations and problem solving through home visits and other forms of police outreach; crime mapping; registries of uncivil behavior, and Neighborhood Community Policing Councils. The capital city's Community Prevention Brigade works with youth at risk, an Ecological Brigade trains youth in environment fields such as maintenance of potable water systems, and an education center serves current and ex-gang members. A Youth Provincial Coordinating Council was set up in 2006 to coordinate the disparate agencies working on youth issues and has further cut youth crime through efforts at school reintegration and related projects like "You Choose" to help keep kids away from drugs and crime. Of the city's 400 youth estimated to be at risk, officials say these many programs reach up to 90 percent of them. Residents note the visible reduction of crime and fear, and many officials involved in community policing say with satisfaction that parents actually reach out to them for support with their kids.[36] In Mendoza, the stalled 1999 security reform has been replaced by smaller but more successful efforts such as "A School for Fathers", which supports parents, as well as municipally run youth centers for alcohol and drug treatment. But perhaps most significantly, the country's largest and most violent province, Buenos Aires, has created neighborhood, municipal, and departmental Security Forums with unprecedented civilian power to evaluate the police and implement security plans. Focusing on the province's most excluded sectors—the critically poor, informal laborers, and people between 18 and 25 years of age[37]—the forums have established dozens of youth centers and programs in public spaces. Greater local autonomy for mayors has further expanded community-oriented youth policing. For example, the mayor of Morón used city facilities for after-school programs and seminars on civil rights for youth.[38] Unlike the great majority of municipal officials in the province, Morón's mayor was elected without rising up through the Peronist party machine, which dominates provincial politics and is closely connected to the police. This unusual electoral trajectory gave him the popular trust needed to develop programs that channeled citizen complaints about police activity.

Without clear structures and political support, though, community policing risks unleashing underlying tensions that it is unable to contain.

Youth programs and centers that are inadequately staffed or financed are likely to aggravate both community complaints over public space as well as young people's frustration with the government. Since socioeconomic causes of crime such as poverty and unemployment are beyond the police's power to solve, programs to address those causes are often limited. Crime reporting dropped 35 percent in one Venezuelan city after a local distillery employed gang members, for example, but only 1 percent of participating youth found work in other businesses (World Bank 2007). By holding out the possibility of a transformation in citizen security, community policing is criticized around the region for creating expectations and goals that can not possibly be met. Few citizens or police officers in high-violence areas have the time, incentive, or experience to embark on visionary experimentation, turning the space opened by community policing into a vacuum filled by superficial rhetoric or, in many cases, by coercion, intimidation, and violence by cliques of citizens and police whose attachment to zero tolerance policing leads to a reflexive resistance to community policing. In some cases, community policing can also become a channel of abuse and vigilantism by participating citizens and police officers. Even in Costa Rica's venerable program, meetings often degenerate into frustrated citizen demands that the police "do something"— revealing that communities require basic law enforcement before they can move on to new forms of it.

Honduras's community policing program demonstrates all of these weaknesses and unanticipated impacts. Police community meetings in Tegucigalpa tend to mostly involve showing videos and giving pamphlets to residents, while those in the San Pedro area often stall over delays in following up on basic infrastructural problems such as street lighting. In the Pacific coast city of Choluteca, even the community forums touted by the Zelaya government as a new beginning often lapse into exasperated directives from national officials with almost no input from citizens, local officials, or street police. More seriously, the head of a "model" community policing program in Honduras was detained for involvement in the killing of youth, while the head of a citizen policing group in La Ceiba says that they attack local delinquents.[39] With continuing economic and political uncertainty, moreover, citizens rightly doubt that support for community policing will continue. A citizen survey in Honduras's four main cities revealed serious doubts—especially by young people—over the state's commitment to community policing and a reduction in police violence and corruption.[40] Only 14.3 percent of youth respondents said that community policing controlled *maras*, compared to 38.1 percent for those over 25 years of age, and just 4.8 percent said that community policing lessened violence, compared with 23.9 percent of those over 26. Less than 15 percent of youth said that they knew of participation by NGOs—a key measure of the citizen inclusion essential to community policing—compared to 33.7 percent of those over 26. Assessing their overall experience, 57.1 percent of youth said that their opinion of the police had improved, compared to 81.5 percent of older respondents. Such age gaps indicate that community policing is providing reassurance and support to older people, but failing to tackle the youth alienation, violence, and socio-economic misery that fuels the country's extreme levels of fear and criminal violence.

Conclusion

Few issues are as challenging to Latin American democracy as crime, and few populations are as representative of that challenge as youth. Youth violence, gangs, drug use, and criminal activity have dominated media coverage, political discourse, and legislation throughout the region. And while community policing offers a way out of the current policy impasse, it too is vulnerable to the same pressure and limitations that have made general policing ineffective. In particular, as this chapter discussed, the efforts that would be needed to address the conditions that lead to youth crime are impeded not only by the sheer extent of issues that those efforts would have to encompass—from domestic violence to the international drug trade—but by the tendency to fall back on responses with immediately visible results. Lowering the age of responsibility, repressing youth gangs, and intimidating young people in public space are concrete steps that sacrifice long-term approaches in exchange for short-term improvements. As they compound institutional and political weaknesses without bringing sustainable change, though, the gradual exposure of these policies' ineffectiveness will hopefully open the way to a policing of youth that addresses crime as well as its causes. Repressive and preventative policing can be combined, for example, by using both better information and social programs to target the most dangerous offenders for prosecution and at-risk youth for support. By using the resources of the community, as some of the region's best programs show, the power of policing to stop youth crime does not have to compromise on the protection of youth rights.

Notes

1. Homicide is the second leading cause of death for the 10–19 age group in 10 of the 21 countries with populations over one million.
2. In 11 of 17 countries surveyed in a 2005 study by the *Universidad Centroamerica*, El Salvador.
3. Youth here considered were those between 12 and 24 years, and the number includes Latin America and the Caribbean.
4. Covering those between 16 and 24 years of age (Fawcett 2003: 14).
5. Statistics cited in Government of the Province of Buenos Aires (2004: 3).
6. *Sistema de Información, Evaluación y Monitoreo de Programas Sociales* (SIEMPRO), at http://www.siempro.gov.ar, 2002. [accessed November 1, 2007].
7. "Policía identifica a 32 menor reincidentes", *La Nación*, July 9, 2004.
8. Íñigo Herraiz, Juventud sin rumbo, *Adital*, July 29, 2004.
9. *Policía Nacional de Ecuador* (2003: 46). The higher number is for 2002, and the lower number is for 2003.

10. The terms *pandillas* and *maras* are often used interchangeably, but a *pandilla* is officially defined by *Ley de Policía y Convivencia Social*, Articles 90–91 as "a group of adolescents from 12 to 18 years," while *maras* are considered to be more organized, violent, powerful, and criminal—often with leaders older than 18 years of age (Government of Honduras 2002).

11. Author interviews with prosecutors, judges, and police, 2001–2006.

12. "Edad punible," *La Prensa* January 26, 2003, and "San Pedro Sula, como en zona de Guerra," February 13, 2003, cite polls showing crime to be Hondurans' main concern and demonstrating high support for Maduro's policy.

13. Author interviews with the warden, officials, and prisoners in Centro Penal Barrio Inglés, February 24, 2004, and in the Centro Penal San Pedro Sula, March 1, 2004.

14. "La venganza de los marginados," *El Progreso,* March 31, 2005. The estimate of 100,000 was made by the Honduran Congress.

15. In contrast, the Christian Youth Association puts the number at 125,000, 55 percent between the ages of 15 and 17 years and 14.6 percent between 12 and 15 years, (Human Rights Comissioner 2001).

16. Author interview, Álvaro Romero, Security Minister, June 13, 2006.

17. As former Security Minister Guatama de Fonseca put it, the police have adopted the view that "the shortest road to terminate crime is to terminate criminals." (Author interview, July 21, 2003).

18. *See* Casa Alianza at www.casa-alianza.org/EN/about/offices/honduras/.

19. These estimates from author interview with street workers; with Gustavo Zelaya, Legal Director, 2003–2006, and with youths on the streets of Tegucigalpa, July 16, 2003.

20. Author interview, Security Minister Oscar Álvarez, Tegucigalpa, July 18, 2003.

21. Personal communication, DGIC Department of Statistics, February 2004.

22. Some human rights commission officials estimate that over 80 percent of detainees are beaten and that such cases are not investigated by overwhelmed judges and prosecutors. Author interview, Víctor Parelló, Human Rights Commissioner for the Northern Region, San Pedro Sula, February 20, 2004.

23. Author interview, Aída Estella Romero, July 22, 2003. Eduardo Villanueva, publica prosecutor, added that "there are neither human nor logistical resources," to handle "the enormous quantity of cases." (Author interview, Tegucigalpa, July 15, 2003).

24. Author interview, Ramón Custodio, National Human Rights Commissioner, July 4, 2005.

25. Author interview, María Luisa Borjas, former UAI Chief, Tegucigalpa, July 18, 2003.

26. Author interview, Elia Ramírez de Zelaya, June 16, 2006.

27. Author interviews, officials and inmates in El Porvenir penal center, El Porvenir, and Barrio Inglés penitentiary, La Ceiba, February 23, 24, and 25, 2004.

28. Author interviews, Centro Penal San Pedro Sula; San Pedro Sula, March 1, 2004.

29. Author interview, Carla Luque, IHNFA, June 12, 2006.

30. Data from Carola Mittrany, "Gun Free Towns Project cuts homicide rate drastically in El Salvador's San Martín," www.comunidadsegura.org [accessed November 1, 2007].

31. This is the case of San Pedro Sula Valley city of Choloma, for instance, where regular community meetings are held. There were nine murders in January 2002 but only four per month in the first 4 months of 2003, and 17 robberies in January 2002 but none in the first 4 months of 2003 (Author interviews, community policing meeting, Choloma, February 19, 2004; and Carlos Chinchilla, Executive Director, *Comunidad Más Segura*, Tegucigalpa, July 22, 2003; see also "Presidente Maduro inaugura programa "Comunidad Segura" en Choloma, Cortés, 3 de mayo de 2003," at: www.casapresidencial.hn/Security.).

32. Author interviews, Gloria Robaina of the National Citizen Security Progam; and Gabrial Courtoisie, Center for National Rehabilitation, August 2003.

33. Author interview, Ana Durán Salvatierra, Vice-Minister of Governance and Police; San José, June 19, 2006.

34. Author interview, Alberto Li Chan, Police Commissioner and Coordinator of Community Security, June 2006.

35. Author interview, Colonel H. James, Police Commander, La Paz Department, December 22, 2004.

36. Survey of La Rioja city residents, CUNY Collaborative Grant, 2005.

37. Author interview, Martha Arriola, Subsecretariat of Community Participation, Security Ministry, Buenos Aires Province; July 2007.

38. Author interview, municipal officials and youth center participants, Morón, June 2004.

39. Author interview, Celio Santos, El Confite, Honduras, February 25, 2004. Criminal justice officials report thousands of unreported vigilante attacks since 2002 (Author interviews: Eduardo Villanueva, Tegucigalpa, July 15, 2003; Walter Menjivar Mendoza, Head Prosecutor for the Northern Region, February 26, 2004).

40. Funded by the 2004–2005 CUNY Collaborative Grant project, *Police Reform and Community Policing in Latin America*, directed by Mark Ungar and Desmond Arias, John Jay College and, conducted with the Centro de Documentación de Honduras (CEDOH).

Bibliography

Arriagada, I. 2001. *Seguridad Ciudadana y Violencia en América Latina*, paper presented at the XXIII Latin American Studies Association Congress, Washington DC.

Bandeira, A., and J. Bourgois. 2006. *Armas de Fuego: ¿Protección? ¿O Riesgo? Guía Práctica*, Stockholm: Parliamentary Forum on Small and Light Arms.

Bobea, L. 2003. Economía política de la inseguridad y desafíos a las políticas de seguridad ciudadana en la República Dominicana, in L. Bobea (ed.), *Entre el Crimen y el Castigo*, Caracas: Nueva Sociedad. pp. 175–228.

Casa Alianza. 2006. *Violence in Guatemala: A Channel 4 Documentary*, http://www.casa-alianza.org.uk/northsouth/CasaWeb.nsf/CasaNews/Channel, November 2. [accessed November 1, 2007].

Castellanos, J. 2002. El tortuoso camino de la reforma policial, *El Heraldo*, October 8.

Castillo, S. 2004. *Familias Hondureñas Vislumbran Nuevos Horizontes para Sus Hijos*, http://www.casapresidencial.hn/reportajes/200104.php, January 20. [accessed November 1, 2007].

CEPAL (Comisión Económica para America Latina). 2003. *Panorama Social de América Latina 2001–2002: Elevadas Tasas de Deserción Escolar en América Latina*, Santiago: CEPAL.

De Roux, G. 1994. Ciudad y violencia en América Latina, in A. Concha Eastman and F. Carrión (eds.), *Ciudad y Violencias en América Latina*, Quito: Programa de Gestión Urbana. pp. 25–46.

El Achkar, S. 2007. Reforma policial en Venezuela: Una experiencia en curso, in M. Ungar and D. Arias (eds.), *Mejores Prácticas de la Policía Comunitaria en América Latina*, unpublished report draft.

Espinal Díaz, E. 2004. La policía nacional de Honduras, *Diario Tiempo*, January 16.

Fawcett, C. 2003. *Los Jóvenes Latinoamericanos en Transición: Un análisis sobre el desempleo juvenil en América Latina y el Caribe*, Washington: Inter-American Development Bank.

Gentili, R. A. 1995. ...*Me Va a Tener Que Acompañar: Una Visión Crítica sobre los Edictos policiales*, Buenos Aires: El Naranjo.

Government of Argentina. 2001. *Encuesta Permanente de Hogares*, Buenos Aires: Instituto Nacional de Estadística y Censos.

Government of Honduras, 2002. *Ley de Policía y Convivencia Social*, Poder Legislativo, República de Honduras, Tegucigalpa.

Government of the Province of Buenos Aires, 2004. *Cuaderno No. 4: Programa de Respuesta Múltiple para la Prevención Comunitaria de la Violencia*, La Plata: Ministry of Security.

Grindle, M. S. 2004. The politics of education decentralization in Mexico, in Kaufman, R. Nelson, and J. Nelson (eds.), *Crucial Needs, Weak Incentives*, Washington: Woodrow Wilson Center Press. pp. 283–314.

Hopenhayn, M. 2004. El mundo del trabajo y los jóvenes, *Jóvenes: Revista de Estudios sobre Juventud*, vol. 8, no. 20, pp. 54–73.

Human Rights Commissioner, 2001. Inicia La Discusión del Dictamen de Ley Para Rehabilitar, *Boletín Informativo No. 1554*, 16 August.

Kelling, G. L., and C. M. Coles. 1996. *Fixing Broken Windows*, New York: Touchstone.

Kunz, A. 2005. *Percepción social de la administración de Justicia*, Departamento de Investigación, Área de Sociología Jurídica, Documentos de Trabajo, No 132. Universidad de Belgrano.

PAHO (Pan-American Health Organization). 2002. *Violence, a Growing Problem for Public Health*, Washington: PAHO.

Pleitez Chávez, R. 2006. *Violencia y Criminalidad en El Salvador: Obstáculo para el Desarrollo*, San Salvador: Fundación Salvadoreña para el Desarrollo Económico y Social (FUSADES).

Policía Nacional de Ecuador, 2003. *Presentation a Cargo del Señor Jefe de Estado Mayor*, Quito.

Royal Canadian Mounted Police (RCMP). 2006. *Feature Focus: Youth Gangs and Guns*, Ottawa: RCMP Strategic Policy and Planning Directorate.

Sanjuan, A. M. 2003. Dinámica de la violencia en Venezuela: Tensiones y desafíos para la consolidación de la democracia, in L. Bobea (ed.), *Entre el Crimen y el Castigo*, Caracas: Nueva Sociedad.

Small Arms Survey, 2007. *Guns and the City*, Geneva: Small Arms Survey, http://www.smallarmssurvey.org/ [accessed June 2 2009].

Solís Robles, A. 2004. Analizan situación de las pandillas juveniles en nuestro país, *La Prensa Libre*, November 12.

UN-Habitat. 2004. *The State of the World's Cities*, Nairobi: UNCHS.

UNICJRI (United Nations Interregional Crime and Justice Research Institute). 1995. *Criminal Victimization in the Developing World*, Publication 55, Rome: United Nations.

USAID. 2005. *Reflections on Community-Based Policing Programming in Guatemala*, Washington: USAID.

Vieira, C. 2005. *Edad de Imputabilidad en Tela de Juicio*, Inter Press Service (IPS), August 19.

WHO. 2007. *Violence and Injury Prevention and Disability (VIP)*. Department of Injuries and Violence Prevention of the World Health Organization, Geneva: WHO, http://www.who.int/violence_injury_prevention/en/ [accessed November 1, 2007].

World Bank. 2007. *El Desarrollo y la Próxima Generación*, Washington: World Bank.

Contributors

Dominique P. Béhague is Lecturer in Medical Anthropology at the London School of Hygiene and Tropical Medicine. She works on public health issues, including in particular youth violence and reproductive health, as well as the politics of international public health and policy making, in Brazil and in Benin. Her recent research, funded by The Wellcome Trust, uses ethnographic and epidemiological approaches to explore the influence that social, political, and health care changes in Pelotas, Brazil, are having on the life course and health of young men and women, particularly as it relates to mental health and violence.

Héctor Castillo Berthier is Senior Researcher in the Institute of Social Studies at the *Universidad Nacional Autónoma de México* (National Autonomous University of Mexico, UNAM). His publications include work on urban problems, such as garbage, wholesale food markets, youth, gangs, and popular culture in Mexico and Latin America. Héctor has combined academia with activism, serving as under secretary (*subdelegado*) for Social Development for the borough of Álvaro Obregón in Mexico City between 1998 and 2000, and as director of the *Circo Volador*, see www.circovolador.org. This project was awarded one of twelve Dubai International Awards for Best Practices by UN-Habitat. He is presently working on a research project on youth gangs and other forms of youth organization for the *Unidad de Estudios sobre Juventud* (Youth Studies Unit, UNESJUV) at the UNAM.

Graham Denyer Willis is a PhD candidate in the Department of Urban Studies and Planning at the Massachusetts Institute of Technology (MIT). A Canadian urban sociologist, he has undertaken primary research on the *Primeiro Comando da Capital* (PCC), the social construction of violence, and the hollowing of public security in São Paulo, Brazil. He continues to research violence in urban settings, particularly as it relates to non-state armed groups, violent state actors, democracy, and state formation.

Gareth A. Jones is Senior Lecturer in Development Geography at the London School of Economics and Political Science and coeditor of the *Journal of Latin American Studies*. From 2005, he codirected a 3-year project entitled *"Being in Public": The multiple childhoods of Mexican "street" children*. Gareth was a Member of the Expert Panel for Study of Street Children and Violence in Latin America organized by The Consortium for Street Children, which advised the *State of the World's Street Children: Violence* report (2007), and cowrote the UN Youth Unit Briefing Paper on *Youth on the Streets* (2008).

José Luis Rocha Gómez is Senior Researcher at the Central American University (UCA) in Managua, Nicaragua, and Research Coordinator of the Central American Jesuit Refugee Service. His work focuses on issues relating to youth gangs, local government, disaster prevention and management, the coffee industry, and migration. His publications include *Una Región Desgarrada: Dinámicas Migratorias en Centroamérica/A Region Torn Apart: The Dynamics of Migration in Central America* (2006); and *Bróderes Descobijados y Vagos Alucinados: Una Década con las Pandillas Nicaragüenses 1997–2007* (2008) (with Dennis Rodgers), also published electronically in English as *Gangs of Nicaragua* on the website http://www.gangresearch.net).

Dennis Rodgers is Senior Research Fellow in the Brooks World Poverty Institute at the University of Manchester and Visiting Senior Fellow in the Crisis States Research Centre at the London School of Economics and Political Science. He is a Cambridge-trained social anthropologist, and works on issues relating to violence and urban development in Nicaragua and Argentina. He has been carrying out participant observation fieldwork on youth gang violence in a Managua slum since 1996, and has published extensively on this topic, as well as on others relating to urban development more broadly.

Monique Sonnevelt is in the Department of Cultural Anthropology at the University of Utrecht, conducting her doctoral research entitled *Living at Odds: Urban Violence, Social Class, and Social Exclusion in Guadalajara, Mexico*. Monique has also conducted research on policing in Managua, Nicaragua, for the Dutch Ministry of Foreign Affairs in collaboration with Utrecht University. Previously, her Masters involved work on the ex-paramilitary forces and their role in the 2003 elections in Guatemala.

Cordula Strocka works as Programme Officer for the Youth Empowerment Partnership Programme (YEPP) at the Free University of Berlin, Germany. She is a psychologist by training and holds a PhD in Development Studies from the University of Oxford. Her doctoral research became a book: *In Search of Identity: Youth Gangs in Ayacucho* (2008). Cordula has worked for several years in Bolivia and Peru, researching youth gangs, youth organizations, street children, and child labor.

Mark Ungar is Associate Professor of Political Science at Brooklyn College and of Criminal Justice at the Graduate Center of the City University of New York. Publications include the books *Elusive Reform: Democracy and the Rule of Law in Latin America* and *Violence and Politics: Globalization's Paradox,* as well as articles on democratization and criminal justice. He is also author of a forthcoming book, *Policing Democracy: Overcoming Obstacles to Citizen Security Reform in Latin America,* and is currently completing an edited volume on community policing. Ungar also works as an advisor on police reform with several international organizations and Latin American governments.

Jon Wolseth is Visiting Assistant Professor of Anthropology at Luther College. He has conducted in-depth ethnographic research on youth violence and religious movements in Honduras and on violence and drug use among street populations in the Dominican Republic. His previous publications include work on the relationship between Pentecostalism and gang violence, the cultural politics of youth, and the intersection of social exclusion and grief. He is currently working on a monograph about street youth in Santo Domingo.

Verónica Zubillaga holds a doctorate in Sociology from the *Université Catholique de Louvain* (2003). She is Professor and Researcher at the *Universidad Simón Bolívar* (USB) and at the *Universidad Católica Andrés Bello* (UCAB), and is associated with the *Laboratorio de Ciencias Sociales* (LACSO) in Caracas. Her research interests and writing include urban violence in Latin America, youth, masculinities, and qualitative methods.

Index